Governing Migration beyond the State

Governing Migration beyond the State

Europe, North America, South America, and Southeast Asia in a Global Context

ANDREW GEDDES

OXFORD
UNIVERSITY PRESS

OXFORD
UNIVERSITY PRESS

Great Clarendon Street, Oxford, OX2 6DP,
United Kingdom

Oxford University Press is a department of the University of Oxford.
It furthers the University's objective of excellence in research, scholarship,
and education by publishing worldwide. Oxford is a registered trade mark of
Oxford University Press in the UK and in certain other countries

Published in the United States of America by Oxford University Press
198 Madison Avenue, New York, NY 10016, United States of America

British Library Cataloguing in Publication Data

Data available

Library of Congress Control Number: 2020951650

ISBN 978-0-19-884275-0

DOI: 10.1093/oso/ 9780198842750.001.0001

Printed and bound by
CPI Group (UK) Ltd, Croydon, CR0 4YY

Acknowledgements

The research upon which this book is based was made possible by the generous support of a European Research Council Advanced Investigator Grant for the project Prospects for International Migration Governance (MIGPROSP, Project no. 340430). It's difficult to overstate the significance at a personal and professional level of ERC support. I was hugely grateful and fortunate to have it and to benefit from the responsibilities and opportunities that it provided. Between April 2014 and August 2017 the MIGPROSP project was based in the Department of Politics at the University of Sheffield. Between September 2017 and its end in March 2019 it was housed, after I became its Director, at the Migration Policy Centre at the European University Institute in Florence, Italy. A key advantage of generous ERC support was being able to recruit a fantastic team to help develop the project. In Sheffield, Dr Leila Hadj Abdou, Dr Marcia Vera Espinoza, Jason Freeman, and Dr Gabriela Ibarra made important contributions to the project's development, to keeping things on track, and to generally being great people to be around. Special thanks are due to Leila, who joined the project at its outset, more or less stuck it out until the end, and brought a vision and commitment that helped define the scope and purpose of the work. Michaela Bruckmayer, Luca Lixi, Laura Foley, and Andrea Pettrachin all successfully completed their PhDs as part of the MIGPROSP project and were a continual source of ideas and inspiration for the project. When I moved to EUI, Dr Leiza Brumat joined the team. Leiza played a key role in a conference held in Buenos Aires in October 2018 under the auspices of the MIGPROSP project that brought together more than 100 scholars working on Latin American migration governance. The project also profited from the participation of Professor Diego Acosta and Professor Nicola Phillips as external collaborators. Diego made a vital contribution to the work on South America, and his book *The National versus the Foreigner in South America* (Cambridge University Press, 2018) is a definitive study of migration and citizenship to which the MIGPROSP project proudly contributed. Elements of the book were presented at the Sussex Centre for Migration Research and the London Migration Research Group. Thanks to Paul Statham and Sarah Scuzzarello at the University of Sussex and Eiko Thielemann of the LSE and Fiona Adamson of SOAS for the kind invitations.

I also had the honour of presenting an earlier version of the arguments in this book as the Yves Mény Lecture at the Robert Schuman Centre for Advanced Studies at EUI. Grateful thanks are due to Brigid Laffan, the Director of the Schuman Centre, for the kind invitation. At EUI, Aurélie Boursier and Ciara Burbridge provided administrative backup supplemented by wisdom and kindness. As the book neared completion, the research assistance provided by Eleonora Milazzo made a critical difference to creating a manuscript that had some semblance of order and structure. Federica Bicchi, Leiza Brumat, Leila Hadj Abdou, Feline Freier, Nicola Piper, and Gabriella Sanchez provided feedback on parts of the manuscript, although all errors of fact, interpretation, or omission are mine alone. Thanks also to Victoria Garin Giménez who prepared the Index. Last but not least, thanks are due to my family, who bore the MIGPROSP project with good grace, most of the time. The manuscript was completed during the Covid-19 lockdown, when the value of being at home with people I love was made very clear. The book is dedicated to Federica, Jacopo, and Beatrice (and Penny, our dog).

Andrew Geddes

Florence, April 2020

Contents

List of Figures   ix
List of Abbreviations   xi

1. Governing Migration beyond the State   1
   Introduction   1
   The organization of migration governance   8
   Studying migration governance   9
   Beyond the state   12
   The regional level   15
   Actors in migration governance   17
   How the research was done   19
   Organization of the book   22

2. Repertoires of Migration Governance   24
   Introduction   24
   Migration governance repertoires   27
   The meaning of migration governance   30
       How can we figure out what's going on out there?   37
       Why do something when we don't know what effect it will have?   41
       How can we choose our priorities?   43
       Who are all these people at this meeting?   45
       Does that make sense to us?   48
   Is governance Eurocentric?   51
   Conclusions   53

3. Southeast Asia: The 'Temporariness of Migration'   55
   Introduction   55
   Drivers and characteristics   57
       Labour migration   59
       Forced migration and displacement   62
   The Andaman Sea 'crisis'   65
   What kind of region?   70
       Flexible engagement   74
   The Bali Process   80
   Conclusions   83

4. *De jure* and *de facto* Openness in South America   85
   Introduction   85
   Drivers and characteristics   87
       Forced migration   93

A liberal tide? 97
What kind of region? 102
Conclusion 108

5. The Normality of Crisis in the European Union 110
Introduction 110
Drivers and characteristics 112
Free movement 116
Migration and asylum 118
What kind of region? 123
The effects of crisis 127
The politicization of migration governance 132
Old and new actors 134
Making sense of public attitudes 135
Conclusions 138

6. North America: A Region without Regionalism 139
Introduction 139
Drivers and characteristics 141
What kind of region? 156
Crises and their regional effects 162
Conclusion 168

7. Prospects for Global Migration Governance 170
Introduction 170
The meaning of the global 172
A global migration governance repertoire? 175
Origins and emergence 182
Regime complexity 187
The Global Compacts 188
Conclusion 191

8. Conclusions 193

Bibliography 203
Index 223

List of Figures

1.1. Intra-regional migrants in ASEAN, 2019   13

1.2. Intra-regional migrants in the EU, 2019   13

1.3. Intra-regional migrants in MERCOSUR, 2019   14

1.4. Intra-regional migrants in the ex-NAFTA region, 2019   14

3.1. Trends in intra-regional migration in ASEAN, 2010–19   58

3.2. Immigrants and emigrants in ASEAN, 2019 (thousands)   58

4.1. Trends in intra-regional migration, 2010–19   89

4.2. Share of intra-regional migrants by country of destination, 2019   90

5.1. Immigrants and emigrants in the EU, 2019   113

6.1. Trends in intra-regional migration in the ex-NAFTA region, 2010–19   141

6.2. Share of intra-regional migrants by country of origin, 2019   142

List of Abbreviations

ACMW	ASEAN Committee on Migrant Workers
ASEAN	Association of South East Asian Nations
CBSA	Canadian Border Services Agency
CONASUPO	National Company of Popular Subsistences
CPA	Comprehensive Plan of Action
CUSMA	Canada—United States—Mexico Agreement
DACA	Deferred Action for Childhood Arrivals
DAPA	Deferred Action for Parents of Americans and Lawful Permanent Residents
DHS	Department for Homeland Security
DREAM	Development, Relief, and Education for Alien Minors
EAM	European Agenda on Migration
ETA	Electronic Travel Authorization
EU	European Union
FRONTEX	European Border and Coastguard Agency
GCIM	Global Commission on International Migration
GCM	Global Compact for Safe, Orderly and Regular Migration
GCR	Global Compact on Refugees
GFMD	Global Forum on Migration and Development
ICE	Immigration and Customs Enforcement
IIRIA	Illegal Immigration Reform and Immigrant Responsibility Act
ILO	International Labour Organization
IOM	International Organization for Migration
IRCA	Immigration Reform and Control Act
MERCOSUR	Southern Common Market
MIGPROSP	Prospects for International Migration Governance
MPP	Migration Protection Protocols
MRA	MERCOSUR Residence Agreement
NAFTA	North American Free Trade Area
ODP	Orderly Departure Program
TCNs	Third Country Nationals
T-MEC	Tratado entre México, Estados Unidos y Canadá
UNASUR	Union of South American Nations
UNEP	United Nations Environment Programme
UNESCAP	United Nations Economic and Social Commission for Asia and the Pacific

UNHCR	United Nations High Commissioner for Refugees
UNODC	UN Office on Drugs and Crime
UNTOC	UN Convention against Transnational Organized Crime
USMCA	United States-Mexico-Canada Agreement
WHO	World Health Organization

1

Governing Migration beyond the State

Introduction

Migration governance occurs in the shadow of uncertainty where facts, values, and beliefs elide. In October 2019, the European Commissioner responsible for migration, Dimitris Avramopoulos, and the German interior minister Horst Seehofer travelled to Ankara to meet with Turkey's interior minister Süleyman Soylu. European Union (EU) leaders were concerned about increased numbers of 'irregular crossings' by would-be migrants, of whom there were a reported 12,000 in September 2019. People were travelling the short distance by boat from the Turkish coast to nearby Greek islands. The *Financial Times* reported that 'the numbers of arrivals remains far below its October 2015 peak, when 210,000 people crossed between Turkey and Greece in a single month', but went on to note that the increase had 'caused alarm among political leaders worried about the impact that a further surge could have on EU nations' (Peel and Pitel, 2019). Consider this last phrase for a moment: EU leaders were reported as being alarmed about what might happen if numbers of migrants increased. This alarm might be well founded, but then again, it might not. The point is that a representation of a possible future event shapes actions based on a perception of what has happened in the past, of what was going on at the time, and of what might happen in the future. Generating alarm amongst EU governments was their fear of a further surge in numbers that played a key role in the EU 'migration crisis' that was at its height in terms of numbers of arrivals in 2015 and 2016 and had a major destabilizing effect on European governments and the EU.

Also in October 2019 it was reported that more than 865,000 Venezuelans had moved to Peru, leading the National Superintendent of Migration Roxana del Águila to describe the migration as 'crisis-like behaviour' (Rochas Sánchez, 2019). For Águila, the focus was the behaviour of migrants, but the Peruvian foreign minister, Gustavo Meza-Cuadra, also observed that the crisis was of state capacity to deal with large numbers of displaced people. Meza-Cuadra said that solutions were needed at a regional and global level (Redacción EC, 2019). Crises focus attention on underlying representations

Governing Migration Beyond the State: Europe, North America, South America, and Southeast Asia in a Global Context. Andrew Geddes, Oxford University Press (2021). © Andrew Geddes. DOI: 10.1093/oso/9780198842750.003.0001

of why people move, but also of governance capacity and what governing systems across various levels (national, regional, international) should be doing.

In the same month, the United Nations High Commissioner for Refugees (UNHCR) published a report entitled *Refugee Movement in Southeast Asia 2018–June 2019* that called for greater efforts to create safe and legal pathways for people in need of protection while also calling for greater efforts at regional level to develop 'a more predictable and coordinated response' (UNHCR, 2019a). The report was framed by reference to the 2015 'Andaman Sea crisis' (see Chapter 3) and centred on calls by a key international organization, the UNHCR, for stronger, coordinated action at a regional level, with a particularly important role for the Association of South East Asian Nations (ASEAN). Uncertainty—or a lack of predictability—is viewed as a characteristic of migration but also of governance responses.

In early 2019, the US government introduced what it called 'Migration Protection Protocols' (MPP), which, as the then Secretary for Homeland Security, Kirstjen Nielsen, put it, was 'an unprecedented action that will address the urgent humanitarian and security crisis at the Southern border [and] help to end the exploitation of our generous immigration laws. The MPPs represent a methodical common sense approach, exercising long-standing statutory authority to help address the crisis at our Southern border' (Department for Homeland Security, 2019). Leaving aside for now these references to urgency, US generosity and, once again, crisis, the practical effect of the MPPs was to force asylum seekers to wait in often dangerous border towns on the Mexican side of the border. The MPPs were seen as a way for the US government to move towards its wider goal of a 'safe third country agreement' with Mexico that would prevent people from moving across Mexico to the US to seek asylum and thus cut off a route to protection for many people, particularly from Central America. When reporting on how many would-be asylum applicants simply abandoned their quest for protection when reaching the US border because of the obstacles put in their way, the *New Yorker* magazine wrote that 'From the standpoint of the Trump Administration, such high rates of attrition were a welcome by-product of a more overt aim: deterring future asylum seekers from making the trip north in the first place' (Blitzer, 2019). Put like this, 'deterrence' can be understood as a governance effect because it informs a policy approach that is based on a representation of the causes and effects of migration that then feeds back to decisively influence the journeys and experiences of migrants.

Each of these vignettes presents a way of representing the governance of migration beyond the state. All focus on events understood and defined by elite governance 'actors' as crises, more on which soon. Each also illustrates how these elite actors of various types (such as national governments, international organizations, and regional organizations) that are involved with varying degrees of power and influence in migration governance try to make sense of what, for them, can be troubling issues that combine uncertainty with risk. Risk can be understood as the potentially negative effects of decisions, is inherent in choice, depends on the ordering of options in some meaningful hierarchy, and is related to the values placed upon possible outcomes by decision makers.

Migration governance actors respond to risk and uncertainty by drawing from what this book characterizes as *repertoires of migration governance*. These repertoires centre not on the more observable effects of governance (such as laws and policies) but on what actors *know how to do* and *what they think they should be doing*. These repertoires comprise knowledge claims (they are narratives); develop through interaction with others (they are social); can be based on intuitive or emotional responses to issues (they are affective); have a symbolic component, which means that actions are taken that are designed to appease or placate rather than resolve (they are performative); and don't have a beginning and an end (they are ongoing). Through their operation and effects, these repertoires have powerful effects on migrants and their lived experiences.

The book also develops a distinctive argument about the relation between 'crisis' and 'normality'. Rather than crises as drivers of migration governance, it is representations of what is 'normal' embedded within migration governance repertoires that shapes migration governance in Europe, North America, South America, and Southeast Asia and, ultimately too, prospects for global migration governance. Understandings and representations of normality can provide an anchor or starting point against which assessments are made. These are subjective assessments that centre on understandings and representations of the causes and effects of migration now and in the future, as well as of the key risks and uncertainties associated with it. This focus on decision-making under conditions of risk draws from prospect theory, which is a behavioural theory of choice attuned to analysis of real-life situations and scenarios to which significant risk is attached (McDermott, 2001; Mercer, 2005; Tversky and Kahneman, 1979). Prospect theory postulates that in situations of gain individuals are more likely to be risk-averse, and in situations of loss they are more likely to be risk-seeking. De Vries (2018: 36) highlights the importance of what she calls 'baseline' assessments that mean that '[w]hen deciding to opt for a change from, or to remain with, the status quo, people weigh up the benefits they derive from the status quo, the *existing* situation, to an alternative state, the expected *changed* situation'. Risk aversion can reinforce the status quo 'because the disadvantages of leaving it loom larger than the advantages' (Kahneman et al., 1991: 163). In her application of prospect theory to US foreign policy, McDermott (2001: 4) characterizes prospect theory as 'profoundly situationalist' because 'risk-taking...evolves out of a cognitive response to a situation that constrains the ways options are interpreted and choices are made'. There can be risk and uncertainty about the scale and direction of future migration flows; openness and closure in migration governance, such as openness to certain flows and closure to others; and scope for migration governance beyond the state, involving various forms or types of cooperation, with scope too for 'pooling' of sovereignty in some areas. There are, of course, many ways to understand and represent international migration—as 'pulled' by labour markets and welfare states in destination countries; as impelled by fear and violence; as motivated by hope and opportunity—but the point is that all provide a frame or way of seeing international migration that helps to define the nature of the issue or challenge and the responses that develop to it (as defined). Also, of course, some representations are more powerful than others because of the actors that hold them and their ability to make or shape responses.

This book's actor-centred approach focus is on elites, defined as those who seek to make, shape, or influence policy. This doesn't negate the structural economic, political, social, demographic, and environmental factors that can cause or drive international migration, but highlights how there is uncertainty about the causes and effects of these structural changes that require interpretation and representation. These representations rely on information, facts, and evidence, but are also be shaped by the beliefs and values held by individuals and organizations that will necessarily influence how facts, information, and evidence are understood and represented. This means that the focus for this book is on the 'representation of facts' that are 'represented both in what people think and in what they say' (Mercier and Sperber, 2017: 111). The representation of facts can coalesce into knowledge of, about, for, or against international migration that is 'produced through interaction and communication, and its expression is always linked to the human interests that are engaged' (Moscovici, 2001: 2).

The idea of a migration governance repertoire draws from and builds upon work on migration governance that focuses on 'narratives' (Boswell et al., 2011; Carling and Hernández-Carretero, 2011; Pécoud, 2014). Boswell et al. (2011: 4) analyse the development and use of knowledge claims about migration and view narratives as 'the factual beliefs espoused by policy-makers and others engaged in policy debates'. For Pécoud (2014), narratives are a way to understand how dominant constructions of migration as a political issue emerge and how they are then diffused through the practices of international migration governance. Understood like this, a narrative is 'the growing corpus of reports' emanating from organizations involved in the governance of international migration (ibid.: 3). In related work, Boswell (2009) shows how expert knowledge can serve various purposes that are not only to inform policy choices (so-called evidence-based policymaking), but to also substantiate choices that have already been made—which could be thought of as policy-based evidence-making—or legitimizing the role of certain institutions and actors. Similar to Boswell's approach, there is other work that looks 'behind' the more visible manifestations of governance to examine the ways in which narratives can 'stabilize' governance because they provide 'the assumptions needed for decision-making in the face of what is genuinely uncertain and complex. They can be representationally inaccurate—and recognizably so—but still persist, indeed, thrive' (Roe, 1994: 51). Weick (1995, whose work this book draws from quite extensively) studied 'sense-making' in organizations to argue that accuracy is nice but not always necessary and that what matters is plausibility. The word plausibility has an obvious reference to performance and to an audience—to whom is the claim plausible? This may be other organizations, migrants, or the general public, but highlights the importance of the mutually constitutive relationship between organizations and the environment in which they operate. It is possible for there to be a plausible narrative about migration and its effects that may contain elements that are accurate, but that is not necessarily entirely accurate and may, as a result, be partial or misleading. Or put another way, 'incompetent practice might be more "successful" in bringing results than virtuoso performance' (Adler and Pouliot, 2011: 8).

A repertoire of migration governance brings together work on decision-making under conditions of risk, framing, and sense-making. It builds upon the idea of 'narratives' as knowledge claims about migration by adding four further elements. These are, first, the *social* content of inter-organizational relationships that can lie behind the representation of facts arising from interactions where positions are justified and challenged. Second, an *affective* content involving responses to migration at a more emotional level as well as an emotional attachment to ideas and positions (Brader et al., 2008; Erisen et al., 2019). Third, the use of the word 'repertoire' itself evokes ideas of *performance*. It can, for example, be important to be seen to do something even if it is sometimes largely symbolic (Edelman, 1985; Goldberg, 2018; Sears, 1993). Symbols are important because, as Edelman (1985: 1) observes they can 'sustain and develop' individuals or 'warp' them. These two need not be mutually exclusive: individuals can be sustained and developed in warped beliefs. Symbolic politics should not be seen as empty gestures because they can have powerful effects. 'Build the wall and make Mexico pay for it' may not have been a realistic policy proposal, but Donald Trump was elected president of the United States. Performance also plays a deeper and more embedded role in what have been called 'international practices'. In this understanding, 'practices are socially meaningful patterns of action which, in being performed more or less competently, simultaneously embody, act out, and possibly reify background knowledge and discourse in and on the material world' (Adler and Pouliot, 2011: 6). These types of practice are central to the day-to-day work of the organizations that are the focus of this book. Fourth, migration governance repertoires are ongoing because they don't have a beginning and an end. This means that, through their actions and inactions, actors both shape and are shaped by the environment in which they operate while through interactions they learn more about their own identities and about their accounts of the world (Thurlow and Helms Mills, 2009a).

Repertoires contain ways of knowing, ways of deciding, and ways of acting or behaving that can 'stabilize' migration governance systems. Paul and Roos (2019) show, for example, how ideas about 'resilience' within the EU contained certain assumptions that, while questionable, became part of the EU's way of representing and responding to crisis with a consequent stabilizing effect. A result is that governance both as a set of practices and as the ideas that animate these practices can have 'political ordering effects' by establishing categories that structure the debate (Paul, 2019). Migration governance is replete with categories that can be normatively questionable but stabilize the field, at least from the perspective of elite policy actors.

Perceptions and their effects are central to the analysis that follows. There are seminal works in the study of international relations that explore the causes and effects of perceptions and misperceptions, most notably Jervis's (2017) study of US-Soviet relations during the Cold War. Jervis (2008: 294) also argued that 'to understand international behaviour we need to look inside the "black box" of the state, and indeed to study the goals, beliefs and perceptions of the decision-makers'. This book seeks to develop and apply this insight by opening the black box of international migration governance. The aim is to look not at the outputs or outcomes of governance systems but at the representations that shape actions. Actions emerge from distinct organizational contexts and the performance of roles, which means that they are 'embedded in an organizational context, repeated over time and space, constituted by knowledge about the exploitation of potential force, and articulated as part of a complex set of other social performances, which may require learning and training' (Adler and Pouliot, 2011: 7). Representations of migration—of its causes, its effects, and of risks and uncertainties associated with it—have powerful effects on what is done and not done. Organization has been understood as the mobilization of bias, which means that this book is about the causes and consequences of bias as it shapes and is shaped by representations of migration (Schattschneider, 1960). For an issue such as international migration, which is highly diverse and where facts and values combine in the shadow of uncertainty, it seems unlikely that perceptions are either wholly accurate or entirely inaccurate. It's also the case that a misperception or a partial perception if powerfully held—or held by the powerful—has powerful effects.

This book is not seeking to evaluate the veracity of perceptions but, rather, to identify their sources, their effects on the behaviour of the actors that hold these perceptions and their effects on other actors that are affected by them, particularly migrants. A central claim is that these perceptions can and do have powerful effects that can be labelled 'governance effects' that are themselves constitutive of international migration. What is meant by 'constitutive' is that (mis)perceptions, (mis)representations, and (mis)judgements of what is going on 'out there'—for example, of why people are migrating and the effects of migration—can shape or inform subsequent actions. Understood like this, international migration is not simply an exogenous shock to governance systems. It is manifestly the case that these self-same systems through their actions and inactions, inclusions and omissions, perceptions and misperceptions, representations and misrepresentations, and judgements and misjudgements play a powerful role in defining and shaping international migration.

The examples at the start of this chapter introduced in one way or another a regional lens, but Europe, North America, South America, and Southeast Asia are highly distinctive regions with very different types of regional structure. The four core questions addressed by this book can, however, be applied to all four regions, which, put straightforwardly, are: how do migration governance 'actors' of various types make sense of the challenges that they face? How do these representations then inform or shape subsequent actions? How do these then affect prospects for migration governance beyond the state? And how do these representations also affect migration itself through the categories, classifications, and associated practices that are developed? Nestled beneath these broader questions are the empirical issues of how these dynamics play out within different regions based on the assumption that context really matters and also that ubiquitous terms such as 'state', 'migration', and 'governance' can actually mean quite different things in these differing contexts.

The organization of migration governance

Migration governance is necessarily an organizational process. There are many and various organizations involved, but all are shaped by their environment and, through their actions, have effects on the environment in which they operate (Ansell et al., 2017b). While we have extensive knowledge of the outputs (laws, policies, and the like) of migration governance systems, we know less about the organizational characteristics of these processes. Yet much work on migration governance makes assumptions about these processes and has major organizational implications because it often points to evidence of policy failure understood as (usually) states not being able to attain their proclaimed policy objectives (Andersson, 2016; Castles, 2004; Lavenex, 2018). Scholars have identified a gap between what political leaders say and what they do (Hollifield et al., 2014), although, as we all know from our personal and professional lives, there can often be a gap between what we say and what we actually do, so perhaps we shouldn't be surprised by this. Scholars have identified a potentially serious implication of 'gaps' in migration governance because persistent gaps can mean sustained policy failure that would be a serious indictment of any organization and probably mean that its survival would be jeopardized. Similarly, sustained policy failure would seem to mean that key organizations fail to understand the environment in which they operate—they don't know what's going on or fundamentally misunderstand it.

This failure could also be reformulated: is there a failure to understand the environment or is the environment itself highly uncertain and unpredictable so that representations of the causes and effects of migration might be partial, suffused by values and beliefs, and, as a result, contested? Tetlock (2017) distinguishes between learning-friendly environments with shorter-term and more quantifiable outcomes compared to less learning-friendly environments where outcomes are much harder to quantify. International migration seems to correspond with a less learning-friendly environment: there is significant uncertainty, a low level of predictability, relatively high levels of risk, while values will shape how 'the facts' are viewed.

What could this mean for the kinds of expert judgement by actors in migration governance systems upon which this book focuses? Tetlock (2017) used Isaiah Berlin's prototypes of the fox and the hedgehog to argue that some decision-makers are like foxes in that they know many little things, draw from a more eclectic range of sources, and are better able to improvise. This doesn't mean they can predict the future, but that their predictive ability is better than hedgehogs who know one big thing and are inclined to 'toil devotedly within one tradition and reach for formulaic solutions to ill-defined problems' (p. 2). While, generally, when making predictions, Tetlock found that experts performed no better than non-experts; he also found that foxes tended to outperform hedgehogs. Strikingly, although perhaps not surprisingly, a dramatic, single-minded, combative hedgehog ideologue 'makes the best TV' when compared to the nuanced arguments of a fox (Tschoegl and Armstrong, 2008). The evidence in this book does at times seem to suggest tendencies to hedgehog-style thinking such as attachment to particular traditions, ways of thinking, or ways of doing things. This can, for example, be based on a representation of what has worked in the past, or at least didn't go too badly wrong, which is then used as a guide to the future. Or it could be the idea that migrants are 'pulled' towards major destination countries by labour market and social welfare effects, which, in turn, can lead to measures to deter such migrants. As later chapters show, both do form important parts of actually existing migration governance repertoires that centre on what actors know how to do and what they think they are expected to do that have narrative, social, affective, performative, and ongoing components.

Studying migration governance

The study of international migration in its many and various forms and of its governance tends to focus on two very broad questions. The first is: what are the causes and effects of international migration? The second is: what are the causes and effects of migration governance? This book's focus is squarely on this second question—and, more particularly, on forms of migration governance beyond the state. A core contention of this book is that, by addressing this second question, we can also understand more about the first. This is because migration governance as an organizational process plays a key role in constituting the migration issue by creating categories that include some people and groups while excluding others.

To address this second question means focusing on the role of organizations, because migration governance is necessarily an organizational process. As with all organizations, those involved in migration governance—and as we see in later chapters, there are many organizations involved—must address two basic questions: what's going on 'out there' and, having come up with some kind of answer to this first question, what should we do next? Put another way, migration governance understood as an organizational process means picking up and responding to cues and signals from the environment in which these organizations operate and then making sense along with other actors in order to decide upon a course of action. The book draws heavily from work on sense-making, which is an enactive account of cognition that takes as its starting point interactions between individuals and which is thus social (De Jaegher and Di Paolo, 2007; Weick, 1995). The point to take forward is that the meaning of international migration as a social and political issue is contingent on the operation and effects of governance systems, their ways of knowing, deciding, and acting. The categories and associated practices that emerge are governance effects that contribute to political ordering (Paul, 2019).

The standard definition of international migration tells us that it means movement from one state to another for a period of more than twelve months. This very broad definition encompasses a huge and diverse array of motives for migration, the main being for employment, to study, for family reasons, or to seek refuge, although each of these can be broken down into subcategories. But all of these are a result of decisions made largely in destination countries, although regional and international organizations also produce norms and standards. Around 3.5 per cent of the world's population are international migrants. Thought about like this, international migration is a rather unusual experience. But, thought about more widely, many of us will have family members that are migrants or whose family histories contain migration.

While there are important differences between migration labelled as 'voluntary', such as labour migration, and that which is involuntary or forced, such as asylum-seeking, this book includes them both under the broad heading of international migration. Putting them together could be seen as controversial at both a practical and an academic level because of the different factors that can motivate forced displacement compared to migration for work or family reasons that are assumed to be more voluntary, as well as the very different national and international legal frameworks that apply to both (Crawley and Skleparis, 2018; Feller, 2005; Long, 2013). The reason why this book prefers to keep them together is because of its contention that governance systems themselves, through their operation and effects, define, sustain, and change migration types. Introducing an *a priori* distinction between voluntary and forced migration does not mean that the important differences between them cannot be drawn out, but would hinder the capacity to show how the categories of voluntary and involuntary migration are contingent on the operation and effects of governance systems and that the boundaries can be contested. The status of asylum seekers or refugees is defined by international law, but has also been heavily contingent not only on how states interpret this framework, but also on how they operate systems of territorial and extraterritorial regulations and controls that can prevent people getting to the places where they could make a claim for asylum (FitzGerald, 2019). Categorizations such as labour migrant, asylum seeker, and family migrant are not inherent qualities or characteristics of individuals; they are classifications and categorizations that are heavily dependent on organizational processes. This is not to say that these categorizations are necessarily bad or wrong, but to note that they reflect decisions made by one group of people about others (Bowker and Leigh Star, 1999).

There is another distinction that also needs to be considered and that can also be thought of as a governance effect, which is the term 'mobility'. As we will see, regional organizations can seek to promote 'mobility' or 'free movement' for citizens of their member states (Geddes et al., 2019). Technically, international migration is a form of human mobility, namely, that part of it that involves crossing state borders, as opposed to internal migration within states. Mobility and free movement can still mean crossing state borders but have acquired a political meaning in certain regional groupings where there are efforts to promote greater mobility by citizens of its member states. This is most clearly evident in the EU where its own citizens (itself quite a significant development) have a legally enforceable right to free movement. In South America, the Common Market of the South (MERCOSUR) has established a Residence Agreement that does not create South American citizenship or provide a right to move freely but does create common rules governing residence for those that do move. In Southeast Asia and North America, there are much more minimal provisions. For the purpose of the analysis that follows, a distinction is made between migration and mobility that is primarily based on this more political representation of mobility as a (typically) facilitated regional process.

To sum up, migration governance as an organizational process can and does have powerful, constitutive effects that can change or constrain the behaviour of a wide range of public and private actors involved in migration governance, such as states, international organizations, regional organizations, civil society organizations, academic organizations, and think tanks as well as organizations representing the interest of business and workers. A key point is that to understand how this happens means thinking about the organizational logics that inform or shape their actions. At the risk of overloading with jargon, it is accurate to characterize migration governance as 'multi-organizational' and 'multilevel', but this book's purpose is not just to map this multiness or to count organizations, but to study how these shape actors' representations of the challenges they face and how these representations can affect action. This leads us to a second key focus for this book, which is forms of migration governance 'beyond the state', to which we now turn.

Beyond the state

Why study migration governance beyond the state? After all, it seems fairly clear that it is states that determine access to their territory and do so in ways that could at times seem relatively unencumbered by international or global rules and processes. We also know that there are many different types of states, with significant variation in their sovereign authority, modes of legitimation, and capacity. International migration is clearly an issue that cuts across state sovereignty, legitimacy, and capacity and demonstrates how states relate to each other as a result of migration processes. These can connect state actors at a transgovernmental level or non-state actors at a transnational level (Keohane and Nye, 1977). Transgovernmental processes operate at a state level and on the production of binding rules and other forms of cooperation such as capacity building. (Abbott et al., 2000). Transnational processes involve non-state actors and can centre on the social, economic, political, and cultural connections between the places migrants leave and the places they move to (Vertovec, 2009). While migration governance has become more transgovernmental and transnational, this doesn't mean that states and national governments are somehow written out of the equation; far from it. What it does mean is that there are forms of governance beyond the state that can in some circumstances bind states and other actors through the creation and enforcement of new rules and—more commonly—can seek to build capacity or change behaviour through persuasion (Betts, 2011).

The book also demonstrates that actually existing migration governance beyond the state often occurs at a regional level, but regional organizations come in many different forms. This book focuses in particular on four regional organizations: ASEAN, MERCOSUR, the EU, and the US-Mexico-Canada agreement or what used to be known as the North America Free Trade Area (NAFTA).

The regional level is emphasized because international migration is also regionalized. We may be distracted by the word 'international' to think that most migrants move long distances. In fact, migrants often move to neighbouring or nearby states rather than undertake lengthy and potentially expensive journeys. As Zolberg observed in 1989 when exploring the effects of the end of the Cold War on international migration:

> One might anticipate a regionalization of migration pressures from each 'south' to its particular 'north', determined not only by geographical proximity but also by political and economic linkages which contributed to the formation of migratory networks.   (Zolberg, 1989: 404–5)

There is major variation between the regions that are the focus for this book. Figures 1.1 and 1.3 uses data on the migration stock as a proportion of the population to show that migration in both South America and Southeast Asia

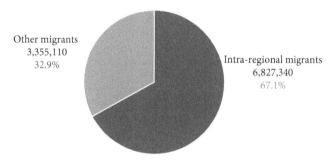

Figure 1.1 Intra-regional migrants in ASEAN, 2019
Source: UNDESA 2019.

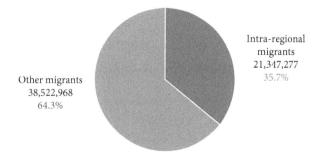

Figure 1.2 Intra-regional migrants in the EU, 2019
Source: UNDESA 2019.

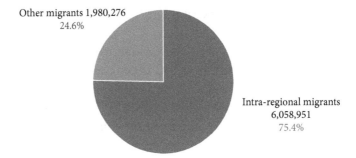

Figure 1.3 Intra-regional migrants in MERCOSUR, 2019
Source: UNDESA 2019.

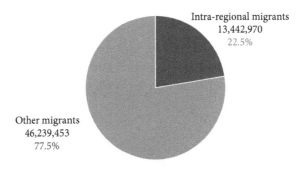

Figure 1.4 Intra-regional migrants in the ex-NAFTA region, 2019
Source: UNDESA 2019.

is strongly intra-regional. This is less the case in the EU and what was known as NAFTA, as shown in Figures 1.2 and 1.4, although, the EU has created a distinctive, comprehensive, and supranational framework to guarantee free movement rights to citizens of its member states (who are also EU citizens), while in North America, the US has been a major destination for global migration, but the largest group is from Mexico, and the regional dynamic has been a powerful shaper of responses.

A distinction between regionalization as a social process and regionalism as a more formal governance process is important because, as we see in the chapters that follow, migration itself may be regionalized, as it is in South America and Southeast Asia, but this does not necessarily mean that there is regional governance of migration. Regionalization captures the effects of proximity and interdependence in regional settings and how political, economic, social, and cultural linkages between states can become consolidated in migration networks that are not necessarily matched by formalized regional migration governance (Börzel and Risse, 2016). In Southeast Asia, Chapter 3 provides evidence of regionalized migration flows with a strong gendered component from that region's 'south' (i.e. poorer countries) to its 'north' (i.e. richer countries), but there are only very limited provisions for formalized regional migration governance. In North America, Chapter 6 shows a powerful regionalized effect linked to proximity, interdependence, and social, economic, and political connections, but there is no formal regional migration governance.

The regional level

A core argument made by this book is that it is more likely that global norms and standards are regionalized rather than regions becoming globalized. What is meant by this is that regions 'localize' global norms and standards by making them consistent with regional norms and standards (Acharya, 2004). The UN's Global Compact for Migration, agreed in December 2018, contains fifty-four references to the regional (including subregional and cross-regional) and recognizes the centrality of regional processes to attainment of migration governance beyond the state (United Nations, 2018).

The four regions analysed in this book (Europe, North America, South America, and Southeast Asia) provide significant variation in patterns and flows of regional and extra-regional migration flows, in the balance between relative openness and closure in migration policies and in the degree of interstate cooperation on migration. Focusing on the regional level also creates significant scope for analysis of variation in these migration effects and characteristics in countries and regions with higher and lower levels of economic growth, existing migration flows that have become embedded within migration networks, and experiences of intra- and interstate conflict and governance system breakdown, as well as demographic changes evident in population ageing in some countries and younger age profiles in others. The point of the analysis that follows in this book is not to map flows or to document policies, but to look at how these more objective structural factors are understood by actors in migration governance systems in these regions or, as put earlier, how facts are represented assuming that they are unlikely to possess a single, objective meaning.

Regions can be understood as political constructs that centre on and/or seek to promote social, political, economic, or organizational cohesiveness (Cantori and Spiegel, 1970). They are highly diverse in form, sit between the national and the global, are reflective of the multilevelling of international politics and of the multidimensional complexities of international governance. Typically, a regional organization is a grouping of states that are geographically proximate, leading to perceived common interests derived from location and associated interdependencies. They tend to seek broad-based cooperation on a range of issues, but particularly security, trade, and economic cooperation (Börzel and Risse, 2016; Katzenstein, 2015).

There are many different types of regional organizations, which, as Hurrell (2007: 241) observes, means 'the underlying distinctions matter greatly and much regionalist analysis is muddled precisely because commentators are seeking to explain very different phenomena or they are insufficiently clear about the relationship amongst the varied processes described under the banner of "regionalism"'. A reinvigoration of the study of regionalism after 1989 led to a focus on 'new regionalism' understood as an 'open' rather than protectionist regionalism and defined as 'the processes by which actors, public or private, engage in activities across state boundaries and develop conscious policies of integration with other states' (Gamble and Payne, 1996: 4). There have been waves of regionalism with varying levels of political commitment from member states as well as at time a profusion of regional organizations. In South America, for example, there has been reference to aplethora of regional organizations or 'spaghetti bowl' (Carranza, 2000; Margheritis, 2016; Riggirozzi and Tussie, 2012).

There are important differences in the form and scope of regional integration, but some convergence between regions has been identified in terms of border management and security. Andreas (1998: 591) identified a more complex and paradoxical dynamic at the boundaries between developed and less developed countries, where:

> the expansion of cross-border economic activity and the decline of geopolitical tensions are paralleled by a rapid expansion of border policing and rising tensions over prohibited cross-border flows. This is evident, most strikingly, along the United States-Mexico border and along the EU's external borders. These borders are increasingly protected and monitored, not to deter armies or impose tariffs on trade, but to confront a perceived invasion of 'undesirables', particularly illegal immigrants, drug traffickers, and other clandestine transnational actors.

To summarize, regions are central to migration governance beyond the state for three main reasons. First, they are a significant locus for action, albeit their actions on migration can take very diverse forms. Second, they mediate the relationship between the global and the national to the extent—as this book shows—that it is not regions that become globalized, but the global that becomes regionalized, i.e. rendered consistent with regional norms and standards. Third, regions themselves can be—and are—active producers of norms and standards related to various types of migration.

Actors in migration governance

As with the focus on migration governance 'beyond the state', a focus on 'actors' might also raise some eyebrows. After all, it seems fairly clear that international migration is driven by powerful structural factors. Two in particular stand out. The first and perhaps key motive for international migration is relative inequalities of income and wealth. The second key motive is the effects of conflict either within or between states. To label these economic and political factors as 'drivers' is overly simplistic because it's not always the case that a potential driver actually drives migration. It could be that economic change or conflict actually makes it more difficult for people to move, so that people are voluntarily or involuntarily immobile (Carling, 2002). Also, to identify a driver says nothing about the 'three Ds': the distance that migrants move, the direction of their movement, and the duration of the migration. The effects of economic and political change will also interact with other factors, including the role of connections within migration networks that can become consolidated over time and link places of origin and places of destination (Fussell, 2010; Loebach and Korinek, 2016; Massey et al., 1993). Demographic factors are likely to make a difference too, particularly the age structure and gender composition of a population. Finally, environmental change and the effects of the climate crisis can also affect migration. While this book does not focus specifically on climate change and migration, one point is worth emphasizing. As explained more fully in the next section, more than 400 interviews were done over a four-year period to support the analysis in this book. In each interview, respondents were asked to identify what they saw as the main causes of migration. Overwhelmingly, these were identified as economic and political, which is hardly surprising. We then asked if respondents thought these drivers might change in the future. Here, what was striking was that climate was often raised as a factor across all four regions, but, importantly, as one that was projected into the future. Our conclusion was that this actually told us something important about migration governance systems. This is that, while there is evidence that climate changes are currently shaping migration, there are reactive tendencies in migration governance systems—why do something *now*?—that push responses into the future.

These economic, political, social, demographic, and environmental factors are all clearly structural, and there can be no dispute that they will play a key role in shaping migration, but one key justification for the actor-centred perspective developed in this book has already been made. It is that migration governance is always, everywhere, and necessarily an organizational process. These organizations typically have a street address and the capacity to act. People working in these organizations will draw from their existing representations of migration and their own values (and those of their organization) to try to make sense of and respond to signals and cues from their environment and do so in way that helps to sustain the organization itself. This means that international migration in its various forms is interpreted by organizations in relation to their own cultures and their relationships with other organizations.

This leads to a second, linked justification, which is that there is significant uncertainty about the operation and effects of these potential migration drivers as well as the effects of interactions between them. It may be that migration data are incomplete, although it is not simply a matter of gathering more and better evidence, because there will be divergent beliefs and values that shape how data are understood and inform judgements. There will be also significant uncertainty now and in the future about the scale and effects of international migration as well as disputes about the social and political meaning of migration in its many and various forms that cannot be resolved by appeals to 'the facts', because the facts are contested. This means that actors of various types play a highly significant role in migration governance because they must respond to signals and cues from their environment and decide upon a course of action. As already noted, it could favour what Tetlock (2017) identified as the hedgehog, with his or her 'big idea', and give them a greater impact than foxes, which are keen to draw out all the nuances. Obviously, too, some actors are more powerful than others. Throughout this research, we will see the continued prominence of state actors, particularly national governments, but they are not the only actors, and the way they see things can change as a result of political change and also through interactions.

This focus on actors and their organizational settings should not be taken to mean that autonomy is ascribed to these organizations. Rather, they are 'situated actors' bound by their own organizational histories and cultures and by their relationships to other organizations (Bevir and Rhodes, 2010;

Eule et al., 2018). When these situated actors try to make sense of international migration, they draw from their own experiences either as individuals or within an organization and from their interactions with other individuals and organizations. As Bevir and Rhodes (2010: 432) put it, 'agency is possible, but it is always situated in a particular context'. Chapter 2 pays careful attention to these contexts, and the associated repertoires of migration governance and of what they make possible in terms of both actions and inaction.

How the research was done

The previous sections might suggest that the bar has been raised quite high: to develop an actor-centred perspective on migration governance in four world regions that would require access to these organizations and interviews with key actors within them. Responding to this challenge was enabled by support to this book's author from the European Research Council for a five-year project entitled Prospects for International Migration Governance (MIGPROSP) that ran between 2014 and 2019. During this research, 409 interviews were conducted during three phases of research with actors of various types in migration governance systems in twenty-four countries across the four regions, plus research with EU actors in Brussels and in international organizations located in Geneva and New York. In addition, considerable secondary information was gathered to support the analysis. This took the form of both primary and secondary material, including official documents and policy and position papers as well as the extensive academic literature. There was also a specific interest in events deemed or designated to be crises. These were seen as focusing events with potential powerful impacts on migration governance repertoires, although a key finding offered by this book is that it is representations of the normality of migration that play a key role in configuring responses to crises. During the course of the research, the MIGPROSP team also participated in a number of expert meetings on various aspects of migration governance. This does, of course, also highlight that the research team itself—as do many other academic researchers—formed part of the organizational field that was being studied.

The core of the research in terms of the approach and the guiding questions was the same for each region, but given the differing regional structures, there were some variations in practical application. The purpose of the analysis was not to develop country-level case studies, and it was also not possible to travel to every country that is a member of each of the four regional groupings, so selections were made in order to secure a sample that represented exposure to migration flows, centrality within the regional organization, and/or recent experience of migration law or policy development. Prior to the interviews, a media analysis was conducted at national level in the selected countries with two leading newspapers over a three-month period, with the aim of identifying prominent voices in the debate. This was done to ensure that representatives of organizations were interviewed that played a key role in shaping the migration policy field and thus avoiding biasing the selection of interview partners based on preconceptions held by the research team. That said, it is also the case that some of the main actors that are highly influential in shaping the field might not always be represented in the public debate, which meant that the research team also based the selection on previous academic literature and expert interviews with regional specialists in order to gather information on major actors. Interviewees were anonymous, with a commitment to maintain the confidentiality of the views that were expressed in the sense that no individuals can be identified. This means that throughout the book there is frequent reference to the interview material with information on the place of the interview and its date and the organizational location of the individual. Because, in some countries or institutions, there are not many people that deal with migration, the precise role is not specified in order to ensure participants' anonymity.

There was variation within regions in terms of the actor composition of the governance field, but organizations could be grouped into the following main types: state actors, primarily national governments and associated ministries and agencies; regional actors (and, in the EU, various organizational units within them); international organizations with specific migration responsibilities (such as the UNHCR or the International Organization for Migration, IOM) or with international migration as part of their responsibilities (such as the International Labour Organization, ILO); business organizations; trade unions; other civil society organizations such as groups representing migrants or promoting migrants' rights; and academic researchers and think tanks.

Two waves of interviews were conducted, allowing follow-up interviews with actors interviewed during the first wave, or with representatives of the same organization if the interviewee from the first wave was not available. In the first wave, during which 302 interviews were conducted the questions focused on the following themes:

- incidents or events that affected the interviewees own representation of migration;
- representations of the causes and effects of migration;

- representations of whether these causes and effects were likely to change in the future;
- representation of key risks and uncertainties associated with international migration and strategies to deal with them (as defined);
- sources of knowledge and information about international migration;
- key organizations with which the interviewee interacted and the perceived value of the interaction.

The research was influenced by the absence or presence of formal regional structures. In North America, for example, interviews were conducted at state level in Canada, Mexico, and the United States, but there was only a very limited NAFTA Secretariat comprising member state delegations and focused on dispute resolution (a feature maintained in NAFTA's successor organization; see Chapter 6). In Europe, by contrast, interviews were conducted in twelve EU member states (Austria, the Czech Republic, Denmark, Germany, Ireland, Italy, Malta, the Netherlands, Poland, Sweden, Spain, and the UK), plus extensive interviews at EU level with the main EU institutions (Commission, Parliament, and Council) and the delegations in Brussels of key member states. In Southeast Asia, there were interviews at the ASEAN Secretariat in Jakarta, plus fieldwork in Indonesia, Thailand, and the Philippines. For the Southeast Asian work, interviews were also done in Australia, given its strong presence in the Southeast Asian region. In South America, there is a small MERCOSUR bureaucracy, while interviews were also conducted in Argentina, Brazil, Chile, Colombia, Ecuador, and Peru. Interviews were conducted in the interviewees' first language where possible, although this was not always feasible. Interview data were, however, gathered in English, German, Italian, Portuguese, and Spanish. Documentary material was also gathered in those languages.

The second wave of 107 interviews was more focused on the perceived effects of specific representations and interventions. There were differences in the specific questions between countries and regions, but the interview would focus on an interviewee's evaluation of a specific action or intervention: what was the thinking behind the response? How effective was the response judged to be? We also asked whether specific events, such as a conference, seminar, or other form of interaction or something that the interviewee had read or seen had also shaped or perhaps even changed their perspective.

The final, third phase of the research centred on validation workshops with smaller groups of twelve to fifteen actors that had previously been interviewed during the research. At these validation workshops, a facilitated conversation was held between members of the project team and small subgroups of four or five participants, with the aim of validating key project findings. In practical terms this meant returning to key project themes: representations of the causes and effects of migration; the management of risks and uncertainties; and the circulation of knowledge and ideas.

Common to all three phases was our intention not to simply ask people to describe to us the latest policy initiative or new legal framework. We could gather this information separately from other sources. We wanted to learn more about the causes and consequences of knowledge and know-how; the impacts of expectations about role; and how the cognitive processes and the biases inherent within them can affect the capacity for migration governance systems to adapt or not.

Organization of the book

Some of the parameters of the book's framework having been established, its basic organizational structure can now also be introduced. Chapter 2 develops the conceptual framework more fully, particularly the idea of migration governance repertoires. The aim here is to develop the core insight into migration governance as an organizational process by discussing the ways in which a better understanding of know-how and of expectations about role can allow the opening of the migration governance 'black box' and to understand more about what 'drives' governance. This is then followed by four chapters that explore regional dynamics in very different regions. Chapter 3 looks at Southeast Asia and at two key regional groupings with major implications for migration governance: ASEAN and the Bali process. The chapter shows that a representation of the normality of migration that centres on its supposed 'temporariness' is a central, structuring component of the migration governance repertoire. Chapter 4 analyses developments in South America with a particular focus on the MERCOSUR grouping and what has been seen as its noticeably progressive approach to migration. A distinction is made between de facto and *de jure* openness, which, in turn, are shown to be closely related to underlying conditions of governance. Chapter 5 assesses the European regional context and the EU's role as a highly developed regional framework guaranteeing free movement rights to citizens of its member states as well as developing competencies for aspects of migration and asylum. It is shown that a migration governance repertoire in Europe is shaped by concern about the potential for large-scale and potentially uncontrollable flows. Again, as in other regions, the intention is not to evaluate whether these concerns are justified, but to show how they can be understood as a governance effect. Chapter 6 analyses development in North America, where formal regional governance structures are weak, but regional effects are strong and stretch also into Central America. In ways that are similar to developments in Europe, the idea of large-scale flows and the need to deter them has become a central component of the migration governance repertoire and that strict enforcement with a strong security focus predated not only the Trump administration but also the 9/11 terror attacks. Chapter 7 extends the analysis to the global level to explore the prospects for global migration governance. Consistent with influential work on global migration governance, it is shown that the key element of a global framework is the effect on the behaviour of participating actors, including states. There are global processes, but their effects vary. While the creation of rules is relatively rare, it is quite common to see attempts to build capacity or to try to persuade states and other actors to change the way that they behave. While the global migration governance repertoire tends to focus on elite-driven cooperation, it is also shown that the idea and practice of globalization and of 'the global' are increasingly contested in ways that question functionalist accounts (Triandafyllidou, 2018). A concluding chapter (Chapter 8) then synthesizes key findings and considers their implications for both research and practice.

2

Repertoires of Migration Governance

Introduction

This chapter specifies the idea of *migration governance repertoires* within which migration governance understood as an organizational process requires actors of various types to organize their experiences both of migration and of the wider environment within which they operate. The organization of these experiences shapes actions on migration. The chapter outlines the core concepts and ideas, but to avoid becoming too abstract also uses some of the empirical material derived from some of the more than 400 interviews that were done during the research for this book. This helps to illustrate the practical application and relevance of repertoires of migration governance beyond the state and to prefigure the more detailed focus on migration governance in Southeast Asia (Chapter 3), South America (Chapter 4), Europe (Chapter 5), North America (Chapter 6), and global migration governance (Chapter 7) that follow. As with all quotes used in this book, the purpose is not to evaluate the veracity of representations, but to use them as examples of how actors in migration governance systems try to make sense of what's going on 'out there' and about what they think they should do next. As a further point of clarification, the aim is neither to add to existing studies of the 'gaps' that can emerge between decision-making and implementation nor to assess migration policies in terms of, for example, the effects of policies on flows or the extent of convergence. There are already important studies that do this (Boucher and Gest, 2018; Helbling and Leblang, 2019; Hollifield et al., 2014). Instead, the aim is to open the 'black box' of governance to address some prior questions about what actors know how to do and what they think they should be doing. This should not be taken to mean that migration is understood in this analysis as just something that happens in peoples' imaginations as opposed to the more observable outcomes of these processes. Clearly, there are powerful economic, social, political, demographic, and environmental factors that shape and can drive international migration. The point is that the operation and effects of these potential drivers are uncertain and require interpretation

Governing Migration Beyond the State: Europe, North America, South America, and Southeast Asia in a Global Context.
Andrew Geddes, Oxford University Press (2021). © Andrew Geddes. DOI: 10.1093/oso/9780198842750.003.0002

and representation by governance actors in organizational settings, which is where questions about know-how and expectations fit in.

As was made clear in the Chapter 1, whether subnational, national, or international, migration governance is always and everywhere an organizational process. While the focus for this book is on migration governance beyond the state, it would be mistaken to understand these various levels in morphological terms as though they were separate and distinct from each other. There are actually and not surprisingly intense connections across levels: migration governance beyond the state is also a forum for responding to issues that resonate at local and national levels too. This avoids artificially imposed distinctions between the various levels as though they can be neatly distinguished from each other.

To analyse migration governance requires understanding how, as a structure, process, and set of ideas, migration governance is constituted. This constitution of migration governance is necessarily linked to the representations held by actors within these systems of the causes and effects of international migration. Changes in underlying economic, political, social, demographic, and environmental systems as well as interactions between them can cause people to migrate, but these changes and their effects are complex and uncertain. This means that interpretations and representations of the consequences of the effects of change in these systems become central to migration governance and to the associated repertoires.

We now look more carefully at the idea of a migration governance repertoire. For an account to be developed that analyses the effects of interpretations and representations means going beyond a focus on the outputs and outcomes of governance processes, or *what actors do*. This is, of course, important, but a shortcoming of focusing only on what actors do—on the more visible outputs or outcomes of governance systems—is that this tells us relatively little about the organizational processes that produce these outputs and outcomes. To build upon these contributions and to look more closely at these organizational processes it is necessary to also think about two other characteristics of migration governance:

- What is it that actors in migration governance systems *know how to do*? What is meant by this is the ways in which experiences, facts, information, data, and evidence influenced by values and beliefs can coalesce through interactions with other people and organizations into knowledge of, about, for, or against international migration. This emphasizes cognitive and social dimensions of migration governance.

- What do these actors *think they should be doing*? What is meant by this is how these actors understand, interpret, and represent cues and signals from their environment. These cues and signals will interact with existing beliefs and values embedded in organizational settings to steer perceptions of the issues. Signals and cues include knowledge of, about, for, or against international migration, but also about other wider social expectations about role that may, for example, be linked to representations of public attitudes to migration or to struggles for resources and attention with other organizations not dealing with migration. Expectations about role do involve knowledge claims and social interactions but can be affective, performative, and ongoing.

The word 'governance' has loomed quite large over the analysis so far. The chapter's second substantive section puts in place some foundations for the idea of a migration governance repertoire by saying more about what is actually meant by the term governance by drawing from what Pierre (2000) called its 'dual meaning': the conceptual representation of change in underlying systems and efforts to manage or steer the effects of these changes. Or, put more colloquially, 'What's going on "out there?"' and 'What should we do next?' Deciding what to do depends on understanding what's happening. Links between reasoning and actions—and justifications for those actions—are integral to the operation and effects of governance systems. When we turn our attention to migration governance more specifically, there is clearly a high level of uncertainty about the causes and effects of international migration both now and in the future. This means that it is important to focus not only on the more practical and observable manifestations of governance, but also on the interpretive settings within which actors make sense of migration and of the context in which they operate. To label these as interpretive settings is a deliberate choice of words. Trying to make sense of what is going on 'out there' is not a precise science. This does not mean that ignorance prevails; far from it. The actors that we focus on this book are often highly experienced and well informed about international migration in its various forms; but, being experienced and well informed can also mean understanding the degree of uncertainty and risk attached to decisions. This can also induce a reluctance to act, because extensive research shows the allure of the status quo (Kahneman et al., 1991; Samuelson and Zeckhauser, 1988).

After looking more closely at the concept of governance, the chapter's third section develops the idea of a migration governance repertoire by asking five intuitively expressed questions that confront actors in 'everyday' migration governance systems and to suggest some of the ways that these actors may then go about trying to address these questions. The questions are:

- 'How can we figure out what's going on 'out there'?
- 'Why do something when we don't know what effect it will have?'
- 'How can we choose our priorities?'
- 'Who are all these people at this meeting?'
- 'Does that make sense to us?'

Asking these questions in these more intuitive ways allows the analysis to draw out conceptual themes but also to relate them to actors' know-how and expectations about role and to the narrative, social, affective, performative, and ongoing components of migration governance repertoires.

Finally, the chapter also considers how well ideas about governance travel beyond Europe and considers the risks of Eurocentric analysis that could be particularly relevant when European regional integration is highly developed but is far from being a template that is followed in other regions (Acharya, 2012; Lombaerde et al., 2010; Sbragia, 2008). We also see that regions are less commonly vehicles for the diffusion of global standards than they are mechanisms for what Acharya (2004) calls 'localisation' so that 'the global' is rendered consistent with regional norms and standards that could suggest that 'governance' acquires different meanings.

Migration governance repertoires

A very basic question that informs this book's analysis is what migration governance actors of various types in Europe, North America, South America, and Southeast Asia think that they are doing, but it is plausible that there could be significant variations within and between regions in answers to this question. This could include variations in representations of the causes and effects of international migration, as well as in views about whether and how these could change. A further element of variation is in how these actors view the key risks and uncertainties associated with international migration and in how their organizations try to deal with these risks and uncertainties, as understood, and then try to decide what to do next. A wider contextual difference is very likely to be the very different social, economic, and political situations in which these questions are addressed, as well as the role that the regional and other forms of international cooperation might play.

The study of migration governance does tend to have a strong applied focus on specific practical issues and problems, which also often brings with it attempts to address or evaluate the strengths or shortcomings of particular policy approaches. This also means that much research on migration governance focuses on observable results, which mean the outputs or outcomes of these processes such as the various laws, policies, approaches, and practices that, taken together, tend to be understood as migration governance. This book changes the analytical focus by recognizing that while these outputs and outcomes are obviously important, studying them is a necessary but not sufficient way of accounting for migration governance. It is necessary because these various kinds of outputs have hugely important effects on migrants, the places they move from, the places they move to, and various points along their journeys. It is insufficient because it says less about the factors that motivated and shaped the decisions made by various kinds of 'actor' within governance systems. To understand why this is the case means making a more basic methodological observation. To understand the outcome of a process requires analysis of the process itself rather than trying to concoct an *ex post* assessment of what might have been happening from only observing the outcome. It is, of course, difficult to access those who make or shape policy, and it could be that motivations can remain hidden or obscured, but this does not seem like a valid reason to not even try to find out more about motivations, aspirations, and goals. This requires asking questions of these actors about the prevailing representations that informed choices, decisions, and actions; the sources of information on which these were based; the effects of limits on time, information, and the available resources that affected representations and actions; and whether decisions or actions were based on particular representations of the causes and effects of migration that may or may not be accurate, but that do have important effects on outcomes. It could, also be that these representations are shaped by longer-standing institutional logics or the approaches that have typically been pursued in the past by particular organizations.

To capture more fully these dynamics of migration governance, this chapter adapts the idea of a 'repertoire' from the sociologist Charles Tilly, whose work extensively documented the dynamics of political mobilization and protest. Tilly (1986: 4) understood a 'repertoire' as being the ways in which individuals or groups make claims of different kinds on other individuals or groups. There has been reference in work on international migration to the importance of repertoires, but this has been in the context of decisions to migrate. Massey et al., (1993: 452) wrote about the ways in which at community-level migration can become deeply ingrained in the repertoire of people's behaviour, with the result that values associated with migration can become part of a community's values. Faist (2000: 196) discusses how transnational communities formed by international migration 'develop a common repertoire of symbolic and collective representations'. In some ways, the meaning of a repertoire for migrants is analogous to its meaning in migration governance processes, because values, symbols, and representations associated with certain representations of international migration clearly also form part of the identity of communities of governance actors too.

An advantage of thinking about repertoires of migration governance is the potential to broaden analysis beyond the observable outputs or outcomes of governance processes to also account for what people know how to do and what they are expected to do. Actions are necessarily shaped by cognitive processes and cognitive biases concerning the nature of the problem, as well as by social expectations about what should or could be done. Actions, cognition, and expectations all share important things in common: in particular, they are formed through social interactions and they arise 'from within a culturally sanctioned and empirically limited set of options' (Tilly, 1978: 151). There is not a blank canvas upon which actors develop their responses to particular issues or challenges. We see, for example, that there have been fairly frequent associations between migration and crisis, but we also see in all four regions that responses to crisis tend to draw from established patterns of responses and actions. When confronted with a new challenge or even a crisis, actors in migration governance systems are likely to ask themselves 'What is this problem like?' or 'Do I have experience of a similar problem or challenge?' The availability of examples—of what comes to mind, of what seems comparable, or lessons from the experiences of others—can have a powerful effect on subsequent actions. The response may prove to be appropriate or effective, but could also be an example of an 'availability heuristic', which means that a judgement about a seemingly novel challenge is configured by previous experiences and expectations that can provide shortcuts for decision-makers (Tversky and Kahneman, 1973). The influence of past experiences means that migration governance repertoires are likely to change only very slowly, if at all. As this book documents throughout the chapters that follow, it is representations of the normality of migration grounded in experience that define responses to 'migration crises', rather than the other way around.

The meaning of migration governance

This section specifies how governance systems play key roles in constituting international migration. This is an observation that is fundamental to the analysis that follows, because migration governance repertoires mobilize knowledge and resources in ways that try to make sense of complex social phenomena. There is a wider methodological point here too, which relates to what is 'dependent' and 'independent' in this analysis. Generally, the analysis in this book tends to see international migration as strongly dependent on governance processes rather than as a phenomenon to which these systems must respond. Put another way, international migration is not something that simply happens to these governance systems because, as will be shown, governance systems themselves through their actions and inactions over time have played and will continue to play a key role in defining international migration in its various forms as social and political issues. Put like this, migration governance can be understood as a response to changes in underlying social and natural systems that can cause international migration; or, put more intuitively, international migration happens because other things change. These can be changes in material circumstances at household level that generate the relative inequalities of income and wealth that can cause some people to migrate (Mincer, 1978). It could be the effects of conflict within or between states that displace people across state boundaries (FitzGerald, 2019). As a practical example, the so-called 'migration crisis' in Europe after 2015 was strongly linked to previous and ongoing European and EU governance interventions not only in migration policy, but in other associated areas such as security and development (Andersson, 2014; Kingsley, 2016). A key point is that while changes in economic and political systems can cause people to migrate, there is significant uncertainty about the effects of these drivers on decisions to migrate, on who moves, the motives for migration, and the direction, distance, and duration of this movement. This is why the representation of what's going on 'out there' is so important to migration governance.

By definition, international migration becomes visible at state borders, whether these be territorial (air, land, and sea ports), organizational (such as labour markets and systems for social protection), or conceptual (boundaries of belonging and identity) (Geddes, 2005). The resultant classifications and categorizations at these various kinds of borders are a result of governance processes and play a key role in defining international migration and delineating between migration types. Governance systems organize international migration and, by doing so, can organize 'in' some types of migration and organize 'out' others. Clearly, migration governance is not some neutral and largely technical process; it is intensely political, because it defines the terms on which migrant newcomers can enter the territory of another state and make claims upon it as well as the measures that can be used both to facilitate and prevent migration. This book was concluded at the time of the global Covid-19 health emergency when massively constrained mobility was the reality for many: by the end of 2020, 93 per cent of the world's population lived in countries that had imposed travel restrictions while 39 per cent lived in countries that had closed their borders (Pew Research Center, 2020). While closing borders was a crisis response, the crisis also showed the centrality of migrants to key economic activities such as the provision of care and food. Other migrants faced terrible conditions in detention or camps where their health needs were neglected with fatal consequences for some. While it is not possible at the time of writing to predict the effects of the Covid-19 crisis on migration and mobility, the arguments put forward in this book would suggest that, rather than induce a step change in response or paradigm shift, responses are likely to be consistent with established ways of doing things. For instance, closing borders on the scale that occurred at the height of the health emergency was dramatic, but built on a pre-existing trend to strengthen and reinforce border controls, walls, and fences that existed prior to the crisis. At the same time, the crisis did also provoke a wider awareness of the economic centrality of many migrant workers and led to a rethink both of what counted as a 'key' occupation and perhaps too of labour migration policies, although that remains a more open question.

The term governance is much used, although often with more attention paid to the adjectives attached to it ('multilevel', 'experimental', 'regulatory', 'pluricentric', 'networked', 'deliberative', to name six) than to the meaning of the term itself. Governance is generally seen as 'a signifier of change', which could mean change in the meaning, processes, conditions, or methods of governing (Levi-Faur, 2012). Peters (2012: 19–22) recognizes the 'ambiguity' of the concept before noting that 'successful governance' has four functional requirements: goal selection with these integrated across all the levels of the system; goal reconciliation and coordination to establish priorities; implementation; and feedback and accountability as organizations must attempt to learn from their actions, although whether the appropriate lessons are learned is a different question.

Underlying goal selection and learning are what was referred to earlier as the conceptual representations of change in underlying systems. These representations involve cognition, social interaction that can promote learning as well as expectations about role. To understand repertoires of migration governance means knowing more about how the causes and effects of international migration are understood, interpreted, contested, and then articulated in action and practices in specific organizational settings. To provide an example, this quote from a representative of a US NGO who had previously worked in the US Department of Homeland Security is a good example of a reflection on the organizational setting in the US federal government:

> it's pretty clear to me that the way the US government works, and I think it doesn't matter who's in charge, when the White House decides that something is a priority it becomes a priority and agencies scramble, offices scramble, people all try to provide the answers that they want, but of course they want the answers yesterday or a week ago...So one of the things that I've been telling people right now is that we have to actually plan now to determine what kinds of programmes and what kinds of approaches are successful that could be offered up immediately or at a time when the White House says, 'Boy, we want to do more on immigration, what should we do?' or, 'We've got a new flood of immigrants coming through, how are we possibly going to manage it and do better than we did last time?' What that shows me is that, at least in the immigration sphere so far, government isn't very good at listening to the agencies and the academics and the thinktanks and all of that about what works and what doesn't work.
>
> (Representative of NGO, Washington DC, September 2018)

As with all quotes in this book, the point here is not to assess whether this view is accurate or not, but to illustrate how this organization of experience can be understood as a 'frame', which is a 'schemata of interpretation...to locate, perceive, identify, and label' (Goffman, 1974: 21). These frames are then used to 'organize experience and guide action' (Benford and Snow, 2000: 614). Framing is 'an active, processual phenomenon that implies agency and contention at the level of reality construction. It is active in the sense that something is being done and processual in the sense of a dynamic, evolving process' (Benford and Snow, 2000: 614). The quote above from the former US government official contains components of a migration frame that are both diagnostic (What is the issue? Is it changing?) and prognostic (What can or cannot be done?).

When analysing the causes and consequences of frames, the variable of interest is an individual's judgements and the ordering of a set of objectives and alternatives (Druckman, 2011: 280). A key insight from prospect theory concerns the importance of what are called 'judgement heuristics' or, put more intuitively, shortcuts in the framing process. The effect of these heuristics or shortcuts is that individuals might reach for an historical analogy, whether it is appropriate or not, when trying to make sense of contemporary dilemmas. As we see later, this might mean thinking about something that was seen to have worked in the past, whether or not it is appropriate to the current situation. They may also be swayed by what they have read in a newspaper or seen on TV. More specifically, a *representativeness* bias assumes the probability that an object or event belongs to a particular category is based on their similarity rather than the statistical likelihood of such an event occurring. An example here would be the use of historical analogy, whether or not appropriate. An *availability* bias judges the frequency of events on the basis of their availability in the memory and can be dependent on the prominence given to an issue by media coverage. An *anchoring* bias occurs when judgements are made based on uncertain data. Research by social psychologists on attitudes to international migration, has shown that the 'anchor' can influence 'judgements about immigration such as estimation of probability or amounts of immigration, negotiation with migrant newcomers, legal judgements and general knowledge' (Navarro and Arechavaleta, 2010: 254).

Benford and Snow (2000) identify two ways in which frames get made. The first is discursive and centred on talk, conversations, and written communications. As will be seen in the chapters that follow, the way that actors frame and make sense of international migration is strongly influenced by the social context within which they operate. Knowledge of, about, for, and against international migration is social. The second way that frames are made is strategic, goal-oriented, and includes building support for a view or course of action. The context for this is also social, as actors are likely to search for 'like-minded' colleagues within their own governments or other governments or with organizations within or outside their own country. The migration governance field has become more densely populated, which means that the frames that underpin migration governance repertoires develop in multi-organizational settings. In turn, this also means that they are subject to power relations and associated inequalities, with the obvious effect that some actors and their representations are more powerful than others. This can also lead to circuits of like-mindedness with confirmation bias, or what Heffernan (2011) calls 'wilful blindness'.

To illustrate the discursive, strategic, and motivational components of frames we can consider ways in which the idea of 'normality' in migration governance is defined by key actors. This is an important point in relation to this book's core argument about the importance of representations of the normality of international migration—as opposed to crises—in defining international migration as a social and political issue in Europe, North America, South America, and Southeast Asia. This is an example from Europe that also resonates in North America. At the end of 2014, an interviewee from an EU agency was asked to reflect on the causes and effects of migration and identified important future challenges, which were described as follows:

> Yesterday at this meeting of the US and the Commission and others... [they] were repeatedly mentioning that this will be the new normal. These 250,000–280,000 irregular migrants a year, that's basically what we have to count on in the foreseeable future. Nothing will change in this regard. I tend to agree, because as long as things are going the way they are going on in North Africa, sub-Saharan African countries, Afghanistan, Iraq, what have you, I don't see an end unfortunately to that.
>
> (EU agency official, Brussels, December 2014)

Whether accurate or not, this view is based on a representation of the effects on migration of changes in the underlying drivers of migration; in this case, the effects of conflict. It can provide an anchor against which assessments or judgements are made. The view was shaped by interactions with others, in this case with US officials. These changes are seen as likely to lead to persistently high migratory pressure that is called a 'new normal', although, as Chapter 6 shows, this is actually very similar to an 'old normal', which means long-standing concerns in Europe (and North America) about the potential for large and potentially uncontrollable migration flows. Whether this is understood as being an 'old' or a 'new' challenge, the key word is 'normal', representations of the normality of migration and the way these shape judgements and assessments of the causes and effects of migration. Interestingly, in terms of the use of language, the European Commission in June 2016 proposed a new framework for working in partnership on migration with non-EU countries and also used the phrase 'new normal' with reference to potential migration pressures. The Commission made a clear link between the framing of the issue (as external migratory pressure) and a set of proposed remedies:

> External migratory pressure is the 'new normal' both for the EU and for partner countries. This requires a more coordinated, systematic and structured

approach to maximise the synergies and leverages of the Union's internal and external policies. To succeed, it needs to reflect both the EU's interests and the interests of our partners, with clear objectives and a clear way forward on how the objectives will be achieved, in terms of positive cooperation where possible but also the use of leverage where necessary. Such an approach will be translated into compacts which will be embedded within the existing and future processes and partnership.   (CEC, 2016: 5)

The two quotes above develop a representation that is diagnostic (the problem of external migratory pressures), prognostic (the need for closer relations with non-EU states), and then also puts forward a motivational argument (the need to build relations between the EU and third countries about migration and other linked issues such as trade, aid, and development). They provide a good example of the roles played by know-how and expectations about role as drivers of migration governance in that they involve attempts to conceptualize the operation and effects of underlying social systems and then to think through their implications for action. In the case just cited, they also centre on this idea of what is 'normal' about international migration, as well as challenges to normality, as it is understood. To show how such views aren't only evident in Europe, a US Congressional staff member put it to us as follows:

> I was talking to some folks the other day. They think the new normal, if you will, of illegal migration is somewhere in the 400,000 range.
>   (Staff member of US congressional representative, June 2015)

This reference to 'talking to some folks' is important because it reiterates the importance of the social context within which representations develop and that can also help to render plausible such representations. Again, the point of using these quotes is not to assess whether or not these views are accurate, but to identify a prevailing representation that influences what actors know how to do and what they think they should be doing. It's also clearly the case that such views expressed by key actors within the EU and US systems, while contested, do have powerful effects.

A further example can be used, although here the representation of normality is rather different and is used by an Argentinian government official to refer to how 'normal people' make sense of the causes and effects of migration. Perceptions of perceptions also shape know-how and expectations about role:

If you talk with normal citizens, there are so many that say, 'We have to stop, we have to first give employment to our people.' You know, it's quite normal in a country which has economic problems. Usually, when you have economic problems, you are looking to see where is the cause of this, and sometimes immigration, it's easy to see immigration as part of the problem. I'm not saying that's objective, it's subjective, but it's part of the perception. I think it's part of the perception.

(Argentinian government official, Buenos Aires, July 2017)

Such representations of normality are based on understandings and representations of the causes and effects of migration. Such representations are important because they organize experiences and shape the context for action. They are also shaped by uncertainty and risk. In many of our conversations with actors in migration governance, reference was made to representations of political risk. A representative of a migration think tank that works closely with European governments put it to us like this when referring to how, in her experience, governments make sense of risk:

That is what's really frightening. You see it in lots of different places. A civil servant will have a different understanding of risk because he has to manage the long-term prospects of an immigration system with a political leadership that's placing pressure to move that line. You have politicians who are terrified that the next move they make is going to see them out of office. Home secretaries have typically been the most fragile, death sentence position.

(Representative of think tank, Brussels, November 2015)

Highlighting the 'internalization' of risk by national governments and resultant behaviour, a European Commission official put it this way:

member states have a different view on this [risk]. They see mainly the risk to their national administrations, so what they bring to the table is very practical. They want to make sure that the system is workable, and then they have some political priorities as well.

(European Commission official, Brussels, December 2014)

Concern about risk has led, within modern governance systems, to a greater use of expert knowledge and quantification in the process of governing (Fisher, 2010). That said, precise quantification of the scale of migration is difficult to generate. There can be fairly clear ideas about, for example, the numbers of asylum seekers because they make themselves observable by making an asylum application. There is much higher uncertainty about the number of irregular migrants. There are also major difficulties projecting into the future and predicting migration flows. This is precisely why representations of what is happening now are likely to have important effects in structuring responses to future migration. In his influential work on sense-making in organizations, which is looked at more closely below in the section 'Does that make sense to us?', Karl Weick (1995: 11) points to the importance of prior representations as the basis upon which approaches to ostensibly new challenges develop, because 'human situations are progressively clarified, but this clarification often works in reverse...an outcome fulfils some prior definition of the situation'.

Sharing information and knowledge exemplifies the social settings within which experience is organized. For example, an Australian government official told us about the circulation of knowledge and ideas within relatively small groups of 'like-minded' states where trust is strong:

> the experience that Australia had was one that we shared in common with New Zealand and Canada. Then, to a significantly lesser extent with the UK, and then even further behind the US. The Anglo countries would caucus a bit at OECD meetings. Then, interesting variations across Europe. The big challenge in the EU countries was that they were dealing with a cohort of migrants that was vastly different to what we were dealing with: primarily humanitarian or refugees.
>
> (Australian government official, Canberra, October 2015)

To summarize, this section has attempted to specify more clearly what is meant by governance and how an understanding of its 'dual meaning' can help to broaden the focus beyond the outputs and outcomes of governance processes to also account for what actors know how to do and what they think they should be doing.

The chapter now moves on to say more about the five intuitively expressed questions identified earlier that confront actors in migration governance systems in all four of the regions assessed by this book.

How can we figure out what's going on out there?

Migration governance is relational; it is about picking up and responding to signals and cues from the environment within which organizations operate. This is a relational process in the sense that signals and cues are used by individuals and organizations to develop an understanding of the challenges that they face and then try to figure out what they should do next. Figuring things out and making interventions mean that organizations also shape their environment.

These signals emerge from a complex environment from which the demands may be inconsistent or even contradictory. In such a situation, the choices that are made and the solutions that are proposed do not emerge fully formed from the environment based on indisputable facts, which is why framing is so important. As Schön (1983: 40) put it, practitioners recognize that, while defining the issue or problem is a necessary condition for technical problem-solving, this definitional process is not only a technical problem. He goes on to note:

> When we set the problems, when we select what we will treat as the 'things' of the situation, we set the boundaries of our attention to it, and we impose upon it a coherence which allows us to say what is wrong and in what directions the situation needs to be changed. This means that problem setting is a process in which, interactively, the things that will be the focus for attention are defined which then shapes the ways in which they will be attended too.

If, for example, international migration is seen as being driven by powerful pull factors such as good job prospects or generous social protection in destination countries, then responses could develop that seek to deter such movement. This is, in fact, quite a powerful and prevalent representation in Europe and North America. The Austrian foreign minister Sebastian Kurz in March 2016 spoke about the large number of migrants making Mediterranean sea crossings to European countries, particularly Greece, in 2015 and 2016:

> These people don't come to Europe because they want to live on Lesbos. They come here because they want to enjoy the living standards and benefits they are guaranteed in countries like Austria, Germany and Sweden...Don't get me wrong, I don't blame these people; I can understand them, because many politicians have triggered false hopes.   (Oltermann, 2016)

Kurz was identifying a pull factor. Whether accurate or not, this representation based on the interpretation of signals and cues has powerful effects on know-how, on expectations about role, and on what is done.

Unsurprisingly, our extensive interview material demonstrates very clearly that there is general agreement that the environment 'out there' is complex, with different forms and types of migration, varying types of response to these different migration types and significant differences between national- and regional-level responses. But just saying that something is complex is unlikely to be an effective strategy, because political systems constantly generate a demand for action or at least being seen to do something even if it is largely symbolic. That said, as already noted, symbolic politics is not an empty gesture because it can have powerful effects. This demand for action is particularly acute if an issue is high on the political agenda. For governance organizations, being seen to fail is serious, because it undermines that organization's credibility and, ultimately, its ability to sustain itself. It could even provoke a legitimacy crisis for the wider institutional system. Research on policy failure sees it as involving what has been called 'a degeneration of policy learning' (Dunlop, 2017: 20). This can involve whether or not actors in governance systems update their beliefs, but also the raw material on which these beliefs are based that can provide particular representations of what the issues are and similarly what the range of possible actions could be.

In the academic literature, there is a fairly widespread view that migration policies fail to achieve their objectives. For Castles (2004), decision-makers may not understand the phenomena with which they are dealing, can be poor at absorbing research evidence into decision-making, and may be subject to the influence of hidden agendas. For Hollifield et al. (2014) failure arises from a gap between restrictive rhetoric from political leaders who overstate their capacity to attain restrictive policy objectives and the reality of continued immigration. In contrast, Acosta Arcarazo and Freier (2015) identify a 'reverse policy gap' in South America, where progressive rhetoric about more open migration policies does not easily translate into on-the-ground implementation.

These perspectives on failings and gaps focus on an observed divergence between intended objectives and outcomes. This may not be confined only to migration policy. The literature on policy implementation tells us that it may well be more likely that a policy fails to achieve its objectives than that it actually successfully attains them all (Pressman and Wildavsky, 1973). This is because policy decisions are made at one place, at one point in time, and by one group of people, while they are implemented somewhere else at a different point in time and by different people. Not surprisingly, a lot can go wrong, which suggests that we shouldn't necessarily be surprised if policies fail to achieve their objectives. It could also be that success and failure are not aggregate categories and are not evenly distributed across the policy process from talk to decision to action, so that some actors may benefit, while others may lose out across these various stages (Brunsson, 2003). Looking at how policy decisions are made and the influence of organized interests, Freeman (1995) has argued that the concentrated beneficiaries of migration such as the employers of migrants that are a relatively cohesive group with a strong incentive to organize can win out over the general public as the more diffuse bearers of costs with lower organizational capacity. The result can be immigration policies that are more open and expansive than public opinion would appear to support.

A more basic methodological problem with a focus on outputs or outcomes is that motives are ascribed to actors based on the observed outcomes of a process rather than the characteristics of the process itself. This means that, if a policy fails to achieve its objectives, this could be because of the motives of decision-makers or their knowledge of the issues. Decision-makers might have inadequate knowledge, possess biases that are not consistent with evidence, fail to consult widely enough, or could say one thing and do another. These may all be true, but organizational settings shape know-how and expectations about role, and it is difficult to understand their effects only by observing the outcome or output of a process. To illustrate this point, imagine a situation that has nothing to do with migration governance but illustrates the more general point. Two cars have just collided with each other. You arrive on the scene slightly after the incident, as too do some other passers-by. Everyone, you included, might have a view on what caused the incident, but it is likely to be very difficult to work out what actually caused the incident. In fact, you and all the other people who arrived on the scene shortly after the incident may well have very divergent views on what might have happened. One driver may be a young man, another an elderly woman, which could trigger preconceptions. There may also be some conversations among onlookers during which people change their assessment in line with the reasoning of others (who also didn't see what happened). This does not mean that migration policy is analogous to a car crash, but it does help to illustrate the point that it is hard to observe the outcome of a situation or process and be confident that we could explain what led to that outcome. We may well end up making an educated guess based on experience, hunches, or some prior beliefs, which may be accurate. Even if we did directly observe the incident, prior beliefs about, for instance, young male drivers could still play a crucial role in how we interpret something, even if it happens before our eyes.

To sum up, figuring things out can be very difficult because the causes and effects of migration are complex, not easily observable, and plagued by significant uncertainties and risks, while representations of evidence and data are shaped by values. This doesn't mean that the decision-making is characterized by ignorance. Those that spend most of their working lives dealing with these issues—including the elite governance actors but also the academics who do this kind of study—probably have a fairly good understanding of the issues, but there are knowledge gaps and biases as well as the power of established ways of thinking about and doing things, plus the impact of values and beliefs. The sources and limits of knowledge—as well as its effects—will be shaped by experiences and representations of past and current events as well as of future challenge that all—both retrospectively and prospectively—provide the filters for interpreting cues and signals from the environment.

Why do something when we don't know what effect it will have?

Uncertainty about the effects of change in the underlying social and natural systems (economic, political, social, demographic, and environmental) that can cause international migration can lead to a status quo bias because of risk aversion. This doesn't mean that the existing situation is viewed as ideal or even as particularly desirable, but it can mean that doing something might be seen as even riskier. Yet, at the same time, there can be pressure to act or at least to be seen to do something (a performative component of migration governance repertoires), particularly if migration is high on the political agenda, so that there is a perceived public demand for something to be done. Actions may lead to activity but not to change; but just saying, 'It's complicated' is unlikely to be enough. This also means that interventions and the representations on which they are based can have intended and unintended effects on the environment.

Migration governance is not simply an *ex post* response to migration; it plays an important role in shaping the phenomena it is regulating or steering. This means that there are elements of endogeneity within migration governance systems that centre on how representations are developed of the causes and effects of migration. Endogeneity has a further implication, which is that migration governance can be a cause as well as an effect of increasingly 'turbulent' tendencies in governance that can be understood as how 'the collision of politics, administrative scale and complexity, uncertainty, and time constraints' affects the things that are done and the things that are not done (Ansell et al., 2017c, 1). Governance is becoming quicker as 'speed compresses time frames and accelerates activity'; more complex as organizations and institutions become more closely linked to each other, 'intricately nested and overlapping' (ibid.: 4); and more conflictual as battles for resources intensify with these conflicts producing more uncertainty—becoming a vicious circle.

Migration governance exemplifies these tendencies and is not only reflective of turbulence but can also generate turbulence. In Southeast Asia, for example (Chapter 3), a representation of international migration as 'temporary' (temporary foreign workers and temporary protection for the displaced) has defined what is understood as the 'normality' of international migration leading to the irregularization and criminalization of migration (Piper et al., 2017; Spaan and Naerssen, 2018). Irregularity and, by association, criminality are then represented as a cause of turbulence in the migration governance system that is associated with the dynamics of migration. In fact, it is more accurately associated with the political ordering of the 'normality' of international migration. Put another way, an outcome fulfils a prior definition of the situation.

The potential for turbulence can be linked to complex systems within which there can be significant variation, inconsistency, and scope for unexpected or unpredictable outcomes. That this turbulence is both endogenous and exogenous to organizations means that organizations themselves can play an important role in generating turbulence: '[t]his is particularly relevant for public sector organizations led by a political leadership and accountable to legislatures' (Ansell et al., 2017c, 8).

It could be the case that turbulence provokes profound institutional change, but it may also lead to reactive modes whereby past experiences deemed successful are used to shape responses to current events. Later chapters will show reactive tendencies and a status quo bias in migration governance. This view is reflected in a somewhat jaded quote from a European Commission official:

> it's very much, it goes in cycles...we hear the same discussion now that we heard 10 years ago. And we see the same responses now that we saw 10 years ago. It didn't work then so I don't think it will work now. The normal 'strengthen the borders', Schengen, controlling, etc. I just don't think that's the right...it's too simplistic I think.
>
> (European Commission official, December 2014)

Our interviews also suggest that actors in migration governance systems, particularly at a political and official level within national governments, have concerns about the consequences of interventions because they are unsure of the effects and fear of unintended and negative consequences. The quote below, expressed with irony, from a US government official illustrates this point:

> One is it's [immigration policy] so reactive. Two is, 'Well it seems to be limping along just fine so why rock the boat? If we rock the boat somebody might see us and want to, like, you know, make even more changes.'
>   (Department of Justice official, Washington DC, June 2015)

Similarly, a Department for Homeland Security (DHS) official in the US linked change to turbulence that was seen as a cause of reactive tendencies. Turbulence in this case was associated with fears of the effects of 'opening the floodgates' to new migration flows:

> I think there's a reluctance to do anything that might make the flood start again. So maybe a risk averseness. Well, so we don't know what stopped the floods. So anything—all of the actions we took we're hesitant to change, because any one of them could have been the one.
>   (DHS official, Washington DC, June 2015)

Doing something can have effects, but so too does choosing not to do something. Choosing not to act is closely tied to what actors know how to do and also what they think they should be doing as part of a migration governance repertoire. A status quo bias can have powerful effects if, for example, it leads to a strong focus on reinforcing border controls. This illustrates how a prior representation of the situation shapes current and future actions.

How can we choose our priorities?

International migration is ambiguous, complex, and diverse, which means that the challenges to governance that are associated with it can also be ambiguous, complex, and diverse. Ambiguity means that 'most of what we believe we know about elements within organizational choice situations, as well as the events themselves, reflects an interpretation of events by organizational actors and observers. Those interpretations are generated within the organization in the face of considerable perceptual ambiguity' (March and Olsen, 1976: 19). Ambiguity also means that problems and choices can be decoupled, because, as Ansell et al. (2017a: 45) put it, there are 'enduring tensions within organizations which produce ambiguity about what problems, solutions and consequences to attend to at any time, and what actors are deemed efficient and legitimate'.

Actors in migration governance systems deal with four main forms of ambiguity. First, those arising from competing pressures, which could be, for example, a demand from business for migrant labour while there are political demands for reduced immigration. A second derives from the inherent complexity of the issues encompassing very different motives for migration, effects of that movement, and diverse social, economic, and political responses. The third reason is linked more generally to limits on the ability of organizations to respond to their environment. This is not necessarily because they are ignorant of the phenomena with which they must deal, but because there are constraints on time, information, and resources, or what has been called 'bounded rationality' (Simon, 1955). But more than this, and fourthly, rationality may be bound not only by limits on time, information, and resources, but also by prior representations and expectations that influence responses to ostensibly new challenges. The 'shadow of the past' can loom large over those who seek to make or shape migration policy. For example, particular organizations have their own histories, experiences, and viewpoints that will shape reactions. As was noted earlier, what people know how to do and what they think they should be doing are likely to produce options that are shaped by the organizational context that produces them or, as Tilly (1978: 151) puts it, choices and actions are 'culturally sanctioned and empirically limited'.

There can also be a distinction between what is said and what is done. As will be seen in subsequent chapters, a common feature across all four regions is gaps between decision-making and implementation that are illustrated in this quote from a German government official:

> the problem is that the implementation of the legislation varies a lot in Germany. We have … a number of different public bodies are involved. Take immigration authorities, for example—we have over 500 immigration authorities in Germany and they implement the legislation very differently on the ground.   (German government official, Berlin, June 2015)

There are also 'political' instances of decoupling linked to the complexity of the institutional environment, as well as the number and range of actors and the diversity of institutional logics (Boswell, 2008). This can lead to 'garbage can' models of organizational choice, where an organization is understood as 'a collection of choices looking for problems, issues and feelings looking for decision situations in which they might be aired, solutions looking for issues to which they might be the answer, and decision makers looking for work' (Cohen et al., 1972). Decisions can rely less on rational assessments of the evidence than on chance, timing, and who happens to be present at the time.

Ambiguity means that decision-making preferences are powerfully driven by interpretations of the effects of external environments (or 'what's going on out there'). This might be a representation of the various drivers of migration and their perceived causes and effects, but could also be a representation of organizational constraints or perhaps also the perceived causes and effects of anti-immigration sentiment. The result is that decisions and actions may be loosely coupled or become decoupled because of 'gaps' within the decision-making system. This also means that the links between problems and choices is interactive rather than linear because it is informed by ongoing evaluations of the effects of actions and by the social context within which these assessments are made.

Political and symbolic considerations can play a key role in decision-making that can lead to an emphasis on being seen to do something rather than actions necessarily achieving their intended effects. This is captured by the idea of a migration governance repertoire having a performative component that can include the more symbolic manifestations—being seen to do something—but is also more deeply embedded in the everyday practices of organizations. Expensive investments in border security and associated technologies, despite evidence that these might have limited effect or even be counterproductive, are an example of the importance of political and symbolic considerations, but, of course, there can be electoral pay-offs for political leaders that talk tough about control. Obviously, this final point should not be discounted, because a political leader may well think that a particular intervention is successful if it conveys to the electorate a sense that security concerns are being dealt with. It also helps us to see that 'success' and 'failure' are not aggregate categories: a 'success' for some actors may well be a 'failure' for others.

Who are all these people at this meeting?

Migration governance beyond the state is a densely populated field. There are lots of conferences, meetings, workshops, seminars, and other gatherings. Some are more informal and can involve meetings in bars and restaurants as well as more formal, official settings. Participants include national governments, regional and international organizations, interest groups, civil society organizations, and academic researchers. Migration governance beyond the state can thus be labelled as pluricentric or plurilateral because it involves lots of organizations in many different locations (Oelgemöller, 2011). This is not to say that the logic of decision-making is plural. Certain interests and voices, particularly those of national governments, tend to be much more powerfully present within what have been called transgovernmental networks, which can be understood as networks that link governance actors across national boundaries (Raustiala, 2002).

The centrality of an organizational perspective on migration governance becomes even more evident when considering these tendencies to 'pluricentric' or 'multilevel' migration governance. Multilevelness means involvement of more, not fewer organizations. As subsequent chapters show, the precise constellations of actors and organizations do differ across regions, as too can the balance between state and non-state forms of authority in migration governance systems.

Focusing on multilevelness does not write the state out of the analysis. States remain central to migration governance, not least because the borders of states define international migration as a social and political concern. To capture the centrality of states, Levi-Faur (2012) discusses 'state-centred governance' that, despite changes in the state (such as limits on capacity and an increased role for private actors) also recognizes their continued centrality. Similarly, Offe (2009) talks about the 'resilience' of the state. While states are clearly key actors in migration governance, comparison at regional level of institutional settings can show how state and non-state actors potentially operate across multiple levels of governance. This creates the potential for institutionalized modes of coordination to produce decisions at regional level that can be both binding and implemented (Scharpf, 1999) or have a more informal character (Börzel, 2016).

Multilevelness is a much-observed characteristic of migration governance, with the implication that power and authority can be 'rebundled', with involvement by more, not fewer organizations. As Ansell et al. (2017a: 27) put it, 'Governance is not characterised by a move away from organizations, but rather by the entry of new kinds of organizations into an increasingly crowded field.'

To give an example of how the field is crowded, consider this quote from a European Commission official prompted by an initial reflection on relations with Egypt to then describe cooperation between the EU and countries in the Horn of Africa. Within it, we can see cooperation between the EU and African Union, forms of bilateral and multilateral cooperation, the linking of

emerging issues to existing agendas, the development of a regional consultation mechanism (the Khartoum process), plus, beneath the surface, a layer
of official-level cooperation as draft texts are worked through to support
higher-level political meetings:

> That's why the Egyptians like it, with all the meaning. That's why we said,
> 'Listen, why don't we actually use that same venue and occasion to then also
> bring in our EU Horn of Africa initiative?' Which is what it was initially
> called and then we turned it into the Khartoum process. 'All the people will
> be there. It's sponsored by you, African Union, and we want you to retain an
> important role in this.' We had signals that everybody would come, includ-
> ing Eritrea. That's actually how it happened. The first formal starting point of
> the Khartoum process was a senior officials' meeting that happened back to
> back with the African Union conference in Khartoum in mid-October on
> trafficking and human beings and smuggling. In that senior official meeting
> we actually brought the draft declaration. We had a first exchange with all
> delegates on the text and then the ambitions and what it would actually
> mean, how it would be implemented and all that. Then there were bilateral,
> very heavy negotiations from October to the end of November in between
> Khartoum and Rome. We then arrived in Rome where the declaration was
> endorsed at the ministerial level. Now we are actually starting to, as I said,
> prepare the first projects.
>
> (European Commission official, Brussels, December 2015)

The role of informal, non-binding settings is also important because of how
these can be venues for 'like-minded' states to interact and to share ideas and
information. A particularly notable instance of this is the Five Country
Conference of Australia, Canada, New Zealand, the UK, and the USA, which
was described thus by an Australian government official:

> In terms of broader governance, we've got a thing called the Five Country
> Conference...and there are several arms to that. So we've got an immigra-
> tion arm, we've got a borders arm, we've got an intelligence arm. So that's
> countries with similar thinking around settlement and migration. We have
> similar programmes, if you like, we share information. Every year we have a
> two- or three-day get together, we work through what's happening in the
> world, what are we doing and responding, how can we work better around a
> whole range of issues, around the movement of people of our countries, the
> conditions under which they move, etc. To the point where there are open

discussions around…There is probably a day in the future where a visa to America is a visa to Australia, is a visa to Britain, because we're getting so good at connecting our systems.

(Australian government official, Canberra, October 2015)

Organizations can also play an important role in creating multilevel and multi-actor systems by, for example, seeking to include civil society and private sector organizations within consultations and dialogues, as this quote referring to the situation in Southeast Asia exemplifies:

We work with a huge amount of organizations, obviously the UN agencies on various different levels. Civil society has always been a big partner across the region here. We don't work as much with the private sector as we could and should probably. We're trying to put more emphasis on that, recognizing that they can really be in some cases the drivers of change.

(Representative of international organization, Bangkok, October 2016)

There are, of course, major differences in the formal and informal constitution of migration governance within different regional settings, but migration governance is multilevel, which means more actors and more organizations and demonstrates the centrality of the organizational dimension of migration governance. This means that actors in migration governance systems may well be wondering who all these people are. Over time, they'll get to know people better and, also over time, probably identify those that have similar views, which, in the ongoing process of migration governance, might confirm or challenge representations of international migration.

Does that make sense to us?

Migration governance is enactive of what can be called 'sensible environments' that provide actors with a plausible but not necessarily accurate account of what's going on 'out there' (Pye, 2005; Weick, 1995). Actors in migration governance systems try to frame their experiences as meaningful, particularly in situations that are uncertain or ambiguous. They then use the organization of experiences to guide actions. This means that migration governance itself can be enactive of sensible environments that are shaped by the practical activities of people engaged in concrete situations of social action (Weick, 1995). To enact a sensible environment requires a combination of cognition and interactions with other actors to inform learning as well as social expectations about role. Sense-making is an enactive approach to cognition that depends on the social context (Thurlow and Helms Mills, 2009). By making sense of their environment, actors in migration governance systems also create or enact this environment.

Issue-framing has a social dimension that involves interactions and the sharing of ideas in ways that are both ongoing and extracted by signals or cues from the environment within which organizations operate. This can then form a basis for action or, in an unstable environment, inaction or confusion, as this quote from an Australian government official dealing with resettlement of displaced people demonstrates:

> The policy space is just constantly changing. So, we just get across one policy and start to think about that and come up with solutions. Numbers go up, and then the next government says, 'Oh, well, we're actually not going to increase it to 20,000. You're back down here.' Then, a year later, 'We'll take in an extra 12,000 from Syria,' and gearing up, and the policy in how you treat those different cohorts. There are a lot of pilots and individual policy responses that are very appealing to government, because they can make quick gains for just a few clients. It just makes it very hard for government and public servants as a whole to move forward and get better outcomes in the longer term.
>
> (Australian government official, Canberra, October 2015)

This takes us back to the question at the start of this section: 'Does that make sense?' Asking this question opens the door to an important body of work in organizational studies on 'sense-making', which, as an approach to the study of repertoires of migration governance, highlights the roles played by cognition, learning, and also the social expectations that are held about role (Weick, 1995).

Sense-making is grounded in identity construction, as identities [of actors and organizations] are constructed through interactions, as 'no individual ever acts like a single sensemaker' (Weick, 1995: 18). In practical terms, this means the sharing of information within and between organizations, which can also include the like-mindedness exemplified by this point made by an official of an EU member state:

> So we will have a likeminded dinner tonight,...Austria is one of them, Sweden, Germany, the UK, France, Belgium, the Netherlands. That's it. We

discuss what we should say and how we should react at the following meeting, trying to get a common approach to the issue. Because on this issue we think more the same than a lot of other countries.

(EU member state official, Brussels, December 2015)

Constellations of like-mindedness in Europe, North America, South America, and Southeast Asia do vary and aren't stable, but like-mindedness highlights the importance of sharing information among those who see issues in more or less the same way. Sense-making is retrospective, as people can only know what they have done after they have done it. Reflective action and history can also lead, as shown earlier, to a reluctance to act because of the fear of unintended effects.

Actions themselves create an environment that previously didn't exist, because they establish boundaries, draw lines, create categories, and label. These processes are social, which means that it is essential to focus on the social processes that shape interpretations and interpreting: '[i]n working organizations decisions are made either in the presence of others or with the knowledge that they will have to be implemented, or understood, or approved by others' (Burns and Stalker, 2000: 43). This means that the considerations that form the basis for decisions need to be shared with others or acceptable to them. The chapters that follow provide numerous examples of the influence of social settings, as well as the importance of both formal and informal modes of cooperation.

A further important characteristic of sense-making is that it is ongoing, because 'people are always in the middle of things' (Weick, 1995: 43). This means that migration governance beyond the state doesn't have a beginning and an end. There is no telos or final destination. Instead, the complexity associated with various kinds of governing organizations beyond the state that are non-hierarchical, functionally differentiated by migration type, and, at times, overlapping either in their territorial or functional scope is likely to persist.

Sense-making is focused on and extracted by cues, 'simple, familiar structures that are seeds from which people develop a larger sense of what may be occurring...control over which cues will serve as a point of reference is an important source of power' (Weick, 1995: 50). Sense-making is driven by plausibility rather than accuracy or, as Weick puts it, 'accuracy is nice but not necessary' (1995: 56) and what counts is 'plausibility, pragmatics, coherence, reasonableness, creation, invention and instrumentality' (1995: 57). To return to a point made in Chapter 1, such a setting could favour the 'hedgehog' with his or her 'one big idea' and a tendency to reach for formulaic solutions (Tetlock, 2017).

Framing and sense-making can be linked within migration governance repertoires to allow assessment of the ways in which actors form a representation of their situations—of what they know how to do and what they think they should be doing (Fiss and Hirsch, 2005). Repertoires containing elements of framing, and sense-making also enable connections between thought and action, as sense-making can be understood as 'the practical activities of real people engaged in concrete situations of social action' (Boden, 1994: 10). The result is that:

> connecting framing and sensemaking better enables us to examine how structural factors prompt and bound discursive processes, affecting when and where frame contests emerge...If framing focuses on whose meanings win out in symbolic contests, sensemaking shifts the focus to understanding why such frame contests come into being in the first place, as well as how they are connected to "hard" structural changes, and over which territory they are fought.   (Fiss and Hirsch, 2005: 29, 31)

To sum up, actors must ask themselves if what they are doing makes sense not just as individual or personal justification, but to validate their views and beliefs with others about what is going on 'out there'

Is governance Eurocentric?

This section raises another question and a possible objection to a focus on governance, which is the potentially damning assessment that analysis of migration governance is irredeemably Eurocentric. Analysing governance and, indeed, using the word itself, could presuppose ideas about relations between the state and society and between public and private actors that emerged from a European and EU context and make less sense elsewhere. If so, analysing 'migration governance' brings with it a perspective fuelled by Eurocentric assumptions and an associated social, economic, political, and cultural matrix that may well not fit with the ways in which these issues and associated tasks are understood in other regions. It could also involve projections of a one-size-fits-all vision of neoliberal governance and its imposition, as happened in South America (Remmer, 1986). In Southeast Asia, Acharya (2004) identifies the importance of 'localisation' at a regional level of global norms and standards so that the global is rendered consistent with the regional, rather than the other way around. In South America there are representations of *gobernabilidad* or governability, which has been understood as a specific issue for migration (how to make it 'governable' (Braz, 2018; Domenech, 2013; Mármora, 2010)) but also as a more general concern that relates to underlying economic, political, and social conditions as they affect *gobernabilidad* (Camou, 2001; Mayorga and Córdova, 2007).

The origins of governance as a field of study are clearly located within a European cultural matrix, most notably in the way that state–society and public–private relations are conceptualized (Draude, 2007). It is likely that the cultural matrix that underpins the study of governance and its practice is likely to be experienced and understood in different ways in different regional settings shaped by the historical and social factors that give meaning to that setting and to the role of governance actors within them. Governance could also be viewed as an imposition if it is associated with the demands of other states or certain kinds of templates for action or 'good governance' that emerge from regional or international settings within which certain powerful states and other influential actors and their ideas tend to predominate. Non-Eurocentric migration governance can entail very different assumptions about the meaning of borders, relationship between public and private actors, the ways that these are regulated, and the role and presence of rule- and law-based forms of authority. At the very least, this means not seeking to transport a particular form of regional integration modelled on the EU experience to other regions.

There are grounds for thinking that a governance perspective that emphasizes its dual meaning (*pace* Pierre, 2000) does open some potentially fruitful ground to explore the dynamics of migration governance beyond the state, because it can problematize the state and its role, account for contextual factors across levels, and be sensitive to potential limits to state- and regional-level authority and capacity, as well as the effects of a proliferation of actors organized across various levels. Building on this the idea of a migration governance repertoire seeks to provide a framework for comparative regional analysis that is sensitive to the variation between regional settings, which is precisely why it seeks to understand more about cognition, learning, and expectations about role.

The more difficult question is how to go about doing this. The lens through which issues and problems are viewed will be shaped by the position from which they are viewed. This affects researchers who write books like this one just as much as it does the participants in governance processes that are the subject of this book. There is no simple answer to this question; rather, there is a need to be aware of the problem and what it might mean. Clearly, different people can learn different things in ostensibly similar task environments. If we are interested in how actors in different regional settings learn, then it is relevant to explore the impact of the environment in which these actors operate on the ways in which they deal with the tasks that they face. There are fascinating examples of how this might occur. One of the most influential is developed by Herbert Simon (1975), who uses the Tower of Hanoi puzzle to show that there can be multiple answers to the question 'What is learned?' The puzzle comprises three vertical poles or pegs and a number of disks of varying sizes that fit onto these poles. The task is to move all the disks from one pole to another without ever placing a smaller disk on top of a larger disk. Simon shows that, even when tasks are relatively simple, a variety of learning strategies develop that inform the ways in which the task is dealt with. We could take this as a warning to illustrate 'the diversity of behaviour that may be hidden under a blanket label like "problem-solution process" even in a very simple task environment' (ibid.: 268). This isn't a solution to the problem of Eurocentric analysis of governance, but, rather, it is an attempt through the development of an idea of a migration governance repertoire—and the understanding of governance that informs it—to be aware of the problem, to be aware of the potential constraints imposed upon analysis that seeks to be comparative, and to develop tools and strategies that seek to overcome at least some of these constraints.

Conclusions

Migration governance is everywhere, always, and necessarily an organizational process. This chapter has developed a framework for analysing migration governance beyond the state that seeks to account for this organizational dimension, which centres on two core concerns: how these organizations make sense of the environment in which they operate (what's going on 'out there') and, on the basis of the representations that are developed, to try to decide what to do next, with inaction a distinct possibility. To seek to capture the diversity of context in Europe, North America, South America, and Southeast Asia and at global level, governance is defined as possessing a dual meaning as the conceptual representation of change in underlying social and natural systems and the efforts to steer or manage the effects of these changes. There is likely to be major variation in how these are understood as issues in the context of governance beyond the state, particularly at the regional level that is this book's focus. Central to the approach that is developed is the idea of a migration governance repertoire that goes beyond analysis of the observable outputs or outcomes of governance systems to consider two additional factors: what do actors know how to do and what do they think they should be doing? By doing so, the chapters that follow seek to understand more about how cognition, learning, and social expectations about role enable or limit migration governance beyond the state. Chapter 3 explores the migration governance repertoire in Southeast Asia.

3

Southeast Asia

The 'Temporariness' of Migration

Introduction

While there are clear and tangible limits to formalized regional migration governance in Southeast Asia, this chapter shows that regionalized migration flows that cross national borders have led to an array of bilateral and multilateral processes within and beyond the region. Together, these processes constitute a repertoire of regionalized migration governance in Southeast Asia that is associated not only with what actors do—the more visible manifestations of migration governance—but also with what they know how to do and what they think they should be doing. More particularly, the migration governance repertoire in Southeast Asia centres on a powerful connotation of 'temporariness' held by key migration governance actors, particularly at state level but with resonance beyond the state. This means that migrants are understood and represented in policy debate as *temporary* foreign workers or, if displaced, in need of, at best, *temporary* protection. This also results in approaches to migration governance in key Southeast Asian destination countries that connect migration in its various forms with irregularity, illegality, and criminality. This attribution of meaning to migration is constitutive of 'normality'—of what is understood as normal—in Southeast Asian migration governance within a regional framework that does not easily enable formalized, supranational regional engagement. Responses to intermittent 'crises' draw from powerful or prevalent representations of normality and induce a status quo bias. Those that do contest this imputation of temporariness, particularly civil society organizations, have found it hard to get a secure foothold in national and regional decision-making processes.

The twin foci for this chapter's analysis of migration governance beyond the state in Southeast Asia are, first, the ten-member ASEAN founded in 1967 that has some, albeit very limited migration provisions (the members are Brunei, Cambodia, Indonesia, Laos, Malaysia, Myanmar, Philippines, Singapore,

Governing Migration Beyond the State: Europe, North America, South America, and Southeast Asia in a Global Context.
Andrew Geddes, Oxford University Press (2021). © Andrew Geddes. DOI: 10.1093/oso/9780198842750.003.0003

Thailand, and Vietnam). ASEAN's role is limited to schemes for mobility for certain categories of professional workers, while, as an organization, it combines principles of non-interference in the sovereign affairs of its members and adheres strictly to consensus-based decision-making (Acharya, 2004; Jones, 2011). And, second, the regional consultation processes, particularly the Bali Process set up in 2002, which established a more informal, state-led setting for discussion of migration-related issues that also involves Australia, its concerns, and its approaches in Southeast Asian migration governance (Curley and Vandyk, 2017; Douglas and Schloenhardt, 2012; Kneebone, 2014).

In Southeast Asia, relatively high levels of regionalization, including migration to, from, and within the region are accompanied by relatively low levels of formal regionalism. Such is the significance of migration to, within, and from the region that the United Nations Economic and Social Commission for Asia and the Pacific (UNESCAP) observed that 'International migration is a major driver of social and economic change in the contemporary Asia-Pacific region' (UNESCAP, 2016: 9). This is true, of course, but this chapter's analysis turns this statement around to look at how these social, economic, and political changes powerfully shape migration. Irrespective of the deeper and more embedded role that migration clearly plays in Southeast Asia, the imputation of temporariness is an effect of governance, or, put another way, is enactive of a 'sensible environment' that provides a plausible, although not necessarily accurate account of the causes and effects of migration in Southeast Asia. This frame or representation then plays out in very real ways as it shapes migration patterns and flows, the rights and status of people that migrate, and associated social and political mobilizations. The complexity of migration flows is mirrored by the growing complexity of migration governance, with an increased number of participants in various types of organization operating within what Acharya (2017) calls the 'ASEAN multiplex'. Recurrent crises linked to conflict-induced displacement have reaffirmed rather than shifted existing regional approaches and the emphasis on temporariness (Petcharamesree, 2016).

Interviewed in Manila in November 2016, a representative of an international organization identified the nascent nature of regional cooperation in Southeast Asia and also captured both the wariness and ambiguities associated with approaches to both migration and regionalism in Southeast Asia:

> I think there's a growing acknowledgement of the need to manage this [migration]. I think it's a rather limited and weak process. Compared to what you can see, perhaps, in Latin America, or in Europe for that matter.

So, it is also a function of how Asia thinks of international cooperation, how careful they are of integration.

(Representative of international organization, Manila, November 2016)

Drivers and characteristics

While Acharya's idea of an ASEAN multiplex captures the complexity of governance, within these governance systems are located actors of various types trying to make sense of what is going on 'out there': principally, why are people moving and what are the effects of this movement? How can organizations of various types respond to the risks and complexities associated with international migration in its various forms? The representations that emerge are not formed on an individual basis; rather, they are shaped by established ways of doing things, past experiences, organizational hierarchies, and interactions with others. They can also be deeply contested. The causes and effects of international migration in Southeast Asia, as in other regions, occur in specific places and play out over periods of time. This means that there are important spatial and temporal dimensions, because, as Lee and Piper (2017: 229) observe, 'Temporality shapes migrants' whole experience from pre-departure to after-return, frames the migration industry/market including the middlemen/broker practices, and establishes the foundation of governmental (of both destination and origin) policies and transnational governance structures.' There is also a powerful spatial focus, as migration has been a key vector for urban development.

While there are substantial migration flows to, within, and from the region, policy frameworks at national and regional level remain underdeveloped. While not the main focus for this chapter, emigration to countries outside the region is an important phenomenon in Southeast Asia and has been pursued by the Philippines, Indonesia, and, more recently, Vietnam as a state-led export strategy (UNESCAP, 2018).

The growing and regionalized complexity of the Southeast Asian migration system is highlighted by Hugo (2014: 45), when he notes that the number of immigrants in ASEAN countries increased by almost 80 per cent between 2000 and 2013. By 2013, intra-regional migration between ASEAN countries amounted to 68.9 per cent of immigration, with the largest countries of origin being Myanmar, Indonesia, Malaysia, Laos, and Cambodia. Together, these five countries accounted in 2013 for 64.5 per cent of immigrants in ASEAN countries (Hugo, 2014: 45). Similarly, Tuccio (2017: 144) notes how intra-regional flows 'skyrocketed' between 1990 and 2013 from 1.5 million to 6.5 million migrants. Figure 3.1 for the period 2010–19 shows growth in numbers of intra-regional migrants.

Figure 3.2 shows total numbers of immigrants and emigrants in ASEAN countries to illustrate the distinction between those countries that are predominantly sending and those that are destinations.

A regionalized dynamic outside formal regional migration governance processes is shaped by relative inequalities of income and wealth within the region as migration occurs from ASEAN's south to its north, underpinned by income and wealth disparities within the region as well as by migration

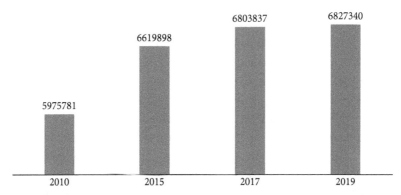

Figure 3.1 Trends in intra-regional migration in ASEAN, 2010–19
Source: UNDESA 2019.

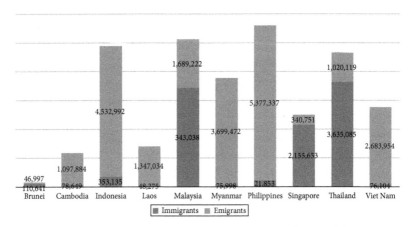

Figure 3.2 Immigrants and emigrants in ASEAN, 2019 (thousands)
Source: UNDESA 2019.

networks connecting points of departure and destination. IMF data for October 2018 showed annual GDP per capita in Singapore to be around US\$61,000 annually, while in Laos and Myanmar the figure was less than US\$1,500. Similarly, Thailand is an upper middle-income country that borders Cambodia, Laos, and Myanmar, which are all low-income countries, to create an obvious differential (Chalamwong, 2011; Nguyen, 2017). These inequalities intersect with a complex demographic picture that sees growth in the younger-age population in Cambodia, Indonesia, Laos, and the Philippines, while in Singapore, Thailand, and Vietnam there are expected to be higher dependency ratios linked to growth in the elderly population (Tuccio, 2017).

Extensive maritime borders combined with long land borders located in remote mountain areas mean that borders can be porous and difficult to regulate. There are also important organizational borders that are internal to states and regulate access to the labour market and to social benefits. Interactions between external/territorial and internal/organizational borders contribute to irregular migration. While it is difficult to precisely quantify the number of irregular migrants, there are estimates ranging from 600,000 to 1.9 million irregular migrant workers in Malaysia alone in 2015 (Gallagher and McAuliffe, 2016). The boundaries between regularity and irregularity are blurred. During migrants' journeys, situations and circumstances can change, while private actors such as smugglers or recruitment agents also play an important role as intermediaries and facilitators in migration and migration governance.

Labour migration

Temporary migration for the purpose of employment is 'the dominant form of international mobility in the ASEAN region' (Hugo, 2014: 48). Temporary contracts are typically tied to an employer 'offering few if any chances for greater socio-economic freedom of mobility or legal security, such as permanency, let alone citizenship' (Lee and Piper, 2017: 221). As already noted, categorizations and their consequences are an inevitable component of migration policy in a world of states and borders. These categories are an output of governance systems and not an intrinsic quality of migrants themselves. In Southeast Asia, temporary labour migration by foreign workers tends to be predicated on the idea of these migrants as agents of economic development or as a security challenge rather than on their potential as long-term residents or citizens (Piper, 2010). The frequent reference in law and policy to foreign workers rather than to migrants is indicative of this.

Temporary contracts are tied to an employer, with the result that breaking a contract or overstaying means that a migrant becomes an 'illegal' worker. Contracts can be severe, including, for female domestic workers, regular pregnancy tests, with expulsion a real possibility for women found to be pregnant (Constable, 2014; Elias, 2018). Where governance arrangements for labour migration do exist, these tend to be bilateral agreements that often lack provisions that protect rights (Lee and Piper, 2017: 227). The result in destination countries is very little social or political commitment to migrants and minimal space for migrants to be active in the public sphere, while they can also be neglected by their countries of origin.

The presence and scale of an irregular population in ASEAN countries is linked to the absence of formal migration policies. Irregular migration was tolerated by Southeast Asian governments because of a reliance on irregular migrant workers (Battistella and Asis, 1998; Martin and Abella, 2014). As it was put to us:

> there's a bit of a recognition they need this labour but they [national governments] don't want to make it fully regular. There could be ways of improving legal avenues to migration. As to why they don't do that, I honestly don't know…It could also be for economic reasons, maybe it keeps the wages lower.
>
> (Representative of international organization, Bangkok, November 2016)

This tolerance is facilitated by visa-free travel for periods between fourteen and thirty days for nationals of ASEAN member states and compounded by labour market rigidities, such as the high costs of recruitment and the restrictive nature of employment contracts that can cause employers not to use legal employment processes (Kassim, 2012; Tuccio, 2017).

A practical example of the dynamics of irregularity occurred in the aftermath of the military coup in Thailand in May 2014. Cambodians in Thailand were concerned they would be the target of a crackdown, with rumours of attacks or even killings of Cambodians. The *New York Times* reported that 122,000 Cambodians crossed back into their home country in the month after the coup (Fuller, 2014). Soon, however, there was a reaction from the business community in Thailand, who, as it was put to us in November 2016 by a Bangkok-based representative of an international organization, 'very quickly realized how much they depend on those migrant workers to sustain the economy here' (Representative of international organization, Bangkok, November 2016).

Social and economic inequalities that can cause people to migrate both regularly and irregularly to, within, and from Southeast Asian countries interact with power relations at both the household and wider societal levels. There are sharp distinctions between the types of employment into which male and female migrants move, with men moving into sectors such as construction, while female migrants are predominantly located in domestic work. Trends towards the 'feminization' of international migration have been identified that are clearly evident in Southeast Asia (Chin, 1997; Kaur, 2007; Piper and Roces, 2004). While flows are feminized, migration governance is not similarly feminized (Foley, 2020). Temporary schemes do not allow family reunification and, because of the strictly temporary nature of contracts, the integration of migrants is not seen as a relevant policy concern. As the UNESCAP (2016: 10) notes, 'Restrictions on female migration and the undervaluing of female labour puts women at particular risk of irregular migration.' A representative of an NGO in Manila pinpointed the combined effects of temporariness and gendered migration to highlight a potential social cost of migration:

> There are social costs in migration in terms of the family, the relations within the family, in terms of the fact that migrants find themselves in a foreign country, particularly when it comes, as I said, to temporary migration, because temporary migration does not provide for the possibility to integrate. Therefore, basically, you're always a foreigner, and, also, in terms of social benefits, you never acquire the right to own social benefits, really, so these people cannot bank on the future, their retirement time, and other stuff because that is not granted.
>
> (Representative of NGO, Manila, November 2016)

Labour migration in Southeast Asia is predicated on an everyday representation of its temporariness that militates against the development of frameworks to manage or regulate migration, while blurring the boundaries between regularity and irregularity. This framing shapes what key actors, particularly at state level, know how to do and also their expectations about role. The result is empirical and cultural limits on change that contribute to the persistence of a repertoire that remains focused on the imputed temporariness of migration.

Forced migration and displacement

As with economic migration, there is a powerful imputation of temporariness to forced migration and displacement in Southeast Asia that can also be understood as a governance effect. This effect is evident in the move away from an automatic attribution of refugee status to those fleeing conflict, with the idea gaining ground after the late 1980s that many were actually economic migrants. This led to tendencies in the region to label some forced migrants as 'illegal', to seek their return to their country of origin, and to conflate their plight with transnational crime.

Between the end of the Vietnam War in 1975 and the end of 1978, just under 110,000 thousand people left Vietnam by boat (Vo, 2005). In July 1979 a conference in Geneva focused on the issue of Vietnamese boat people and offered protection in the region and then resettlement outside the region with sixty-five national governments pledging up to 260,000 resettlement places. The assumption was that all those fleeing were refugees. Indonesia and the Philippines set up regional processing centres. As Courtland Robinson (2004: 320) notes, the plan was to offer temporary protection in the region:

> Countries of first asylum [in the region], however, expected that no refugees would stay in their countries for more than a specified period. Thus was formalized a *quid pro quo*—temporary or first asylum in the region for permanent resettlement elsewhere—or, as some came to describe it, 'an open shore for an open door'.

Subsequent responses to forced migration have been powerfully influenced by the legacy of the Comprehensive Plan of Action (CPA) implemented between 1989 and 1997 in response to continued displacement caused by the Indochina wars. The CPA offered temporary protection to those displaced in the region, with longer-term resettlement to occur outside the region. By the late 1980s, Thailand and Hong Kong were no longer offering first protection because of inadequate resettlement efforts outside the region (Hathaway, 1993). In January 1988 Thailand had begun a policy of 'push-off' for Vietnamese boat people. Thai government officials were threatened with being fired if they did not reduce the numbers of refugees coming ashore. There were estimates of 500 people pushed back from Thai waters, with at least 100 drowning and others left stranded (Hathaway, 1993: 688). In 1988, ASEAN foreign ministers called for a 'new comprehensive plan of action' to deal with refugees, displaced persons and 'illegal immigrants' (cited in Davies, 2008: 194). The CPA 'was therefore born out of frustration and scepticism' (Hathaway, 1993: 688).

The CPA was based on a view of the changing dynamics of migration. Hathaway (1993: 689) teases out these differences by identifying the importance of boat people being subject to a 'conceptual shift' that was motivated by state experiences of flows, but that also served to then legitimate new responses to asylum seekers and refugees. Davies (2008, 192, emphasis in the original) identified a key argument made by Southeast Asian states 'that asylum seekers should not be considered or even treated as "genuine" refugees *until proven otherwise*'. This meant that those that were deemed 'genuine' were resettled outside the region and those deemed not to be genuine could be repatriated.

By 1989 there were around 200,000 refugees from Cambodia, Laos, and Vietnam in UNHCR camps (Courtland Robinson, 2004: 324), with the effect that 'the seemingly endless arrival of boat people heightened Southeast Asia's resistance to boat people and also increased resistance among resettlement states [outside the region]' (Davies, 2008: 213). ASEAN governments working with UNHCR prepared a draft CPA that was presented, in June 1989, to seventy governments at a conference in Geneva. The plan contained two 'radically new ingredients' (Courtland Robinson, 2004: 320): regional screening and repatriation, including forced return. The role of screening was particularly important because it was linked to deterrence: 'Southeast Asian states' primary concern was not how best to provide refugee protection, but how to deter them' (Davies, 2008: 213). ASEAN governments were also determined that there should be repatriation for those not granted protection.

Central to the shift in approach was a changed representation of the fundamental dynamics underpinning forced migration. This new representation offered a plausible explanation to national governments. To the existing imputation of temporariness were added associations with illegality and transnational crime. The 1989 Geneva conference that led to the CPA was premised on the view that Vietnamese migrants were not automatically assumed to be refugees and that some were actually economic migrants (Hathaway, 1993: 688). This narrative had a political plausibility, but, as Hitchcox (1990: 120) notes, '[s]uch evidence as is available suggests that the attraction of resettlement programmes, of images of a better life, are overemphasized by western observers, who are assessing the importance of so-called pull factors from their own perspective rather than the situation of the potential exile'. Courtland Robinson (2004: 321) argues that it is necessary to distinguish between the CPA's shorter- and longer-term effects, as it 'shored up flagging confidence in the asylum system worldwide, though its long-term impacts on Asian commitments to asylum were neither particularly positive nor potent'.

The CPA ended the supposition of automatic refugee status for those displaced by conflict that had applied after the 1979 conference. Davies (2008: 214) sees it as endorsing the view of Southeast Asian states 'that asylum seekers were illegal immigrants until proven otherwise'. To do this, the CPA set up a cut-off date for those arriving before 14 March 1989, for whom refugee status was assumed. After that date, refugee status had to be proven, with all arrivals screened at processing centres. An Orderly Departure Programme (ODP) was established to create a legal pathway for people from Vietnam to emigrate without taking on risky boat journeys. The overall level of resettlement was, however, impressive. Combined, the CPA and ODP saw around 1.5 million people resettled in the USA, 260,000 in China, 200,000 in Canada, 185,000 in Australia, and 130,000 in France, with around 500,000 people returning to Vietnam (Courtland Robinson, 1998).

ASEAN foreign ministers were key actors in the CPA's development, but the backdrop to the CPA was displacement caused by a declared conventional war, whereas, particularly in the context of displacement from Myanmar, it has been 'too controversial and problematic' for ASEAN to recognize as refugees 'those forced to migrate as a result of fighting, discrimination, human rights violations and ethnic and religious conflicts' (Petcharamesree, 2016: 180). In addition to this, there has also been an effect that was probably unintended by the proponents of international conventions such as the UN Palermo Protocol to Prevent, Suppress and Punish Trafficking in Persons Especially Women and Children. The Palermo Protocol has affirmed the tendency evident since the 1980s of Southeast Asian countries to deal with forced migration as a trafficking and crime issue.

The reach of international protection standards is limited because only Cambodia and the Philippines adhere to the 1951 Refugee Convention. In those that have not signed, the UNHCR conducts status determination in the absence of a national system. States without national asylum systems tend to consider refugees and asylum seekers as illegal or irregular migrants, which means that they are at risk of detention, expulsion, refoulement (return to a country where an individual would be at risk of persecution), and other serious protection risks (Petcharamesree, 2016: 177). For asylum seekers and refugees, protection in Southeast Asian countries tends 'to be *ad hoc* depending on the nationality of the asylum seeker, regional strategic and political considerations and otherwise based on a remote sense of international obligation or humanitarianism left to the discretion of field-level immigration officials or magistrates' (Cheung, 2011: 63).

The Andaman Sea 'crisis'

There is, of course, no simple, objective definition of a crisis. It is a core argument of this book that crises are also likely to draw from established ways of representing the 'normality' of migration. Crises are subjective, which means that how they are identified and labelled and the dimensions of crisis (what it is a crisis 'of') are necessarily linked to social and political processes and to the representation of facts. To develop this point, we now look more closely at the displacement of the Muslim Rohingya minority from the Rakhine province of Myanmar to see how it has reaffirmed rather than altered existing approaches in Southeast Asia both to migration and to regional governance. More specifically, responses have continued to emphasize temporariness, linked displacement to criminality, and, backed away from measures that impinge upon the sovereignty of ASEAN member states. Moretti (2018: 254) sees these as 'pragmatic' and 'informal', but also as heightening the precarity of Rohingya refugees. Responses to crises are shaped by everyday representations of the causes and effects of migration, so that crisis becomes an everyday thing. As it was put to us:

> We would say that we're constantly in crisis…We've got a combination of people who are forcibly displaced in the camp situations, and very protracted situations here in the Thailand and Myanmar border, but actually really large urban populations as well, which creates a very different kind of environment for protection needs, and also for advocacy. You've got a region, also, where the really, really low number of states that are party to the Refugee Convention, or the statelessness conventions, or any of the international frameworks that you might be able to look towards…Then, relatively, well, really quite weak regional protection mechanisms. ASEAN is struggling a lot in this regard. Although there is some language in some of the declarations, it's very difficult to apply that. ASEAN, as you know, has a non-interference policy. Then, basically, no domestic legislation. In most of the countries there's no recognition of refugees or asylum seekers because they're subsumed within the wider categories of irregular migrants.
>
> (Representative of NGO, Bangkok, November 2016)

Responses draw from established repertoires that centre not only on outputs of governance processes, but know-how and expectations about role. In ASEAN this leads to a strong focus on process:

> You get a lot of high-level meetings such as the emergency ASEAN minister-ial meeting where they'll sit down and the ministers will agree to say we're going to share information, we're going to cooperate and then it never becomes a reality because it just doesn't filter down to the working level.
>
> (Representative of international organization, Bangkok, November 2016)

The plight of the Rohingya has long been on the regional agenda in Southeast Asia. The UNHCR estimates that more than a million Rohingya have fled since the early 1990s. A renewed outbreak of communal violence and target-ing of the Rohingya after the summer of 2012 led to increased numbers of displaced people moving to Bangladesh. In 2012, the ASEAN Secretary General, Surin Pitsuwan, urged a collective ASEAN response, but member states were reluctant to regionalize the issue. In early 2015, an estimated 25,000 refugees and migrants that had been displaced to Bangladesh departed by boat from the Bay of Bengal (Gleeson, 2017: 8). They then sailed southeast to the Andaman Sea. There, people smugglers were waiting to ferry people to shore in southern Thailand via small boats. Migrants were reported to be pay-ing between $90 and $370 for disembarkation to Thailand or Malaysia (Gleeson, 2017). From these landing points, people would move to camps on the Thai-Malaysian border, where UNHCR reported that there were serious human rights abuses, with smugglers extorting further payments from the family members of those in the camps (UNHCR, 2016a). Those that disem-barked in Malaysia could face being extorted for up to $2,000 to travel on to the camps on the Thai-Malaysia border (Gleeson, 2017: 9). On 1 May 2015, a mass grave with remains of more than thirty people was discovered. Four days later, three Thai officials and a Myanmar national were arrested and accused of involvement in human trafficking (Petcharamesree et al., 2016: 2). Other smugglers went into hiding, which left around 6,000 asylum seekers and migrants in terrible conditions, effectively stranded on board eight ships in the Andaman Sea (ibid). These boats then headed for shore in Indonesia, Malaysia, and Thailand. On 10 May 2015, 578 people tried to swim ashore in northern Aceh in Indonesia and were rescued by local fishermen. The next day, another boat was towed away from Indonesian waters while 1,107 people from two other boats came ashore in Malaysia. On 12 May, the Malaysians turned away two boats with an estimated 1,200 people on board. It seemed that Malaysia and Thailand were taking it in turns to tow boats into each other's territorial waters (Gleeson, 2017: 9). On 26 May, the bodies of 140 people believed to be migrants from Bangladesh and Myanmar were discovered on the Malaysian-Thai border. The Malaysian deputy interior minister Junaidi Jafaar said that Malaysia had to 'send the right message that they are not welcome here' (cited in Gleeson, 2017: 9), while the Thai prime minister, Prayut Chan-o-cha, stated, 'If we take them all in, then anyone who wants to come will come freely…Where will the budget come from?' (cited in Gleeson, 2017: 9). Cheung (2011: 50) observed that this created 'an apparent impasse between migration control policies and dim prospects for solutions'.

The initial reaction of governments was negative: 'In the earliest and most critical days of the crisis, Indonesia, Malaysia and Thailand reacted unfavourably to the attempted influx' (Gleeson, 2017: 8). The three countries issued a joint statement following a meeting held on 20 May 2015 in response to what was represented as a crisis linked to 'the influx of irregular migrants and its serious impact on the national security of the affected countries' (Joint Statement: Ministerial Meeting on Irregular Movement of People in Southeast Asia 2015). In the statement, there was also an appeal to ASEAN's 'spirit of unity and solidarity'. The three countries pledged to offer temporary protection on the basis that resettlement would be done by the international community. The point, however, as Kneebone (2017: 36–7) notes, is that ASEAN remained passive, reluctant to be seen to interfere in the sovereign affairs of one of its member states. The result was reactive decision-making that, when governments were eventually pushed to do something, drew from established regional scripts embedded within a governance repertoire with a preference for, at best, temporary protection and bilateral rather than regionalized responses:

> The first reaction of governments to the Andaman Sea was to not acknowledge. And then, only when there was pressure from the international community to do something about it in a systematic way. Again, the governments were all panicking and all of a sudden the government of Thailand called…a kind of meeting…looking at these mechanisms and how governments react, and what are the tipping points when they are starting to see. 'Well, maybe we need to come together and find collective solutions. What kind of structure should that have?' That is to be decided in this region, so talking about it, getting governments together, getting various stakeholders together.
> (Representative of regional organization, Bangkok, November 2016)

There was recognition by the three most affected countries (Indonesia, Malaysia, and Thailand) that the arrival of Rohingya in the Andaman Sea was a crisis with various dimensions. While states initially focused on the security dimension, it was also clear that this was a humanitarian crisis, although:

> governments in the region were very reluctant to take on responsibility and playing this kind of, I don't want to say 'game', but they were obviously trying to deflect responsibility and not willing to take responsibility unless other states were taking responsibility.
> (Representative of international organization, Bangkok, November 2016)

The displacement of Rohingya was not formally an ASEAN issue in the sense that, as a regional organization, it had no framework for dealing with these kinds of forced migration flows that included significant numbers of people seeking refugee status. The 'crisis' did, however, focus attention:

> I don't want to sound cynical here but it was incredibly useful for focusing the major government players, the governments of the region, well first of all I guess it focused public perception and then the governments of the region, on the issues of migration and migrant smuggling and human trafficking... It's been a lot easier for us to work off the back of that because suddenly migrant smuggling, which was a crime that no one really knew much about, becomes a priority issue... Whereas before, I daresay most of your average senior government officials wouldn't have really known much about it.
> (Representative of international organization, Bangkok, November 2016)

A key element of this quote is the reference to migrant smuggling. There was involvement by smugglers, but to frame the issue as a problem of smuggling implies a particular representation of the causes and effects of displacement that can contribute to the reluctance of states to take or share responsibility. A linkage between displacement and transnational crime is significant because it forms an important part of the repertoire of migration governance beyond the state in Southeast Asia. This was also facilitated by the conceptual shift at the time of the CPA that, while securing the resettlement of around one million people, also led to questioning of the motivations of asylum seekers and created linkages to irregular migration and criminality.

On 29 May 2015 a meeting of the Indonesian, Malaysian, and Thai foreign ministers agreed to offer temporary protection on their territory 'provided that the resettlement and repatriation process will be done in one year by the international community' (cited in UNESCAP, 2016: 28). Malaysia and Indonesia were prepared to allow migrants to enter their territory, while

Thailand offered 'floating platforms' to assist those rescued at sea (Gleeson, 2017: 9). In July 2015, the ASEAN Ministerial Meeting on Transnational Crime sought 'feasible regional solutions' and to create a trust fund to support relief efforts. By December the number of people had dropped to around 1,600, but the wider point is that normalized representations of displacement and the role of the region played crucial roles in shaping responses to the crisis, as defined. The response was largely *ad hoc* and centred on temporary protection, with resettlement expected to occur outside the region. Australia, Qatar, Saudi Arabia, Japan, Turkey, Gambia, and the USA offered financial support and some resettlement places, although when Australia's Prime Minister Tony Abbott was asked whether Australia would resettle refugees, he replied: 'nope, nope, nope' (Petcharamesree et al., 2016: 3).

There then followed numerous meetings that illustrate the increased multi-organizational complexity of migration governance. There was, for example, in July 2015, an ASEAN Ministerial Meeting on Transnational Crime that sought 'feasible regional solutions' and to create a trust fund to support relief efforts, followed in November 2015 by the Jakarta Declaration Roundtable Meeting on Addressing the Root Causes of Irregular Movement of Persons and then by a special meeting held in Bangkok in December 2015 on Irregular Migration in the Indian Ocean (Petcharamesree et al., 2016: 3). There were also alternative venues to ASEAN that could be used to develop regional responses to migration. One such was the Bali Process, which, after March 2016, was tasked with formulating 'an urgent and collective response' (Gleeson, 2017: 10), but with a focus on 'transnational organised crime' with no reference to resettlement.

In March 2016, Australia and Indonesia in the context of the Bali Process reported on responses to the Andaman Sea crisis and identified a need for stronger regional capacity through the creation of a new regional response mechanism, but political sensitivities in the region made the development of such capacity very difficult. Strikingly, the Australian-Indonesian review did not use the term 'Rohingya', preferring 'mixed populations', and made no recommendations on addressing the root causes of displacement beyond proposing further research (Bali Process, 2016b).

A further wave of mass killings, sexual violence, and destruction of villages that began in August 2017 was, by 2020, estimated by the UNHCR to have displaced 742,000 Rohingya to Bangladesh. More than 40 per cent of those fleeing were under the age of 12.

There are clearly regionalized migration flows in Southeast Asia, but the regional responses are very patchy, with a preference for bilateral and multilateral solutions. To understand why and how these responses are effects of a migration governance repertoire in Southeast Asia, it is necessary to look more closely at regionalism.

What kind of region?

In November 2016, this book's author was in Jakarta and visited the ASEAN Secretariat four times. Each time involved a long taxi journey along Jakarta's congested roads. Before heading off, there would be a lengthy discussion with the taxi driver, showing a map with the ASEAN Secretariat's location high-lighted. Every journey was apparently the first time the driver had ever been to the ASEAN building. Jakarta isn't the easiest city to navigate, and each expedition would usually entail a couple of subsequent stops to ask people for clarification of the directions. On one occasion this occurred literally around the corner from the ASEAN building, although the person that we asked did not seem to know what ASEAN was or where it was located, even though it was a stone's throw away. While by no stretch of the imagination a scientific study, the cumulative effect of these journeys was to suggest that ASEAN had not cut through into public consciousness, at least in Jakarta.

The paragraph above could also probably be read as showing how an encounter with ASEAN challenges Eurocentric assumptions about regional governance. ASEAN regional institutions are not led by ASEAN, but this could be a strength not a weakness because:

> Its role is better described as the hub and the agenda setter, a convening power with a normative and social leadership...ASEAN has used socializa-tion and persuasion to engage not only other Southeast Asian and East Asian countries, but *all* the great powers of the current international order.
>
> (Acharya, 2018: 85)

Ostensibly, scope for migration governance beyond the state in the ASEAN region would appear limited. National policy and legal frameworks for migration and migrants are limited. Compared to regional frameworks for migration governance in Africa, Europe, North America, and South America, commitment to international norms and standards is also weak, with only two countries adhering to the UN Migrant Workers Convention and a further two adhering to the 1951 Refugee Convention. A core purpose of ASEAN is the pursuit of economic development rather than emphasizing democratization or the protection of human rights (Rother, 2012). It is not necessary to be a democracy to be a member of ASEAN.

A key characteristic of the ASEAN region is its 'multiplexity', with national governments and regional organizations, 'but also international institutions, nongovernmental organizations, multinational corporations and transnational networks (good and bad)' (Acharya, 2018: 80). Jakarta may host ASEAN, but regional governance is much more complex than the physical location of the ASEAN Secretariat. The characteristics of a multiplex order are complex linkages and multiple layers of governance: 'Regionalism is a key part of this, but regionalism today is open and overlapping' (Acharya, 2018: 80). Our interviews across Southeast Asia revealed an awareness of the diversification of actors and voices that, as argued in Chapter 2, forms part of the context for sense-making ('Who are all these people at this meeting?'). As a representative of an NGO put it:

In migration governance now, we have to consider all the different actors. We tend to think of only governments as actors, but there are many actors in the governance of migration, in different ways, of course, with different roles...you have to include the international institutions. Then, you have to include the recruiters, the smugglers, the traffickers, and all that, so migration has become a very complex reality in terms of governance.

(Representative of NGO, Manila, November 2016)

Smugglers and traffickers are unlikely to turn up at policy seminars, but the field is certainly more crowded. There is also a wider significance that can be associated with multiplexity. More organizations and more viewpoints can mean competing or even contradictory perspectives on migration governance. In such a setting, signals or cues from the environments within which organizations operate may be unclear. Suggestive of these tensions was a comment made to us by an interviewee working for an international organization in the Philippines who talked about 'paradoxes':

We need to not choose between contradicting objectives. So, we have to deal with paradoxes more. We have to just be more accepting of the existence of the paradoxes in our processes...I think it is just, our organizations are products of another century, and another, almost time-space reality, in a sense. So, it is adapting at a slower pace than it needs to, but it is adapting.

(Representative of international organization, Manila, November 2016)

This sense of dealing with paradoxes and of organizations needing to adapt to changing circumstances can also create new ways of working, but another of our interviewees noted the 'different frames of mind' that can impede cooperation:

> It's really quite interesting when you sit in a meeting, or there is inter-agency work involving your fellow executive officers. You have several different frames of mind. When you're dealing with executive offices, you really have to exercise a very long form, you have to really lengthen your patience over a long period of time. Big time. You have to work with them, to cooperate with them. To share your migration and development lens point of view…but we try to be proactive, and we always work with multilateral organizations working in the country. Like the UN system, Asian Development Bank, the IOM.
>
> (Government official, Manila, November 2016)

The result can be raised or even unrealistic expectations that are confounded by slow progress in formal governance settings:

> Everyone gets excited and thinks something really positive is happening and migration governance is going to improve. Then the momentum goes missing, the government changes whatever and it kind of slips away and we go back into this same circle of Thailand being unable to effectively manage its migrant population.
>
> (Representative of international organization, Bangkok, November 2016)

ASEAN has expanded from its initial five member states in 1967 to a current membership of ten, while East Timor and Papua New Guinea have observer status. The ASEAN+3 forum was initiated in 1996 as a way for ASEAN to liaise with the three East Asian nations of China, Japan, and South Korea. ASEAN's founding treaty made no mention of migration. There were limited provisions in the 1995 ASEAN Framework Agreement on Services, and there are also provisions for visa-free travel for up to one month. There is also limited reach by international agreements. As already noted, only Cambodia and Philippines are signatories of the 1951 Refugee Convention, while only Indonesia and the Philippines are parties to the 1990 UN migrant workers convention. As Rother (2018: 111) has put it, 'regional migration governance efforts…have been characterised by slow pace and limited scope'. Petcharamseree (2016: 187) highlights the reactive nature of migration governance in Southeast

Asia: 'While ASEAN reacts to issues, it is always reluctant to act before an issue becomes a "crisis".' More generally, Jones and Smith (2007) highlight the tendency for ASEAN to be dominated by meetings and procedures, with the effect that it can be understood as 'making process, not progress'. As a representative of an international organization put it to us:

> ASEAN is not easy to work with. We find that...things are very bureaucratic and incredibly slow-moving with ASEAN. It's positive in a sense that the member states are engaged in it and the level of ownership is high but everything is on a voluntary basis and a non-binding basis'.
> (Representative of international organization, Jakarta, November 2016)

Central to any representation of ASEAN's role and operation and thus to the shape and content of migration governance beyond the state in Southeast Asia has been the so-called 'ASEAN way', which Acharya describes as 'a short-hand for organizational minimalism and preference for non-legalistic approaches to cooperation'. This 'ASEAN way' is typically seen to comprise consensus-based decision-making, non-interference, non-use of force, peaceful settlement of disputes, and respect for the sovereignty and territorial integrity of members (although, see Jones, 2011). This way of working was 'not so much about the substance or structure of multilateral interactions, but a claim about the *process* through which such interactions are carried out' (Acharya, 1997: 52, emphasis in original). As it was put to us by a representative of an international organization:

> ASEAN states have a tradition of non-interference and solving problems bilaterally instead of enforcing a regional policy that then it will impose on a member state, if they're not following the policy line. The best example is the reaction that other member states have to Myanmar and its treatment of the Rohingya. So, I think there's certainly a framework for ASEAN to take more of a lead on these types of things, but the political will is still not there.
> (Representative of international organization, Jakarta, November 2016)

The very notion of an 'ASEAN way' is suggestive of regional specificity. In his extensive work on Southeast Asian regionalism, Acharya identifies the importance of local, national, and regional contexts. To do so, he draws from a longer tradition of historiographical research that shows that Southeast Asian societies were 'not passive recipients...but active borrowers and localizers of foreign cultural and political ideas' (Acharya, 2004: 244). Localization is defined by Acharya (Acharya, 2004: 245) as 'the active construction (through discourse, framing, grafting and cultural selection) of foreign ideas by local actors, which results in the former developing significant congruence with local beliefs and practices'.

An effect of localization can be to strengthen and not weaken existing institutions and provide them with new pathways to legitimation. To be localized also requires that there are credible local actors with sufficient influence. These 'insider proponents' such as NGOs can build congruence with outside ideas (Acharya, 2004: 249). The aim is to make global norms appear 'local' and make 'an outside norm congruent with a pre-existing local normative order' (Acharya, 2004: 244). The implications of an emphasis on localization are that 'shifts in the global normative environment alone do not produce normative and institutional change at the regional level at the expense of pre-existing normative frameworks and regional arrangements' (Acharya, 2004: 270). This doesn't mean that regions can't develop, but, if they do, they are likely to proceed by 'the localization of international multilateral concepts, without overwhelming regional identity norms and processes' (Acharya, 2004: 270).

Flexible engagement

The Asian financial crisis of 1997 and lack of a regional response coupled with other events such as democratic transformation of Indonesia after the fall of President Suharto in 1998 led to pressure to modify the 'ASEAN way'. As Jones (2008: 735) put it:

[t]his pressure reflects a growing regional consciousness that the internal and external security of the state have become increasingly interconnected. It also coincides with the recognition, at least among the elites in the more developed states of the grouping, that prospects for regional progress depend on, among other things, the projection of a norm of political accountability into the regional order.

How could ASEAN reconcile its founding principles with measures designed to respond to transboundary issues, including international migration. Instructive in this respect were the failed proposals advanced by the Thai government in 1998 for ASEAN to develop forms of 'flexible engagement' aimed at responding to transnational challenges, including migration. Flexible engagement was a 'formal challenge to the ASEAN way' (Haacke, 1999: 582).

Flexible engagement was represented by its key proponent—the Thai government—as a necessary response to increasing interdependence in the face of new security challenges, including international migration, as well as to enhance democratization and human rights (Haacke, 1999). At the core of the debate about flexible engagement was the implication that it would have required ASEAN to breach its principle of non-interference (Acharya, 2004: 240). The Thai foreign minister, Surin Pitsuwan, developed a proposal to make ASEAN more responsive to transnational challenges and to:

> look beyond its cherished principle of non-intervention … to allow it to play a constructive role in preventing or resolving domestic issues with regional implications. The reality is that, as the region becomes more interdependent, the dividing line between domestic affairs on the one hand and external or transnational issues on the other is less clear. Many 'domestic affairs' have obvious external or transnational dimensions, adversely affecting neighbours, the region and the region's relations with others. In such cases, the affected countries should be able to express their opinions and concerns in an open, frank and constructive manner, which is not, and should not be, considered 'interference' in fellow-members' domestic affairs.
>
> (Thai Ministry of Foreign Affairs 1998, cited in Acharya, 2004: 261)

The idea of flexible engagement connected with global norms centred around humanitarian intervention, human rights, and democratization. The most obvious clash was with the military regime in Myanmar, but ASEAN held to its idea of non-interference and preferred 'constructive engagement' with the Myanmar generals instead of promotion of human rights and democracy.

At the Thirty-First Annual Meeting of the ASEAN foreign ministers in July 1998, Pitsuwan's proposal for flexible engagement was rejected, and, instead, there was reference to the pursuit of 'enhanced interaction', although the term never actually subsequently appeared in any official policy statements (Acharya, 2004: 263). Flexible engagement failed because it was a clear challenge to the ASEAN way, meant that criticism would be public, and could be seen as a collective ASEAN judgement, while it could also remove the ambiguity that had surrounded past examples of interference (Haacke, 1999: 583–5). A further weakness was that flexible engagement was grounded in no obvious regional tradition: 'ASEAN was founded by a group of illiberal regimes with no record of collectively promoting human rights and democratic governance' (Acharya, 2004: 262). This led to a continued preference for problems between countries to be resolved bilaterally. In 1998, for example, eight Indonesian migrants died in detention in Malaysia, which was then condemned by the Indonesian foreign minister as a violation of human rights, but this did not become an ASEAN issue. Instead, the matter was resolved bilaterally at a meeting between the Malaysian and Indonesian governments on the margins of the Asia-Europe meeting held in London in April 1998. Malaysia rejected Indonesia's accusations of human rights abuses, while Indonesia accepted Malaysia's right to deport illegal immigrants: 'quiet diplomacy had been restored and ASEAN had not been involved' (Haacke, 1999: 593). As Haacke (1999: 593) goes on to note, by August 1998 Malaysia had deported 200,000 Indonesians.

The 2007 ASEAN Charter reaffirmed existing commitments to consensus-based decision-making, national sovereignty, and other key aspects of the ASEAN way but added to them 'a novel goal': 'to strengthen democracy, enhance good governance and the rule of law, and to promote and protect human rights and fundamental freedoms'. Jones (2008: 737) sees these as 'two incompatible norms: one that maintains the traditional formula of non-interference in internal affairs as the basis of regional peace, and one that promotes democracy and fundamental freedoms'. The ASEAN Charter also established a target deadline of 2020 for the creation of an ASEAN Community. To assist with this, in March 2009, the heads of government agreed to a roadmap to develop the plan for an ASEAN Community. The ASEAN Community has three pillars: an Economic Community aiming to create a single market, a Political-Security Community, and a Socio-Cultural Community. All were formally established on 31 December 2015. Migration is spread across the three pillars: trafficking is located in the Security Community, mobility provisions for professionals are placed within the Economic Community, while provisions for migrant workers are in the Socio-Cultural Community.

Article 5 of the ASEAN Charter expresses the ambition to 'create a single market and production base which is stable, prosperous, highly competitive and economically integrated with effective facilitation for trade and investment in which there is free flow of goods, services and investment; facilitated movement of business persons, professional, talents and labour; and freer flow of capital'. Within the ASEAN Economic Community there is a framework for free movement for professional and highly skilled workers. For eight employment sectors Mutual Recognition Arrangements have been agreed. These cover accountancy, engineering, surveying, architecture, nursing, medical services, dentistry, and tourism. These MRAs do not cover migration into lower-skilled employment, which, as discussed earlier, is the main form of migration.

By the end of 2018, only two professions, engineering and architecture, had stipulated eligibility, but, as Jurje and Lavenex (2015: 6) observe, this is hardly a frictionless process:

> to obtain the standard certification, the applicant must hold a professional license issued by the regulatory body in the home country, which will then be reviewed by the ASEAN Chartered Professional Engineers Coordinating Committee or the ASEAN Architect Council. If the application is approved, a professional is allowed to work as 'Registered Foreign Professional Engineer' in another ASEAN country, nevertheless subject to domestic rules and regulation.

In effect, the scheme for mobility for professionals provides for registration of a pool of professionals, but it doesn't necessarily mean that the people in this pool can move. When an eligible person seeks to move to another ASEAN country, the receiving member state can ask for an employment contract as the basis for issuing a visa. This is a long way from a free movement framework. Discussing these limited developments and revealing some underlying concerns, a government official in the Philippines put it as follows:

> I honestly don't know if we're ready for that kind of integration... there's actually fear. That we will lose jobs... meaning we will not be able to get as many jobs, because other people from the ASEAN will be able to get jobs from the Philippines away from the locals. That's the fear that they say, or we will lose out in the markets, because many products from our fellow ASEAN countries will penetrate the Philippine market. So that's the way the discussion is right now.   (Government official, Manila, November 2016)

In addition to the limited provisions on mobility for professionals, there are other ASEAN declarations with implications for migration. In November 2004 the ASEAN Declaration against Trafficking in Persons, Particularly Women and Children was agreed but its effects are limited, because the preamble requires members to take measures 'to the extent permitted by their respective domestic laws' (ASEAN Secretariat, 2004).

At the twelfth ASEAN summit in Cebu, Philippines, in 2007 agreement was reached on the ASEAN Declaration on the Protection and Promotion of the Rights of Migrant Workers (ASEAN Secretariat, 2007). Paragraph 4 of the Cebu Declaration states: 'Nothing in the present Declaration shall be interpreted as implying the regularization of the situation of migrant workers who are undocumented.' There are no provisions relating to freedom of association or freedom to organize. In 2007 the ASEAN Committee on the Implementation of the Convention was established, which, among other things, organizes a Committee on Migrant Workers (ACMW) and an annual ASEAN Forum on Migrant Labour, with representatives from national governments, employers, trade unions, civil society organizations, and international organizations such as the ILO and UN-Women. The preamble to the Cebu Declaration made clear that 'the sovereignty of states in determining their own migration policy relating to migrant workers, including determining their entry to the territory and under which conditions migrant workers may remain'. The preamble 'weakens the whole declaration, as it curtails any possibility for any regional approach to migration and migrant workers as each state still has full authority to deal with migrant workers, in spite of the recognition [in the preamble] for the need to address "cases of abuse and violence against migrant workers whenever such cases occur"' (Petcharamesree, 2016: 182). No provisions are made for the temporary contract-based labour migration that is prevalent in the region. Rother (2018) detects a growing presence of civil society actors, but the effects of their presence are more difficult to detect. He concludes that space for the inclusion of civil society is limited both because of the way that ASEAN is structured and because of domestic political contexts in member states. Others see ASEAN as creating space that can indicate directions 'until such times as a more propitious climate has emerged' (Quayle, 2015: 424).

Progress within the ACMW has been slow because of 'the sensitivity of the issue and the lack of consensus among its members (Petcharamesree, 2016: 183). The ACMW has as one of its aims the development of an ASEAN Instrument on the Protection and Promotion of the Rights of Migrant Workers, but the pace of development is glacial: 'the instrument itself, a legally binding instrument, has been in discussion for almost 10 years. What we've tried to do with the ASEAN forum on migrant labour is that while they're negotiating this legally binding document, the AFML allows us to move forward' (Representative of international organization, Manila, November 2016). The document could be seen as a rights-based approach to migration and as an indicator of 'small steps towards recognition of migrants' rights', but there is little space for civil society to engage with ASEAN, even though the expressed aim of the ASEAN Socio-Cultural Community is a 'people-centred' community (Rother and Piper, 2014: 39–40). The ASEAN human rights structure is weak. The ASEAN Human Rights Declaration of November 2012 does not provide a comprehensive human rights framework at regional level as there is no court. The ASEAN Intergovernmental Commission on Human Rights does not have the power to receive complaints or conduct investigations. This reflects an economic framing of migration with less space for rights-based concerns, which will also encounter the very firm emphasis in all relevant ASEAN agreements on the sovereignty of member states regarding both the admission of migrants and the terms of admission:

> So, the advocacy on ASEAN on human rights…both in civil society and governments, especially the progressive element, is actually more difficult… When you put migrant workers as rights…that would be more difficult than if you put migrant workers from the perspective of economic develop-ment, or you put migrants as the reality in development…I think ASEAN may understand it better when migrant workers being framed into economic development rather than rights issues.
> (Representative of a Regional Organization, Jakarta, November 2016)

There are proponents of 'alternative regionalism' that see the democratizing potential of bottom-up engagement (Igarashi, 2011; Rother and Piper, 2014). That said, Rother and Piper (2014) see limited scope for engagement within the ASEAN structure but see more scope through the creation of regional networks such as the Asia-Pacific Refugee Rights Network and the ASEAN Migrant Forum. They also see scope for what they call a 'vertical boomerang', by which they mean that global institutions can be a source of regional change. External norms do, though, need to be consistent with regional ways of doing things that impose cultural and empirical limits consistent with an existing repertoire of migration governance. When talking to a representative of an international organization, we got a sense of the frustration that can be felt by those who actively seek to bring international norms to the Southeast Asian region:

> Whereas I think to really have long-standing change, you've got to alter—I mean it sounds a bit neocolonial but you want mindset change on issues. That's any organizational change, it comes down to mindset change, not that we know better than anyone else but you want to change how people are doing business. The way you do that, you don't do that through training. That's a very poor way of doing it.
> (Representative of international organization, Bangkok, October 2015)

This is a clear reference to the cognitive foundations of the migration govern-ance repertoire and the expectations that are associated with them. A strong government-led dynamic is clearly evident in Southeast Asia, but there are also more complex patterns of regionalization that involve a wider array of public and private actors more or less organized within the ASEAN multiplex. This creates a disjunction between the regionalization of migration flows and the limited scope for regionalized migration governance through ASEAN. There are, however, alternative regional venues. Of particular importance has been the Bali Process, a regional consultation process that provides a more infor-mal and state-led venue for intensified cooperation on aspects of migration, particularly smuggling and irregular migration.

The Bali Process

The Bali Process or, as it is formally known, the 'Conference on People Smuggling, Trafficking in Persons and Related Transnational Crime' is a regional cooperation framework established in February 2002. The Bali Process emerged from a prior IOM-led Regional Seminar on Irregular Migration and Migrant Trafficking in East and South Asia, known as the Manila Process, which produced the 1999 Bangkok Declaration on Irregular Migration. In turn, this created the Intergovernmental Asia-Pacific Consultations on Refugees, Displaced Persons and Migrants (Kneebone, 2014: 599). Kneebone (2014: 600) identifies how the 1999 declaration that eventually led to the creation of the Bali Process connects international migration with irregular migration and makes links to smuggling and trafficking. This frame provided a basis for subsequent action, although, as already noted, the CPA after 1989 had already made strong links between asylum seeking, irregular migration, and criminality. In terms of governance, the Bali Process is informal and does not produce binding outputs.

The Bali Process has been seen as a method to export Australian policy priorities to Southeast Asia. These Australian priorities became evident dur-ing Australia's 2001 general election campaign, when 433 Afghan and Sri Lankan asylum seekers were rescued in international waters by the Norwegian freighter MV Tampa. The Tampa sailed towards Christmas Island, with the intention of transferring the asylum seekers to the Australian authorities, but the Tampa was refused entry by the Australian navy. The captain of the Tampa briefly entered Australian territorial waters. In response, Australian special forces were deployed to order the boat back out to sea. The stand-off lasted for a week. The 433 were sent to detention on Nauru, with family units flown to

New Zealand for resettlement. The incumbent prime minister and leader of the Liberal Party, John Howard, stated in an election speech just days before the vote: 'we will decide who comes to this country and the circumstances in which they come' (Marr and Wilkinson, 2004).

Realizing that the Australian response needed to connect to the Southeast Asian region, the Australian and Indonesian governments co-hosted a regional conference in Bali in February 2002, with delegates from thirty-eight states, observers from a further fifteen countries, plus UNHCR and IOM. Co-chaired by the Australian and Indonesian governments and supported by a Regional Support Office in Bangkok, the Bali Process had by 2020 evolved to include forty-five member countries, seventeen observer countries, and IOM, UNHCR, and the UN Office on Drugs and Crime (UNODC), with a steering group comprising Australia, Indonesia, Thailand, New Zealand, UNHCR, and IOM (Douglas and Schloenhardt, 2012; Kneebone, 2014).

The third meeting of the Bali Process in 2002 indicated a particular framing: voluntary commitment by states 'within the framework of their international obligations' and 'respective national circumstances' (Co-Chairs' Statement, Bali Ministerial Conference on People Smuggling, Trafficking in Persons and Related Transnational Crime, February 2002, cited in Douglas and Schloenhardt, 2012: 6). Alexander Downer, the Australian foreign minister, identified the advantages of the Bali Process for the Australian government: 'the Bali Process doesn't legislate, the Bali Process doesn't force anybody to do anything. What is does is provide a framework, it provides context and it provides priority' (cited in Douglas and Schloenhardt, 2012: 13). Oelgemöller (2011: 114) talks about the 'opaque' character of such processes, which help with the 'moulding of ideas about a shared contentious issue'. Comparing the two, an official from a Bangkok-based international organization referred at first to the Bali Process and then compared it with ASEAN:

> A lot of what we're doing, we're looking for—well things like the Bali Process, the ministers agreed to something that creates the space for you to be able to do what you need to do or what you want to do. It's easier to, for example, get that agreement through the Bali Process in some ways than through ASEAN because ASEAN is very politicized.
>
> (Representative of international organization, Bangkok, November 2016)

The Bali Process met in 2002 and 2003 and was then '"reactivated" and "enhanced"' in 2009, linked to another increase in boat arrivals (Kneebone, 2014: 601). Importantly, the Bali Process, more than ASEAN, became an important forum for dealing with Rohingya displacement, which meant a focus on illegality and criminality in an informal 'transgovernmental' setting. In November 2010, the UNHCR presented to the Bali Process *Ad Hoc* group a proposal for a Regional Cooperation Framework that would provide 'a common set of understandings for dealing with irregular movement and asylum-seekers in a protection-sensitive manner' (cited in Petcharamesree, 2016: 186). The key thing here is that existing understandings were not challenged; rather, they went regional. A Regional Support Office for the Bali Process was established in Bangkok.

Australia has been characterized as a regional hegemon that has 'exported its policies of preventing movement of asylum-seekers, as well as detention' through the Bali Process (Kneebone, 2017: 34). Australia's response to asylum seeking has been externalization to the region through what it called the 'Pacific Solution', which was evident between 2001 and 2008 and then again after 2012. Launched in September 2013, 'Operation Sovereign Borders' was a unilateral response by Australia and not embedded within regional struc-tures. It was military-led, with a focus on intercepting boats carrying asylum seekers before they entered Australian territorial waters. Boats could be towed back, usually towards Indonesia. There was also an increased focus on off-shore processing and resettlement (Curley and Vandyk, 2017: 45). As Larking (2017: 86) notes, 'Australia's bilateral arrangements with regional countries concerning irregular migration are primarily focused on detention, process-ing and resettlement, but it has also entered into a wider range of border and customs management arrangements with individual countries.'

Those who do seek to enter Australia by boat have been intercepted and then processed and detained on Nauru and, until October 2017, on Manus Island in Papua New Guinea. Kneebone (2014: 601) links the Bali Process squarely to Australian priorities and describes it as a method to 'export' Australian policies and priorities. This occurs via what has been described as 'incentivized policy transfer', which includes both financial and diplomatic resources. For example, the 2006 Lombok Treaty on the Framework for Security Cooperation between Australia and Indonesia provides a wider framework of cooperation to deal with 'traditional' and 'non-traditional' security challenges with significant financial aid and technical know-how transferred from Australia to Indonesia in the areas of defence, combating transnational crime, counterterrorism, maritime and aviation security, and intelligence-sharing (Roberts et al., 2014). In return, Indonesia promised to crack down on people smuggling and committed to allowing migrants that were intercepted at sea to disembark on Indonesian territory (Nethery and

Gordyn, 2014: 188–9). Curley and Vandyk (2017: 42) highlight that the Bali Process is a way for Australia and Indonesia to 'contest and amend the norms and practices around the human rights of refugees and asylum-seekers', while seeing the Bali Process as being consistent with Asia-Pacific regionalism, as it relies on informal dialogue and the development of regional norms via socialization.

These perspectives emphasize the transmission of Australian norms to Southeast Asia via incentives. Larking (2017) takes as an example of Australian influence that Indonesia, Malaysia, and Thailand have also all refused to allow boats with asylum seekers to land. If Australia had not already had such an approach, 'there would have been less incentive for Indonesia, Malaysia and Thailand to themselves adopt turn back policies' (Larking, 2017: 91). Clearly, Australia has been a key driver of cooperation, but the CPA in the late 1980s had already eroded the status of refugees and represented them as economic migrants trying to enter via other means. Thailand was already trying to push back boat people in the late 1980s. These regional responses in Southeast Asia had blurred the distinction between asylum seeking and irregular migration. 'External' norms were already localized and rendered consistent with the regional focus that has been to seek temporary solutions to displacement and to avoid measures that impinged on state sovereignty.

Conclusions

A repertoire of migration governance in Southeast Asia centres not only on the more visible manifestations of governance (laws, policies, and the like) but also on what actors within the governance system know how to do and on expectations about role. There are, of course, multiple actors and significant scope for variation in cognitive representations and expectations, but this chapter has demonstrated important features of the Southeast Asian migration governance repertoire. Migration governance beyond the state in Southeast Asia centres on national governments with a clear preference for bilateral and multilateral forums rather than formalized, regional venues. Responses to crises draw from an established repertoire that is likely to lead to informal rather than formalized regional responses. The Southeast Asian region has very limited migration competencies and, even in those areas where it could act, such as higher-skilled mobility, it has proven difficult to secure agreement. More informal settings, such as the Bali Process, have provided alternative, non-threatening (to states) venues. Underlying these characteristics of governance is the powerful effect of underlying issue framing and their contribution to the creation of a sensible environment that makes sense to key actors and provides them with a basis to proceed. This directly contributes to a powerful regional effect that shapes responses to labour migrants (labelled as temporary foreign workers) and to displaced people. The migration governance repertoire is powerfully shaped by representations that migrants are temporary. This is an effect of governance that frames responses and establishes the cultural and empirical parameters of subsequent actions. Deeply rooted, this repertoire is persistent and difficult to change. There is migration governance beyond the state in Southeast Asia with powerful effects, but it is consistent with this repertoire; its imputation of temporariness, as currently constituted, tends to reaffirm rather than to challenge prevalent representations.

4

De jure and *de facto* Openness
in South America

Introduction

South America since the 2000s has been seen as offering a distinctively progressive and liberal counterpoint to prevailing global trends in migration governance. Across the region, there was a period when left-wing governments committed to a new approach to migration, proclaimed a right to migrate, and urged the non-criminalization of migration in ways that were seen as emblematic of a 'liberal tide' at state and regional levels (Cantor et al., 2015). This chapter explores the relationship between these important changes and underlying conditions of *gobernabilidad* or governability to show that migration governance beyond the state in South America has been configured not only by concerns about the 'governability' of international migration in its various forms (Braz, 2018; Domenech, 2013; Mármora, 2010) but also by a concern about governability more generally at both national and regional level (Camou, 2001; Mayorga and Córdova, 2007). Perceptions of governability shape what actors know how to do and their expectations about role and are necessarily linked to the economic, social and political context in which actors operate; to concerns about state legitimacy, authority, and capacity; and to political projects of both left and right that seek to harness these concerns into programmes of government. Scope for migration governance beyond the state is necessarily linked to this context and the ways in which actors of various types make sense of it. Regionalism then becomes entwined with representations of state capacity and of domestic political consensus about the state's role (Petersen and Schulz, 2018: 103).

Consistent with the other chapters in this book, the aim is not to analyse the outputs or outcomes of governance systems—such as the gaps between what actors say they want to do and what happens—but to assess the effects of know-how and expectations about role 'inside' governance processes. By doing so, it then becomes apparent how representations of governability

Governing Migration Beyond the State: Europe, North America, South America, and Southeast Asia in a Global Context.
Andrew Geddes, Oxford University Press (2021). © Andrew Geddes. DOI: 10.1093/oso/9780198842750.003.0004

have shaped underlying perceptions of the normality of migration and have underpinned both openness and closure at state and regional level and thus provided a backdrop to responses to crises. Take for example, this quote from an Argentinian government official referring to both crisis and governability:

> I don't know if there was a crisis of governability, but the causes of the immigration are quite the same like we have in history, but the circumstances or the atmosphere is changing.
> (Argentinian government official, Buenos Aires, July 2017)

'Circumstances' and 'atmosphere' are ways of thinking about the context in which this particular governance actor operated where there is a perceived stability in the underlying causes of migration, but context—or underlying conditions of governability, as understood—changes.

This chapter's analytical focus, like those of other chapters, reverses the usual tendency to focus on international migration as a challenge to legitimacy, authority, and capacity. Instead, the argument is turned around: it is perceptions of legitimacy, authority, and capacity and their association with political projects of both left and right that have given meaning to migration as a social and political issue in South America and to regional-level developments associated with these projects. This includes significant changes associated with the liberal tide since the 2000s. More recently, large-scale migration flows such as those associated with mass displacement from Venezuela clearly present a challenge to governance. Here too responses draw from a migration governance repertoire that shapes what actors know how to do and what they think they should be doing. The 'liberal tide' of progressive migration laws and policies in South America depended on left-wing ideological convergence in many South American countries as well as conscious attempts to position the region as separate and distinct from both the United States as the continental hegemon and regional approaches to migration in the EU, which were labelled as harsh and repressive (Acosta Arcarazo and Geddes, 2013). It also involved attempts to make radical change to migration laws and policies and move away from the existing status quo. As we see, this presents a contrast with other regions where a status quo bias and associated risk aversion have made change difficult. The 'liberal tide' in migration policy was an attempt by left-wing governments to enact significant domestic reform while also establishing a distinctive normative template for regional governance that was consciously set in opposition to US hegemony and also a representation of an EU approach as being hostile to migration.

While there is strong evidence of regionalization in South America, with intra-regional migration flows strongly present, it is also the case that formal regional institutions have come and gone. An element of continuity is provided by MERCOSUR, which weathered the effects of economic crisis in the late 1990s and early 2000s to relaunch itself in the early 2000s, including with the MERCOSUR Residence Agreement (MRA) agreed in 2004, in force since 2009, and which has been seen as a regional manifestation of the 'liberal tide' (Braz, 2018; Brumat, 2016; International Organization for Migration, 2012). MERCOSUR's operational rather than more overtly political identity can help to explain its persistence as a formal regional structure. It is centred on cooperation (not integration) between states that have been reluctant to cede sovereignty. There has been a consistent aversion to pooled sovereignty and supranational institutions, combined with oscillations in attitudes to economic liberalization that help to explain the lower levels of economic integration in South America when compared to the higher intensity of exchanges of goods, capital, and services within Southeast Asia or the EU. Malamud (2018) identifies a distinction between ambitious rhetoric and practical achievements, meaning that South American regionalism 'distinguishes itself from the European version in that narratives substitute for institutions, and agendas replace policies'. South America has, however, been shaped by a long history of cross-border interactions, by powerful and shared political legacies that have been linked to migration, exile, and displacement, and by cultural, social, and linguistic affinities. Analysing the distinctiveness of these developments in South America can help to dispel the myth 'that worthy innovations are bound to happen in the West and only echo in the rest—or that normative advancement in migration issues drips naturally from North to South' (Pedroza, 2017: 141).

Drivers and characteristics

A recurring theme of this book's focus on migration governance is that international migration occurs because of underlying changes in social, economic, and political systems, but these changes do not send clear and unambiguous signals. This is why perceptions and representations of facts are so important for the causes and effects of these drivers, of interactions between these drivers, and of risks and uncertainties associated with them. This reflection from an Argentinian government official provides a practical example of sense-making as an enactive concept where people learn more about themselves and the issues for which they are responsible through interactions with others:

> The complexity of immigration is that it's impacting every different sector of the government. It's not just the immigration service, it's the impact on the economy, on education, on health, on security, on development, in so many places. We are trying to see if we can go forward in a, kind of, inter-ministerial consulate for immigration. It's not just to create the place or the space to interact, it's to create the strength in the people who are going to work in this particular interaction. If you don't have the people with some skills in immigration, sometimes the result could not be the best. It could be the worst. If you're going to talk with people from security and they don't have some skill about the real impact of immigration, the first approach is, 'Hey, come on, stop it. We already have our own problems, we don't want more.'
>
> (Argentinian government official, Buenos Aires, July 2017)

There is uncertainty about the causes and effects of international migration, which interacts with levels of know-how and expectations about role held by actors within governance systems who may have more or less experience of dealing with the issue. This means trying to make sense of migration in the context of organizational and institutional roles and also in relation to broader patterns of governance system development and change. There is a shared awareness among governance actors in South America that there are greater levels of immigration to South American countries compared to the emigration flows that characterized the time when the 'liberal tide' initially began to flow in the 2000s. An official from an international organization captured the complexity of migration in the region and resultant uncertainty for governing organizations when noting that:

> A few years ago, all South American countries were worried about our communities abroad and about how many people were emigrating. Ten years later there are people coming, others are returning and others are moving within the region. And this happened within a few years, so those changes in the migration dynamics translate into uncertainty that has an impact on us.
>
> (Representative, international organization, Buenos Aires, May 2015)

Argentina remains a regional migration hub, but is also experiencing flows from outside the region from African countries and China as well as people fleeing poverty and violence in Africa and the Middle East (da Silva, 2019;

Zubrzycki, 2012). Changes in migration dynamics—both real and perceived—have implications for decision-making and state capacity. A government official in Argentina told us that governing organizations would need to become 'faster and more agile':

> you generate a dynamic of permanent attention to where the thing is moving, there are permanent changes, this circuit of sending countries and receiving countries that previously had a slower circuit and every time it is more vertiginous, it takes you to a much faster and more agile dynamic of decision-making.   (Government official, Buenos Aires, April 2015)

A key focus for this chapter is intra-regional migration, although there has also been a growth in migration from outside the region, with a tendency for such migrants to be framed as unlawful, as Zubrzycki (2012) showed in a study of Senegalese migrants in Argentina. Figure 4.1 shows an increase in intra-regional flows in absolute numbers between 2010 and 2019, while Figure 4.2 presents a breakdown of intra-regional flows as a proportion of the overall total for 2019.

While there are data on flows from outside and within the region, our interviewees referred both to information gaps and to a lack of collaboration both within and between governments. A representative of an international organization based in Peru put it to us like this:

> we lack measurements systems, statistical instruments that allow us to measure the magnitude and volume of migration, but also all the

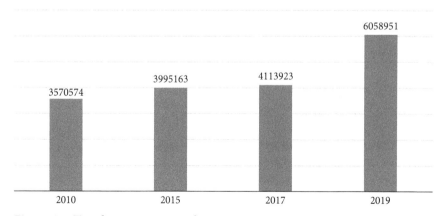

Figure 4.1 Trends in intra-regional migration, 2010–19
Source: UNDESA 2019.

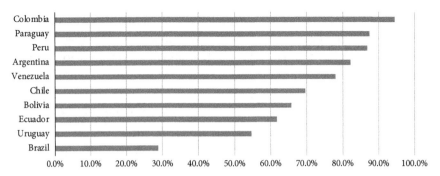

Figure 4.2 Share of intra-regional immigrants by country of destination, 2019
Source: UNDESA 2019.

correlations that are possible in regards to migration. That is one of the main uncertainties that we work with, the lack of information.

> (Representative of international organization, Peru, June 2016)

Similarly, a Chilean government official focused on the uncertain policy-making environment:

> the Chilean state, for different reasons, doesn't have a number and the estimation is vague. Starting from the point that we don't even have the total number of the population and we are working with the census from 2002. So that is a great uncertainty. How many migrants are there? Who are they and where do they come from? . . . currently we are generating policies without information, without full knowledge.

> (Chilean government official, Santiago, July 2016)

These kinds of concerns about knowledge and information gaps and about governmental capacity are not unique, but do play out in quite specific ways at national and regional level in South America and feed into representations of both regional mobility and displacement.

More generally, experience of economic and political change, of instability, and of transformations in South America is a vital underlying component of the ways in which migration issues are understood and also of the extent to which they are understood as regional issues.

In common with other regions, migration in South America is strongly regionalized, while representations of the region itself have been shaped by migration to, from, and within it. Historically, distinctly open approaches to migration were evident in the mid- to late nineteenth century, when, as the Argentinian intellectual Juan Bautista Alberdi (1852) put it:

To govern is to populate in the sense that to populate is to educate, improve, civilize, enrich...But to civilize through the population it is necessary to do it with civilized populations; to educate our America in freedom and in industry it must be populated with populations from the most advanced Europe in freedom and industry.   (my translation)

The words 'civilize through the population' are significant: openness to immigration in the nineteenth and early twentieth centuries was combined with the creation of the 'legal and bureaucratic machinery to cull "ethnically desirable" human stock from the millions yearning to breathe free' (Fitzgerald and Cook-Martín, 2014: 1). South America did, however, then lead the way in an anti-racist turn that saw Argentina, Chile, Uruguay, and Paraguay 'deracialize' their immigration policies in the 1930s and 1940s (ibid.: 334). The nineteenth and early twentieth centuries were characterized by large-scale flows from southern Europe. Between 1856 and 1932, 6.4 million people moved to Argentina, 4.4 million to Brazil, and 700,000 to Uruguay. By 1914, one-third of Argentina's population was foreign-born (Acosta Arcarazo, 2018). Chile, Peru, and Venezuela were also destination countries, albeit not on the same scale. Colombia, Ecuador, Bolivia, and Paraguay tended to be emigration countries.

Existing alongside these intercontinental flows are patterns of short-term, cross-border movements between neighbouring countries in border areas whose roots can be traced to precolonial times that have been facilitated by geographical and cultural proximity and have given rise to commercial dynamism (Durand, 2009; Martínez and Vono, 2005; Martínez Pizarro and Villa, 2005). Migration 'corridors' developed from Bolivia, Chile, Paraguay, and Uruguay to Argentina and from Colombia to Venezuela, although economic and political crisis meant Venezuela became in 2018 the world's major origin country for displaced people (Brumat, 2019a).

Flows of migrants from Europe fell away after the end of the Second World War, but these were compensated by increased intra-regional flows, including seasonal flows by agricultural workers from Uruguay, Chile, Paraguay, and Bolivia to Argentina that had 'precolonial roots...perpetuated with a cultural logic that, in some circumstances, has become transnational'(Cerrutti and Parrado, 2015: 401, 405). Short-term, seasonal, temporary migration has been linked to 'the fluidity of borders, the low cost of migration, and the socioeconomic contexts surrounding informal reception [which mean that] it would be reasonable to expect a high level of circularity and transitoriness associated with migration' (ibid.: 408).

Since the mid-2000s, migration flows to South America have not only increased but also become more diverse in terms of the origins, destinations, and profiles of migrants. As with other 'south-south' flows, proximity and existing migration networks are likely to have a much greater impact on migration, while there is also a greater presence of seasonal flows and cross-border trade as well as migration by people fleeing conflict or ecological disasters (Ratha and Shaw, 2007).

As in other regions and not surprisingly, our interviewees in South America identified economic and political factors as key drivers of international migration. An Argentina-based official from an international organization reflecting on the economic and political context put it to us like this:

> I think the predominant economic model is a model that generates increasing inequality and for this reason, human mobility is inevitable. If the disparities between countries are maintained, added to new factors such as the environment, climate change, etc., there is a tendency to move instead of staying that is growing... not to mention political conflicts.
>
> (Representative of international organization, Buenos Aires, April 2015)

This representation of what drives migration is fundamentally similar to prevailing perceptions in other regions in that economic and political drivers are seen as underlying causes of migration flows, although the adverse effects of neoliberalism and inequality are given greater prominence (Geddes and Vera Espinoza, 2018). International migration is understood as inevitable, linked to the effects of changes in underlying economic and political systems, likely to increase, and subject to uncertainties caused by ostensibly new factors such as environmental and climate change. Levels of development within the region are also seen to affect the scope for the creation of structures and processes such as those governing intra-regional free movement, as this Chilean government official noted:

> The levels of development of countries in the region are very unequal. When we talk about development, we talk about economic development, but also of political maturity... and I think that there is still a lot of inequality in South America and that is very difficult, let's say, to consider a free circulation space if, between the countries of the region, we do not overcome other issues that block free movement inside the region.
>
> (Chilean government official, Santiago, April 2016)

Argentina is the South American migration hub. Migration to Argentina fell after the military coup in 1976 but increased again in the 1990s. Economic crisis in the late 1990s led to increased emigration, but, after 2003, there was a renewed demand for migrant labour in Argentina because of economic recovery and a favourable political environment. Between censuses in 2000 and 2010 the stock of migrants from other South American countries in Argentina increased by 41.4 per cent, or around 1.4 million people (Cerrutti and Parrado, 2015: 402).

To reiterate the point already made about the importance of underlying economic and political changes in shaping the migration governance repertoire in South America, economic and political crisis at the end of the 1990s led to *la estampida migratoria* (the migratory stampede). This saw an estimated 400,000 people leave Argentina, 250,000 move from Bolivia, a further 1 million exit Brazil, 1.9 million leave Colombia, and 1.4 million move from Peru (Ramírez and Ramírez, 2005). The election of left-wing governments and the 'liberal tide' in approaches to migration across South America was powerfully shaped by the effects of economic crisis, subsequent political change, and emigration. As we also see the actor composition of the migration governance field also changed, with, for example, greater involvement by NGOs and academic experts (Brumat, 2016). Only Venezuela, because of oil, and Chile, because of relative political stability, bucked the emigration trend.

Experience of emigration played an important role in shaping the regional migration governance repertoire. Margheritis (2016) identified attempts by South American governments in the wake of economic crisis to actively court their emigrant diasporas, which she saw as a form of state-led transnational governance linked to a 'post-neoliberal' way of governing the diaspora that had strong regional foundations: 'South American-style diaspora engagement invokes collective identities and shared responsibilities to entice migrants self-entrepreneurial and self-disciplinary actions.... [T]he fact they have become part and parcel of a new normative regional consensus makes their reversal unlikely (Margheritis 2016: 8, 10).

Forced migration

South America's migration history has also been powerfully defined by forced displacement caused by political instability, violence, and authoritarian government. Freier (2015: 122–3) identifies historical legacies that shaped the 'asylum condition' in South America by contrasting the 'declarative nature' of the 1951 Geneva Convention whereby a refugee is a person who meets the convention's criteria with what she calls the 'constitutive nature' of asylum in

Latin America, where the status depends upon an asylum seeker proving their actual persecution (rather than well-founded fear of persecution, as per the Geneva Convention) and then being recognized by a government.

Forced displacement caused by dictatorial regimes in the 1970s and 1980s occurred within and beyond the region. Within South America, Argentina was a preferred haven for those fleeing the Strössner regime in Paraguay after 1954 and the Banzer regime in Bolivia, as well as those escaping the military regimes in Chile and Uruguay after 1973. During the period of military rule in Chile between 1973 and 1990, there are estimates of half a million people being forced to leave (Acosta Arcarazo, 2018). Military rule and state terrorism in Brazil between 1964 and 1985 led to around 1.8 million people leaving the country (ibid.). From the late 1980s to the late 1990s, Peruvians were forced into exile in Argentina, Chile, and Ecuador. In Colombia, by 2014, the effects of structural adjustment policies, decreased coffee prices, political instability, and drug trafficking meant that more than 400,000 Colombians had sought refuge in another country. Neighbouring Ecuador hosted an estimated 250,000 Colombians (Pugh, 2018).

In the transition from authoritarian government, Freier (2015) identified a liberalization—defined as being expansive in relation to asylum seekers' and refugees' rights—of South American refugee laws through ratification by all South American countries of the Geneva Convention and its 1967 Protocol. South American countries also moved beyond these provisions with the Cartagena Declaration of 1984. Cartagena was significant because it broadened the refugee definition provided by the Geneva Convention to add five additional elements that provide protection to people fleeing: generalized violence; foreign aggression; internal conflicts; massive violations of human rights; or other circumstances which have seriously disturbed public order (Gurmendi, 2018). Cartagena was initially developed as a response to mass forced displacement from Central America to Mexico but was also shaped by the legacies of mass displacement caused by dictatorships and authoritarianism (Parent and Freier, 2018a). Argentina, Brazil, Bolivia, Chile, Colombia, Ecuador, Paraguay, Peru, and Uruguay all incorporated Cartagena's standards into domestic law.

Mass displacement from Venezuela, particularly after 2014 was widely seen as a defining test of South American openness, the region's position in the vanguard of refugee protection and the effectiveness of regional responses (Acosta et al., 2018). Responses were relatively open to displaced Venezuelans, but this was often *de facto* rather than *de jure* so that people could move and ways were found to allow them to do so without necessarily applying the

Cartagena criteria. This was grounded in governability concerns about issues such as access to social services and employment.

The progressive tide of the 2000s was associated with left-wing governments, but by the mid-2010s the tide had turned and right-wing governments were in power across the region. This did not necessarily mean that right-wing governments would try to restrict entry by Venezuelans; rather, they could demonstrate their opposition to the left-wing Maduro regime in Venezuela by actually being open to those people displaced by it (Brumat et al., 2018). This meant that there were progressive developments even if from ostensibly unlikely sources such as the far-right Brazilian government of President Jair Bolsonaro. In December 2019, Brazil's refugee agency granted refugee status to 21,000 Venezuelans. The Brazilian government decision was hailed as a 'milestone decision for' refugee protection by the UNHCR (UN News, 2019).

There was notable openness across South America—certainly when compared to European responses to increased migration and refugee flows after 2015 (see Chapter 5), although responses were often pragmatic rather than strictly applying the Cartagena provisions. To understand why requires a consideration not only of the scale and rapidity of displacement, but also of the perceived governability of international displacement in South America, given the ways in which underlying social, economic, and political conditions were understood. These underlying conditions are *a priori* not *ex post* factors. While forced displacement is not new in South America, the scale and rapidity, particularly after 2014, of displacement by those forced to flee from Venezuela were unprecedented, resulting from the effects of near total economic collapse and the breakdown of basic social services, including health care. Millions of Venezuelans faced existential threats that impelled migration as a basic survival strategy. Estimates of numbers vary, but by the end of 2020, the UNHCR was estimating, probably conservatively, that around 4.5 million people had left Venezuela, mostly to Colombia, Ecuador, and Peru. Venezuelan migrants often found themselves in desperate circumstances. The northern Brazilian state of Roraima declared a state of social emergency in late 2017 because of an 'intense, unlimited, and disorderly flow of Venezuelans without means or conditions to sustain themselves' (Parent and Freier, 2018b). By the end of 2020, the UNHCR estimated that around 2 million Venezuelans had secured some form of legal stay in another South American country (UNHCR, 2020).

As had happened for Haitians forced to flee after the 2010 earthquake, Brazil initially enacted legislation that allowed temporary residence on humanitarian grounds for Venezuelans and subsequently decided to apply Cartagena to Venezuelans. Peru created a new temporary work/study permit scheme (one year with the possibility of renewal). Colombia offered Border Mobility Cards allowing free travel, followed by access to a temporary stay permit. In Chile, the Ministry of the Interior issued over 20,000 temporary residency permits for Venezuelans. Argentina and Uruguay granted residence to Venezuelans in accordance with the provisions of the MRA. In August 2017, Venezuela was suspended indefinitely from MERCOSUR. That same month, twelve foreign ministers, including those of Argentina, Brazil, and Colombia met in Peru and signed the Lima Declaration, seeking a peaceful resolution of the Venezuelan crisis (Acosta et al., 2018).

While large numbers of Venezuelans have been given a status in another South American country, relatively few have been recognized as refugees. In Peru, for example, Gurmendi (2018) reported that of around 130,000 asylum applications made by Venezuelans by mid-June 2018, only around 200 had been granted refugee status. A Peruvian government official stated that economic reasons in Venezuela, such as lack of food or lack of medicine, did not count as a basis for asylum (cited in Gurmendi, 2018). South American countries appear not be living up to their ambitious commitments, which, according to Freier (2018) means that:

> if countries continue to resist applying Cartagena, they run the risk of reducing their heralded legislation to mere words and window dressing [because] the countries facing the largest numbers of refugees have so far been unwilling to manage the crisis through the lens of refugee and asylum law, choosing instead to handle it through unilateral, temporary, ad hoc mechanisms.

The Covid-19 pandemic had adverse effects on Venezuelan migrants, because many had found work in the informal sector in countries such as Colombia, Ecuador, and Peru but lacked social protection or access to health care. When these countries imposed restrictions or went into lockdown, many Venezuelans lost their jobs and, for some, also their homes, which led to what the Norwegian Refugee Council described as an 'abrupt reversal' in refugee flows (Norwegian Refugee Council, 2020).

De facto openness is linked to underlying concerns about the governability of migration that shape repertoires of migration governance and thus what governance actors know how to do and what they think they should be doing. A sensible environment has been enacted wherein concerns about the effects of granting refugee status to Venezuelans does not necessarily lead to the closure of borders—although more restrictive tendencies were evident as numbers grew—but leads to the development of mechanisms and tools that have offered a path for Venezuelans away from the chaos and hardship of their own country. This can include using regionally agreed rules on residence contained within the MRA in place of protection, as occurred in Argentina and Uruguay. Parent and Freier (2018b) note among South American governments the 'fear that applying the Cartagena standard could lead to a further influx of Venezuelans, putting more stress on already vulnerable public services and stirring up more xenophobic sentiment'. South American countries have been open to people displaced by the situation in Venezuela, but it's also the case that they have not always fully applied their own ambitious refugee protection standards to do so.

Understanding why this is the case is revealing of basic political questions that shape state behaviour and relations between states in South America and are constitutive of a regional migration governance repertoire. What actors know how to do and their expectations about role are grounded in these wider debates about the authority, legitimacy, and capacity of states and their attachment to political projects of right and left that also shape relations between states and the role of regional integration. In more specific terms, these translate into a debate about the governability of migration as it affects the allocation of resources, ideas, and values within and between states. Not fully employing the Cartagena principles could be used as a criticism of the response to Venezuelan displacement as not according with the high standards contained in the Declaration. At the same time, *de facto* openness or the use of alternative frameworks—such as those related to residence, not protection—is grounded in the underlying conditions of governance and concerns about governability. This is not necessarily to provide a normative judgement of these responses and to say whether they are justified or not, or whether they could be more or less open; rather it is to connect regional integration in South America to representations of the authority, legitimacy, and capacity of states that underpin the regional migration governance repertoire in South America. There could be more or less openness, there can also be *de jure* and *de facto* forms of openness that coexist; but whether or not they occur depends on underlying political constellations and their interpretation by the cast of governance actors in South America, which can and does change.

A liberal tide?

The previous section has suggested that South American governments have been relatively open to displaced people, but that the progressive legal frameworks for the displaced that have developed at state and regional level do not necessarily determine responses to Venezuelan displacement. We now extend the analysis to consider schemes for intra-regional migrants. As already noted, in the 2000s South America was seen as a progressive trail-blazer for a more open and rights-based approach to migration, shaped by political change at national level, ideological convergence at regional level, and lauded as a counterpoint to restrictive approaches in Europe and North America (Parent and Freier, 2018b). As Acosta Arcarazo and Freier (2015: 670) put it, 'governmental migration discourses in Argentina, Brazil, and Ecuador shifted from closure and securitization to emphasize migrants' human rights, non-racism, and non-criminalization'. At a discursive level at least, a 'liberal tide' was defined as 'a clear tendency towards abandoning the notion of immigration as a problem or threat towards representing migration in the context of human rights' (Ceriani and Freier, 2015: 29). This has also been seen as a paradigm shift (Freier, 2015). For such a shift to occur funda-mental change would be required in the allocations of material power, as well as in underlying ideas and values. There was certainly rapid economic growth across the region in the early 2000s, plus evidence of policy change in South America and of a distinct approach to migration that developed in the 2000s, but there are limits to the sense in which these can be understood as a para-digm shift, because policy changes remain grounded in domestic politics, with governability concerns that can render them fragile. The relatively open and progressive approach to migration that developed in the 2000s was con-tingent upon left-wing governments and upon the co-existence of *de facto* and *de jure* openness. Together, these demonstrate the relationship between migration governance and underlying social, economic, and political struc-tures in South America that shape the migration governance repertoire.

A wave of new immigration laws were passed by left-wing governments to replace the previous frameworks imposed by authoritarian regimes. These new frameworks were progressive in terms of their rights basis, recognizing the right to migrate and committing to the non-criminalization of irregular migrants, and they also arose from a different kind of migration politics that, while still strongly dependent on presidential leadership, did 'open' the governance process to consult with a wider range of actors, including civil society, business, trade unions, and academics. Ceriani and Freier (2015: 29) sees this as emblematic of 'a different ethos... which has human dignity as a central component'. Together, these were seen to form 'part of a more wide-ranging promotion of equal treatment between nationals and foreigners in a process striving towards some form of universal citizenship', with 'equal treatment as a general rule throughout the region to make migration and citizenship law more enlightened and humane' (ibid.: 3, 6).

Leading the way, Argentina replaced the restrictive and repressive immigration law introduced by the military dictatorship in 1981 with legislation in 2004 that exemplified this progressive turn (Linares, 2017). The 2004 law was strongly linked to the MRA and to a regionalized solution to the regularization of irregular migrants from other MERCOSUR members. Article 4 specified 'the right to migrate as essential and inalienable to the person'. The Uruguayan migration law of 2008 was similarly progressive by, for example, specifying a right to migrate. In both Argentina and Uruguay changes were linked to 'demands made by a strong network of civil society organisations, including NGOS, academics and trade unions' (Ceriani and Freier, 2015: 16-17).

Importantly, this progressive turn, at least at its outset, occurred at a time of large-scale emigration from the region induced by the economic crisis of the late 1990s. The Argentinian law was identifying the kinds of standards that its government wanted to be extended to Argentinian emigrants with, for example, appeals to ideas about 'historic reciprocity' with Spain recalling the large numbers of people who moved from Spain to Argentina. The Argentinian president, Cristina Kirchner, identified Argentina as part of 'a worldwide, morally superior, avant-garde in immigration policymaking' (cited in Acosta Arcarazo and Freier, 2015: 668). Similarly, for refugee protection, the head of the UNHCR legal department for the Americas, Juan Carlos Murillo, stated in 2013 that 'Latin America is the new avant-garde of human-rights based refugee protection' (cited in Acosta Arcarazo and Freier, 2019). Uruguay's 2008 law was more closely aligned with the progressive turn at national and regional level and with the evolving MERCOSUR framework (Lapp, 2017).

The progressive tide was evident in other South American countries. After his election in 2007, President Rafael Correa of Ecuador had similar concerns about the treatment of Ecuadorian emigrants. In Article 416(6) on the principles governing international relations of its 2008 constitution it was stated that Ecuador 'advocates the principle of universal citizenship, the free movement of all inhabitants of the planet, and the progressive extinction of the status of alien or foreigner as an element to transform the unequal relations between countries, especially those between North and South'. While Acosta Arcarazo (2018: 114) notes that 'the precise meaning of this provision is undeniably elusive', Ecuador did introduce in 2008 an open-borders policy that gave anyone from any country the right to enter Ecuador for up to ninety days. The aims were to boost tourism and to fulfil the commitment of Article

416(6). A problem was that it was difficult to get a residence permit after ninety days, which led to increased irregular migration. After six months of this open-borders approach, visa requirements were reintroduced for Chinese citizens and, after eighteen months, for citizens of Afghanistan, Bangladesh, Eritrea, Ethiopia, Kenya, Nepal, Nigeria, Pakistan, and Somalia (Acosta Arcarazo and Freier, 2015: 683).

The liberal tide continued to flow into the 2010s. In 2013, Bolivia and, in 2017, Brazil, Ecuador, and Peru all introduced new migration laws that were characterized as, to varying degrees, progressive (Acosta Arcarazo, 2018; Parent and Freier, 2018b). By the mid-2010s, the ideological convergence that underpinned this liberal tide was beginning to break down. In January 2017 President Mauricio Macri of Argentina, in office between 2015 and 2019, leading a right-wing administration, issued a decree on immigration that was likened by the *New York Times* to a 'Trump-like immigration order' (Romero and Politi, 2017). The decree clamped down on irregular migration by introducing an accelerated three-day fast-track procedure for expulsion and backtracking from key elements of the 2004 law by excluding civil society organizations from policymaking and reinstating the link in both discourse and policy between migration and criminality, which had been expressly rejected by the 2004 law. While subsequently subject to a legal battle in the Argentinian courts, Macri's decree signalled his intention to challenge the progressive turn and to possibly replace the 2004 law. Following his election in 2018, the far-right Brazilian president, Jair Bolsonaro, in response to the Venezuelan refugee crisis had threatened to revoke the 2017 migration law or to create camps for refugees on the Brazilian-Venezuelan border (Caetano et al., 2019). That said, as noted in the previous section, the Brazilian government was hailed by UNHCR for granting refugee status to thousands of displaced Venezuelans.

While shaped by experience of emigration, immigration, and the election of left-wing governments, the progressive turn in South American migration laws and policies that began in the 2000s was also partly defined in opposition to developments in North America and Europe and, at least in rhetorical terms, informed by notions of South American regional identity invoked by the idea of *la patria grande*, a nationalist, anti-imperialist and Hispanic vision of a shared homeland or community for all South Americans (Ugarte, 1922). In contrast, the EU was represented as pursuing harsh and restrictive policies (Acosta Arcarazo and Geddes, 2014). In 2008, the Uruguayan and Chilean presidents, Tabaré Vázquez and Michelle Bachelet, issued a joint declaration that strongly criticized the EU Return Directive for its disregard for human rights and potential to damage relations between Europe and Latin America (Acosta Arcarazo and Freier, 2015: 41). The 'liberal tide' was seen as a wider statement, because it was connected by a 'golden thread' of progressivism that was linked to a vision of the region that stood in 'stark contrast to the "race to the bottom" taking place in other parts of the world' (Cantor et al., 2015: 3).

The wave of new national legislation represented significant change in the form of migration law and policy as well as the practice of migration politics, but qualifying as paradigmatic change also requires change in underlying power relations and in the allocations not only of material resources but also of ideas and values. As already noted, there are constraints on the extent to which narratives and agendas at regional level translate into specific institutions and policies. There can, for example, be limits to practical knowledge and know-how within national governments beyond the ministries that traditionally have responsibility. While the country was a regional trailblazer after its 2004 law, these limits on migration as a 'whole of government' concern were evident in Argentina, as the quotation at the beginning of the section 'Drivers and characteristics' on p. 89 above from an Argentinian government official showed, when he referred to immigration impacting many different areas of government and raising questions about state capacity and know-how. It captures the ways in which state capacity shapes know-how and expectations about role. Ostensible openness to migration can also coexist with gaps between liberal discourses and their translation into laws and policies. One way of thinking about this is as governance systems, primarily at national level, seeking to make the migration issue intelligible as a social and political concern. Domestically, at the level of national governments, the heavy lifting is typically done by interior and justice ministries, while foreign ministries are the key points of contact for bilateral and multilateral relations. This is quite a narrow community of actors when it is borne in mind that the effects of migration can be quite diffuse within national government systems (health, employment, education) and also have major effects on local government. The practical realities of this can be very distinct, from high-level declarations or rhetorical commitments to progressive approaches. An Argentinian government official put it like this:

> I think that we need to balance that with some practical approach too. It's great, I will support this construction or this view of human rights, which is great, and to receive migrants and to dignify people who are arriving in our country and give them access to rights, which is great. But it's not just that. I think that we also have to see the interests of countries, the way that migrants

could insert in new societies, work with them. Not just, 'OK, if you come to our country, you are welcome,' and clap, not just that.

(Argentinian government official, Buenos Aires, April 2016)

This view brings us right back to the issue of the governability of migration and to underlying concerns about the allocations of resources and values within and between South American states. Progressive ideas about non-criminalization and a right to migrate have a clear value and have also had significant influence by, for example, enabling new forms of migration politics that can provide resources for civil society organizations to mobilize in the defence or promotion of migrants' rights. At the same time, high-minded declarations also need to hit the ground. New and progressive migration laws were, for example, also accompanied by efforts to inculcate more participatory modes of migration politics. The other side of this is that this can also mean the inclusion of competing—if not contradictory—views and opinions, which, in itself, is not unusual in any political system. As a Brazilian government official put it:

There is no homogeneity...sectors can change their positions...a country, a civil society or some ministers can very much agree on saying 'Yes, let's liberalize, let's be open, let's have free movement of workers.' But, in that same country, in another sector, they will say no...So, within the same country, we will find contradictions, and those contradictions will emerge when those interests are translated into a document...So there is no homogeneity, there are a diversity of opinions, of positions and there is a clash of interests.

(Brazilian government official, Brasilia, April 2016)

These clashes are embedded in more fundamental questions about the contested meaning of the state, its legitimacy, its authority, and its capacity that, while primarily grounded in domestic politics, have acquired a regional dimension. We now look more closely at South American regionalism.

What kind of region?

It's not unusual for various regional organizations to coexist, but there has been a particular profusion within South America and more broadly within the Americas that has led to it being likened to a 'spaghetti bowl' of tangled interrelationships (Malamud and Gardini, 2012; Riggirozzi and Tussie, 2012).

Some see the variety of regional organizations as leading to discord rather than unity, with strongly contrasting views on the scope and potential of South American regionalism. Malamud and Gardini (2012: 117) write that 'the presence of segmented and overlapping regionalist projects is not a manifestation of successful integration but, on the contrary, signals the exhaustion of its potential'. In contrast, Riggirozzi and Tussie (2012: 1) contend that 'South America became a ready platform for the reignition of regionalism incorporating the normative dimensions of a new era moving beyond American-led patterns of trade integration and that cannot be dismissed as passing.'

What is clear is that, as in other regions, there have been a variety of ways in which migration has been included on the regional agenda. The Andean Community (CAN) has, for example, developed a common passport for its four members (Bolivia, Colombia Ecuador, and Peru) and a common institutional structure, including a court. There is also a regional consultation process, the South American Conference on Migration (SACM). As in Southeast Asia with the Bali Process, regional consultation processes provide informal settings for the exchange of information and ideas. The SACM originated in Lima in 1999, when 'governments recognized the importance of migratory movements within the region and the need for regular consultations on the basis of which future Conferences would be organized' (International Organization for Migration, 2012: 34). Since then, the twelve members (Argentina, Bolivia, Brazil, Chile, Colombia, Ecuador, Paraguay, Peru, Uruguay, Venezuela, Guyana, and Surinam) of the SACM have met annually. A series of non-binding, progressive declarations that emerged from the SACM have been seen to help with the development of domestic legislation and with the formation of a unified position on migration governance beyond the region (Brumat, 2016). There are reflections of the ambitious rhetoric that developed at national level in the declarations of the SACM. In 2013, the SACM's Buenos Aires declaration affirmed that 'the human right to migration and the recognition of migrants as subjects of law must be at the centre of States' migration policies'. The SACM 'claims the unconditional respect of the human rights of migrants and their families', while condemning xenophobia, discrimination, racism, and the utilitarian treatment of migrants and rejecting the criminalization of irregular migration (cited in Acosta Arcarazo, 2018: 1). Settings such as the SACM were also ways for new actors and new voices, such as civil society organizations, to participate in migration governance. Yet, as Finn et al. (2019) observe, the SACM's fortunes are very closely tied to domestic political factors and, given the strong focus on intergovernmentalism and presidential leadership, the SACM, as with other regional consultations, tends to reflect the prevailing mood at state level rather than shape it.

There was a clear resurgence of South American regionalism at the beginning of the twenty-first century that was linked to the populist and nationalist orientation of left-wing governments and to 'post-neoliberal' or 'post-hegemonic' thinking that linked 'domestic growth, equity and regional governance and bringing the regulation of socio-economic relations back to the state' (Margheritis, 2016: 58). Applied to migration governance, this resurgent regionalism had three main components: a commitment to the defence of human rights and citizenship; societal security maintained through border controls and residency rules; and the region being viewed as a route to enhanced bargaining power at the global level (Margheritis, 2016). Change in the ideological composition of governments in South America underpinned 'post-neoliberal' or 'post-hegemonic' regionalism and was consciously defined in opposition to the alleged arch-progenitors of neoliberalism, the USA and EU. Changes in the political composition of governments led Petersen and Schulz (2018) to argue that these and other, earlier 'shifts in the regional agenda are best explained as periods of ideological convergence'. Consequently, the various waves or periods of regional governance require elite-level convergence, with a strong role played by presidents. Petersen and Schulz (2018: 103) go on to argue that to focus only on left-led regionalism (and the 'liberal tide' on migration that was part of it) can distract from the longer historical context and how regionalism has been entwined with state capacity and attempts to build consensus about the state's role. Regionalism thus plays a specific role in South America when 'states can use regional cooperation initiatives to bolster their right to rule' and as a 'tool for legitimizing state activities in specific domains', which means that legitimacy gained through regional cooperation can bolster domestic agendas (ibid.: 103). The strategic use of regional cooperation to legitimize states, bolster their authority, and build capacity can explain various waves of regionalism in South America that are defined or redefined by states on the basis of shared ideas about the role and relevance of the region. Each period or wave in regionalism is path-dependent in that it builds upon but is also constrained by previous waves (ibid.:105).

MERCOSUR was founded in 1991 by the Treaty of Asunción, which aimed to establish free movement for goods, services, capital, and factors of production that could include people, although no explicit mention was made of free movement for people. Developments in the 1990s did play an important role in establishing the context for migration to become a regional issue in the 2000s. In the 1990s democratizing South American countries became subject to the strongly market-oriented approach known as the 'Washington Consensus' propagated by international organizations such as the IMF and World Bank, which brought with it a focus on free trade, economic liberalization, privatization, and deregulation. By the end of the 1990s, as Rand Smith (2014: 164) put it:

> The long and short of how this Washington Consensus played out can be summarized in a word: disappointment. Growth rates did not improve appreciably, and poverty rates and inequality continued to rise. Just as crucially, citizenry newly empowered by (more or less) free elections began to demand accountability from its officials.

This induced a more hostile stance both to economic liberalization and to the US, initially led by Hugo Chavez in Venezuela after his election in 1998: 'The exclusion of the United States enabled the transformation of regional cooperation from a concern with security and free trade to a much wider project' (Petersen and Schulz, 2018:103). Following Venezuela, in Argentina, Bolivia, Brazil, Chile, Ecuador, and Uruguay the left became a governing force and gave additional momentum to a relaunch of MERCOSUR. In terms of formal institutional structures, MERCOSUR has remained relatively weak, 'showing a large gap between an oversupply of laws and a low degree of compliance, and a divergence between scope and level of integration' (Bianculli, 2016: 161).

The MRA, agreed in 2002, formed part of a post-crisis and post-neoliberal relaunch of MERCOSUR (Phillips, 2001). Key to MERCOSUR's relaunch were the ideological convergence associated with political change across the region and the role played by national presidents. Aside from the ambitious rhetoric, the presence of populations of irregular migrants from other MERCOSUR states, particularly in Argentina, was a very practical reason for the MRA. While holding the MERCOSUR presidency in the second half of 2002, the Brazilian president, Cardoso, pushed for an extension of MERCOSUR's social agenda that would include an amnesty for citizens of MERCOSUR states with an irregular residence status in another of the then four MERCOSUR member states. Cardoso's plan was for temporary measures, but the Argentinian government went further and proposed a permanent mechanism that would allow MERCOSUR nationals to access residency (Brumat, 2016). The Argentinian government viewed a more permanent mechanism allowing legal residence as a good way to enhance security by bringing irregular migrants 'in' from the shadows of irregularity and countering exploitation of irregular migrant workers and the potential for them to undercut Argentinian workers (International Organization for Migration, 2012). Support from the Brazilian government created the necessary momentum to secure regional-level agreement. The MRA did not intend to provide a right to free movement and was thus distinct from the EU's more highly developed free movement framework (see Chapter 5). Another important difference from Europe was that the MRA was designed primarily to deal with the issue of irregular migration by effectively regularizing those from other MERCOSUR countries. The MRA allows nationals of MERCOSUR Member States or Associate Member States to obtain a two-year temporary residence permit upon proof of nationality and a clean criminal record covering the preceding five years. Permit holders then have the right to work and equal treatment in their working conditions, access to education for their children, and other civil, social, cultural, and economic rights enjoyed by nationals. They are also granted the right to family reunification, but not political rights. After two years of residence, an application can be made for permanent residence, at which point proof of sufficient resources must be provided (Brumat, 2016).

The MRA's development was strongly influenced by the experience of Argentina, which had previously undertaken regularizations, but these had been ineffective in stemming irregular flows. The solution was to 'go regional', because, as an Argentinian government official put it:

> We then thought of this MERCOSUR criterion, because, 90 per cent of our migrants came from MERCOSUR. Therefore, if we incorporated it as a permanent admission and regularization criterion,... as a regime, then it facilitated [the regularization process], because you were not going to have to prove being a worker or being married or being a student, you only had to prove that you were a national of a MERCOSUR country. We had already thought about it *as an internal matter*, and we were waiting for a moment or an internal situation to present it [to MERCOSUR].
>
> (Argentinian government official, Buenos Aires, April 2015)

The subsequent labelling of the 2006 Argentinian regularization as '*Patria Grande*–MERCOSUR programme' was a reference to the idea of a wider, shared South American homeland. This showed how the regional structure facilitated the attainment of domestic political objectives. Intergovernmentalism does, however, impose limits to regional cooperation, because South American states have not ceded authority to supranational regional institutions to enable them to exercise authority over participating states. There is a MERCOSUR parliament, but it is a consultative, not a law-making body and, while there is a second-instance 'tribunal of revision', it is barely used, because states prefer bilateral resolution, while a 2010 proposal to create a MERCOSUR court remains on the table.

Given its dependence on ideological convergence and presidential leadership, regional cooperation in South America can be volatile, as can be seen through assessment of the rise and fall of the Union of South American Nations (UNASUR) (Sanahuja, 2012). Created in 2008, with Brazilian leadership, UNASUR was closely associated with the post-neoliberal wave of South American regionalism, with its focus on developing a social agenda and common South American citizenship. UNASUR was specifically created outside the Organization of American States, thus excluding the United States. A key UNASUR objective, as stated in its Constitutive Treaty, was to be 'the consolidation of a South American identity through the progressive recognition of rights to nationals of a Member State resident in any of the other Member States, in order to achieve a South American citizenship' (Art. 3.i). To achieve that end, in 2012 a Working Group for South American Citizenship was created (UNASUR, 2012). This Working Group elaborated a roadmap and a 'conceptual report' as the basis for the construction of South American citizenship, which was described as an 'extension, not a substitute, for national citizenships. Likewise, it is the condition of identity, belonging and rootedness to the American continent, its traditions and customs, its diverse cultures, its languages whose primary foundation is the shared history of the Member Countries of UNASUR' (UNASUR, 2014: 14). UNASUR was, however, to fall victim to the rightward shift in South American governments in the 2010s. The vicissitudes of inter-presidential regionalism were evident in 2018, when Argentina, Brazil, Chile, Colombia, Paraguay, and Peru suspended their membership of UNASUR in a move that signalled strong opposition to the Venezuelan regime and a desire for closer alignment by right-wing governments with the US.

As organizations, MERCOSUR and UNASUR had different identities and agendas, as was described to us by an Argentinian government official who contrasted the operational focus of MERCOSUR with UNASUR's political focus:

> From the beginning UNASUR and MERCOSUR had different agendas. While MERCOSUR emerges with an economic emphasis and then develops a social agenda, UNASUR appears from the beginning with a political emphasis, which puts up front the social agenda, the topic of the construction of citizenship.   (Argentinian government official, Buenos Aires, April 2015)

The contrasting fates of MERCOSUR and UNASUR illustrate the importance of political steering and the relationship between regionalism and state capacity. Regionalization in South America has not been matched by formal regionalism, with, as Sanahuja (2017: 118) puts it, 'a clear preference for intergovernmentalism and low levels of institutionalisation, as well as for preserving sovereignty and autonomy in the national realm'. Responses to migration within regional organizations were necessarily shaped by this wider governance setting. This setting contributes to the enactment of a sensible environment that makes sense to the actors involved in that it is shaped by representations of the causes and effects of migration and of the risks and uncertainties associated with it. This environment is also shaped, more generally, by representations of governability as they connect to international migration, to the legitimacy, authority, and capacity of states, and to relations at regional level between states. These political projects can vary, as too can the role of the regional and the forms that regional organization take, but, when applied to international migration, centre on prior concerns about governability that form part of a migration governance repertoire. These prior concerns define issues, problems, and challenges and configure the outputs or outcomes of governance systems.

Conclusion

The chapter connected resurgent regionalism in the 2000s with a set of prior concerns about the causes and effects of migration and with its governability that were shaped by both emigration and immigration. Migration governance was shown to be contingent on wider economic, social, and political conditions or, more particularly, how these became associated with particular political projects and with the space for the regional—and differing visions of the regional—within them. These are constitutive of the 'normality' of migration against which responses to crises are defined.

For a period of more than ten years, there was a conscious, regional effort by left-wing governments to distinguish their approaches to migration (and to social issues generally) from those in the USA and EU. Openness to both regional migration and displaced people from within the region is not necessarily new. Significant migration within, to, and from the region has long been of importance and can also activate governance actors at an affective level, given personal experiences of authoritarianism and exile. There was also a performative element for governments, given the desire to be seen to proclaim on the international stage the distinctive and progressive character of South American regionalism. While the new laws contained important commitments to *de jure* openness enhanced by the MRA, which were evident too in the principles for protection in the Cartagena Declaration, it is also the case that much migration in South America is also indicative of a *de facto* openness and the coexistence of legal frameworks whose application and effects are mediated by prior concerns about the governability of migration at state level and beyond the state. Displacement is clearly a transgovernmental and transnational issue, because millions of people displaced from Venezuela have been able to move to other South American countries, but, more often than not, this has not occurred through the application of the Cartagena principles even though the reasons for the displacement could be argued to fit with the Declaration's provisions. Another significant regional opening was also indicative of a *de facto* openness, because the main driver of the MRA was a desire to regulate already present irregular populations as well as sending a signal to countries hosting South American migrants. *De facto* openness is nested within broader debates about state authority, legitimacy, and capacity and is thus indicative of how governance systems at state and regional levels—through their operation, their effects, and their limits—can shape migration as a governance concern beyond the state. This led to a distinctive representation of the 'normality' of migration—particularly intra-regional migration—that has been distinctively less negative.

5

The Normality of Crisis in the European Union

Introduction

As in other regions, repertoires of migration governance in the EU are shaped by representations of what is 'normal' about international migration—about its causes and effects and the risks and uncertainties associated with it—to provide an anchor that can shape responses to crises. The EU provides a locus for action and mediates the relationship between the national and the global while also being a significant producer of new norms and standards because of its law-making powers. Representations of the causes and effects of migration and of the risks and uncertainties associated with it allow governance actors in Europe and the EU to rationalize what they are doing and to enact a sensible environment that provides a plausible, although not necessarily accurate account of what is going on 'out there'. This has been driven since the end of the Cold War and the onset of EU cooperation on migration from outside the EU by concern about large-scale and potentially uncontrollable migration flows. Whether based on fact or not, these representations have contributed to powerful governance effects. Thinking about the EU comparatively means not looking at the EU as though it were a template for other regions to follow but, rather, as a specific form of regional organization that has mediated the relationship between the national and global.

The EU is a highly developed system of supranational, regional migration governance with laws that bind member states covering free movement for EU citizens, migration, and asylum. The EU is an unusual region because its member states have since the 1950s established a treaty and institutional framework that is 'above' the member states and has the capacity to make and enforce laws that bind member states. European integration can thus be understood as a process by which states cease to be wholly sovereign (Haas, 1970). It is this willingness to cede sovereignty to supranational institutions that is a key and defining feature of the EU. This doesn't write member states out of the equation; they remain key actors. What it does mean is that

Governing Migration Beyond the State: Europe, North America, South America, and Southeast Asia in a Global Context. Andrew Geddes, Oxford University Press (2021). © Andrew Geddes. DOI: 10.1093/oso/9780198842750.003.0005

the EU has evolved into a complex system of power-sharing between member states and supranational institutions that has remade European politics and has important implications for migration, encompassing an internal component (free movement provisions for EU citizens) and the development of common migration and asylum policies for non-EU migrants.

Regional migration governance in Europe has two fundamental elements that, since the Amsterdam Treaty came into force in 1999, have been brought together within the Union's Treaty framework. The first and most long-standing is the development of a free movement framework with origins in the 1950s that, since the Maastricht Treaty of 1992, is associated with the right of EU citizenship held by citizens of EU member states. The second component dates back to the 1980s and began as cooperation on security matters related to migration and has since evolved into a common migration and asylum policy in relation to people that are not citizens of EU member states (known as 'third-country nationals', TCNs, in EU parlance). Crucially, EU migration and asylum policy covers some but not all aspects of migration and asylum. Put simply, EU measures on migration and asylum are primarily oriented towards stemming flows, while the numbers to be admitted and their integration remain matters for member states. EU policy is thus *partial* in that it covers some but not all aspects of policy and *differential* in that its effects have been more strongly felt in some member states than in others. In particular, EU cooperation since the late 1980s has been strongly driven by concern in 'older' immigration countries that newer countries of immigration in southern Europe or prospective member states in central and southeastern Europe needed to have credible border control frameworks.

While there are important linkages between free movement, migration, and asylum, there are also differences in their enactment within European and EU migration governance repertoires. As an article of faith, the European Commission keeps the two separate, because from a legal perspective free movement by EU citizens is not immigration. In the UK, at the time of the Brexit referendum in June 2016, a key achievement of those advocating 'leave' was to connect in the minds of many voters free movement by EU citizens with immigration by TCNs (Dennison and Geddes, 2018a). More broadly, debates about free movement have become linked to organizational boundaries of work and welfare, with the effect of enacting an environment within which the 'market citizen' relates free movement to the EU's core economic purposes (Everson, 1995). For migration and asylum by TCNs, the key reference is to territorial borders and to concern dating back to the 1990s about the potential for large-scale and potentially uncontrollable immigration. Free movement, migration, and asylum became linked after 2015, when large numbers of arrivals to Europe and secondary movement to other member states led to the reimposition of border controls between some EU member states (Börzel and Risse, 2018). As discussed later, the Covid-19 pandemic in 2020 led to a rush to impose new restrictions on travel in Europe to prevent the spread of the disease. While this marked an intensification of restrictions, it built on a pre-existing trend towards greater controls within the EU's free movement framework, or Schengen Area, as it is known.

The chapter shows how representations of free movement, migration, and asylum and their effects help to explain the recursive nature of European and EU responses to ostensibly new challenges—such as the migration crisis of 2015—that draw from repertoires established over a period of more than thirty years. Recurrent crises have consolidated particular representations of what is 'normal' about migration and shaped responses. To do, so the chapter first identifies key drivers and characteristics of migration in the EU, but explores how the operation and effects of underlying structural changes require interpretation of their causes and effects by governance actors. It then specifies key aspects of the EU free movement, migration, and asylum framework. The following section looks at how intermittent crises have played a key role in driving EU and European migration governance, while a final section analyses the impact of high levels of politicization of migration that, distinct from other regions, also had a strong focus on the EU itself as a contested polity.

Drivers and characteristics

Both intra-regional and extra-regional migration are key structural dynamics within the EU, as shown by Figure 5.1, which illustrates the breakdown between intra- and extra-regional flows in all EU member states in 2019, plus the UK, which is now no longer a member. Intra-regional flows are clearly significant, but the 'big five' in terms of total numbers (Germany, UK, France, Spain, and Italy) have also experienced significant flows from non-EU countries.

Powerful underlying structural factors linked to economic and political change can cause migration, but there is uncertainty about their effects and significant risks associated with them. Before looking more closely at some of the empirical aspects of free movement, migration, and asylum in the EU, it is useful to know more about how uncertainty and risk are interpreted and how these can shape governance. Thinking more carefully about the organizational

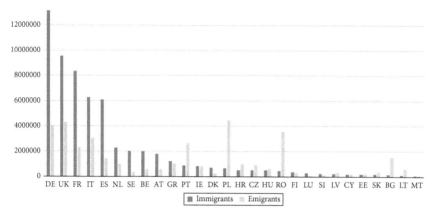

Figure 5.1 Immigrants and emigrants in the EU, 2019
Source: UNDESA 2019.

context means going beyond the clichés that migration is 'a challenge for the EU' or that it is an 'important political issue' and, instead, not only analysing the characteristics of migration, but also thinking about how organizational processes shape and are shaped by migration. Knowing that something is an important issue does not, in itself, suggest an appropriate response, particularly if the issue is contested and there are competing views on its causes and effects. Uncertainty could actually induce reactive tendencies and a reluctance to act, as was observed by an Austrian government official:

> We see a problem coming. The experts tell us its huge and it's cheaper to act earlier than to act later, but still, as a society, I'd say we don't do that. I think there's a word for it, it's cognitive dissonance.
>
> (Austrian government official, Vienna, April 2018)

To label this as cognitive dissonance means that decision-makers are being asked to choose between beliefs and actions that are incompatible, leading to inaction, although an effect of political demands for something to be done combined with uncertainty can also be symbolic politics with a performative component where rhetorical commitments are ramped up without necessarily being translated into actions. Capturing these pressures, a European Commission official put it like this:

> When you are asked to act with a fast pace there is little time to learn from what is working, what is not working. No, you have to make decisions and you have to intervene in terms of reasons, of stepping up interventions and

so on in a short time span. So, from this point of view, it is a challenge because you don't have all the time you would like to have in order to do certain things, have the time to properly evaluate.

(European Commission official, Brussels, November 2017)

Symbolic politics as a performative component of migration governance repertoires also means that officials can be left to 'fill the narrative', as another European Commission official put it:

An essential part of our work is to try to fill the narrative with policy, in a way, because sometimes we get very fancy phrases which our political head-masters say here and there because this is a catchy word where they can look good and look successful. Then we have to fill it with substance. It happens very often. For example, this emphasis on disrupting smuggler networks and trafficking, it came from the top, definitely, as a catchphrase. Then we had to substantiate it with concrete action. There were even some proposals to go as far as developing a rationale/argument for declaring smuggling and trafficking, I think, as crimes against humanity. After substantive analysis by lawyers, by diplomats at expert level, it became evident that this is a no go. We had to think of other specific actions in order to justify this narrative about disrupting smuggler networks.

(European Commission official, Brussels, October 2017)

The context of decision is hugely important, with scope for dissonance in the interpretation of signals and cues from the environment. There are within the EU circuits of information-sharing and interaction that centre on dynamics of 'like-mindedness':

you don't just hold the formal meeting and go back to your hotel room, but we get together again afterwards and discuss things on a much more informal level. That's crucial. It's not just once a month in Brussels… This exchange of ideas across borders, of course that also makes a big impact. Because you get to see another way of looking at things.

(EU member state government official in national capital, April 2015)

Constellations of like-mindedness in the EU vary, but they highlight the importance of information-sharing through interactions and the ways in which social processes shape interpretations, because decisions are made either in the presence of others or knowing that they will have to be implemented, understood, or approved by others (Weick, 1995).

When political leaders make rhetorical commitments to courses of action, it is likely that particular representations of international migration—of its causes and effects—provide shortcuts that help decision-makers to find a way forward. Thinking about the future does, though, often revolve around interpreting lessons from the past. This can mean looking back in time for examples of similar events or situations. Within the EU migration governance system, these shortcuts tend to recur to the potential for large-scale and potentially uncontrollable migration flows and measures that were seen as successful or effective in addressing the problem, as defined.

At a political level, importance is often attributed to the role of pull factors in European countries provided by labour markets and welfare systems. Such views, whether accurate or not, help to enact a sensible environment that informs decisions and relies on plausibility rather than accuracy. It 'organizes in' to the decision-making process particular representations of the causes and effects of migration that inform decisions and actions. The pull factor logic means that it becomes necessary to deter people from making journeys to Europe. There is ample evidence of the power of the deterrence perspective in the evolution of EU operations in the Mediterranean, which, in 2014 during the Italian-led Operation *Mare Nostrum*, had a search and rescue focus, but by 2015 had developed into an approach that was more focused on deterring migrant boat crossings and 'disrupting the business model' of people smugglers. Commenting on restrictions on rescue operations by NGOs, the UN Special Rapporteur on extrajudicial, summary, or arbitrary executions, Agnès Callamard, said:

> This code of conduct and the overall action plan suggest that Italy, the European Commission and EU Member States deem the risks and reality of deaths at sea a price worth paying in order to deter migrants and refugees.
>
> (OHCHR, 2017)

The EU's legal provisions and policy actions are shaped by representations of the causes and effects of migration, as well as by representations of the relationship between migration, in its various forms, and the 'European project'. We can now explore this in more detail by seeing the distinction that is made between free movement for EU citizens and migration and asylum policies for non-EU citizens.

Free movement

While highly valued by EU citizens and one of the EU's most identifiable achievements, free movement was long considered a technical and rather uninteresting issue, although that changed in the early to mid-2010s. As a Commission official put it:

> This field was considered the field for legal nerds...we never managed it really on the agenda of one of the Council meetings...Now we are on top of the political agenda.
>
> (European Commission official, Brussels, December 2015)

In legal, political, and organizational terms within the EU, free movement is separated from migration and asylum. The distinction is important: free movement is a right enjoyed by EU citizens that is guaranteed by supranational law. In contrast, while EU member states cooperate on migration and asylum, the number of migrants to be admitted remains a member state prerogative. From personal experience, a stony silence is likely to descend if a researcher during an interview with EU officials, refers to free movement by EU citizens as migration.

A consequence of the issue becoming more prominent in public debate was the blurring of the distinction in public perceptions between migration (by TCNs) and free movement by EU citizens. This could be a cause of frustration for EU officials:

> It's very much confused, particularly the public perception. From a political and legal and other point, these are two strictly separate things, in particular when it comes to rights and so on. There's a huge difference between EU nationals and third-country nationals.
>
> (EU official, Brussels, December 2015)

The underlying significance of free movement is that EU member states have ceded authority over access to their territory and to the conditions governing entry, residence, and employment of nationals of other member states. In 2018, just under 12 million people, or 3.9 per cent of the EU population were living in another member state. Free movement was largely uncontroversial until the series of enlargements that occurred between 2004 and 2013 that saw the EU increase in size from fifteen to twenty-eight member states. From the right, and, most notably, in the UK, free movement became enmeshed with the 'immigration' issue. From the left, there were concerns free movement could undermine welfare and social standards and lead to the undercutting of labour standards (Hainsworth, 2006; Hansen and Hager, 2012).

The potential for imposition of transition measures that provided a temporary brake on free movement for citizens of new member states was an important aspect of the accession agreement that brought thirteen new member states into the EU in 2004, 2007, and 2013. For a period of up to seven years after accession, restrictions were imposed on the right of their nationals to move freely. Only Ireland, Sweden, and the UK allowed immediate free-movement rights for nationals of the ten states that joined on 1 May 2004. The decision not to impose restrictions taken by Tony Blair's Labour government was hugely significant for the UK. The reasoning behind the decision was twofold. First, there was evidence produced from within the UK government of the potential economic benefits of labour migration. Second, the UK had long championed enlargement and saw endorsing free movement as a way to strengthen relations with new member states in central Europe (Watt and Wintour, 2015). Other member states agreed to a '2 years + 3 years +2 years' formulation that allowed them to review the extension of free-movement rights to nationals of the eight Central and East European countries (Czech Republic, Estonia, Hungary, Latvia, Lithuania, Poland, Slovakia, and Slovenia) that joined the EU in May 2004 with full access to rights after a maximum seven-year period. The UK's decision not to impose transition measures for the new member states contributed to the largest influx of migrants in its history, although these were EU citizens accessing their right to free movement and thus not subject to immigration controls. This paved the way for the heightened political salience of migration and subsequently, for the politicization of 'EU migration' as a key factor in the UK decision to leave the EU taken by a June 2016 referendum (Dennison and Geddes, 2018a).

In terms of formal legal provisions, Article 45 of the EU Treaty provides for the free movement of workers and for equal treatment for those EU citizens that exercise this right. To facilitate free movement, welfare benefits and entitlements are made portable. This, in effect, provides for a form of mutual recognition of social entitlements rather than requiring harmonization of welfare provisions, which would be highly unlikely given the diversity of welfare state types within the EU (Ruhs and Palme, 2018). An EU 'citizens' rights' Directive (2004/38/EC) of 2004 brought into one legal instrument provisions to cover the conditions under which EU citizens can move freely and the rights associated with mobility, including equal treatment for EU citizens and their family members.

For mobile EU citizens there is, over time, a progressive extension of rights. For the first three months, EU citizens and their family members, irrespective of nationality (including registered partners), have an unconditional right of residence. Any EU citizens able to present a valid identity card or passport can enter another EU member state. The only caveat applies if an EU citizen becomes an 'unreasonable burden' on the welfare system of the member state to which they have moved, under which circumstances he or she can be expelled. After three months, there is provision for those who are not economically active to show sufficient means of subsistence and provision for health care. If not, they can be expelled. Finally, after five years of legal residence, an EU citizen resident in another member state is entitled to a permanent right of residence independently of his or her economic status.

The idea and practice of free movement connects to visions of what the EU is, should be, and could become, although, as Recchi (2017) observes, because the beneficiaries of free movement tend to be quite a select group, free movement's 'horsepower' is not sufficient for it to be a locomotive of integration. While there is generally strong support for free movement, there has been debate about the impacts of free movement on welfare systems and labour market standards. Within the key member state governments, particularly France and Germany, there has been less space specifically within governments for Eurosceptic mobilization. In contrast, the UK government was exposed to strong Eurosceptic mobilization, which motivated the decision by the then Conservative prime minister David Cameron in the face of a highly vocal Eurosceptic presence in his own party and growing support for the anti-EU United Kingdom Independence Party to call a referendum on the UK's continued membership, which, of course, he lost (Roos, 2018).

Despite, some contestation, this purposive or teleological component to debates about free movement associates it with the idea of building a European community that transcends national boundaries. While the EU does not have a notion similar to the idea of *la patria grande* in South America because cultural and linguistic affinities are not as strong, free movement does exemplify the EU's continued ambition to promote what its own treaty describes as 'ever closer union between the peoples of Europe' (Everson, 1995).

Migration and asylum

Representations of migration and asylum don't easily fit with a teleological representation of free movement and its relation to the 'European project'. No

European country understands itself as a nation of immigrants, while cooperation on migration and asylum has been driven by concern about the potential for large-scale and potentially uncontrollable migration flows to the EU. Free movement is organized into the European project as a core component of the EU's identity, but migration and asylum have a much more ambiguous relation to the EU project, with a marked determination to organize out—literally and metaphorically—those forms of migration defined by member states through their policies as unwanted, such as asylum seeking and irregular migration.

Even at the peak of the crisis, the main routes for entry to Europe remained 'regular' air, sea, and land ports of entry. In 2015, 2016, and 2017, 2.6 million, 3.4 million, and 3.1 million people, respectively, arrived in an EU member state with a first-issue residence permit enabling entry for motives including employment, family reunion, or study (Eurostat, 2018a). This compares to just over 1 million Mediterranean arrivals in 2015 and just over 362,000 in 2016 (Eurostat, 2019). Those with first residence permits are classed as regular migrants who move for various reasons including employment, to join family, and to study. Those crossing by sea were likely to be labelled as irregular, although many would make a claim for asylum that, if accepted, would give them a legal basis to stay.

In January 2018, 22.3 million people, or 4.4 per cent of the EU population, were citizens of non-EU countries. Germany was Europe's largest country of immigration, with 9.7 million migrants, followed by the UK with 6.3 million, Italy with 5.1 million, France with 4.7, and Spain with 4.6 million (Eurostat, 2019). Spain and Italy saw rapid increases in their immigrant-origin population. Between 2000 and 2005, Spain's migrant population rose by 194.2 per cent (3.1 million immigrants) and in Italy by 54.1 per cent (884,000 immigrants).

Migration has been, is, and will continue to be an important factor in EU population change. EU-wide demographic data consistently show declining birth rates. In 2017, the EU population reached 511.8 million, with slightly more than 3.4 people of working age (aged 15–64) for each person over the age of 65. The effects of population change are not evenly distributed, and arguments for immigration based on demographic change will be mediated by the effects of politics. Italy, for example has an ageing population but has adopted a notably hard-line approach to immigration (Geddes and Pettrachin, 2020). In contrast, Germany has used demographic arguments to inform a more open approach to labour migration into both skilled and lower-skilled employment (Eurostat, 2017). Objective data don't feed straightforwardly into the political process, particularly given the tendency to frame migration as a crisis. As a Commission official put it:

> OK, we need more people to take care of our elderly people, more nurses, so how are we going to get these nurses? Shall we do a deal with, I don't know, Vietnam or Senegal and try to have people that we need and try to have a legal migration framework which also has a return procedure, so you can get a contract for five years and after five years you go back home... The discussion is not happening because everybody is focusing on the current crisis. The perceived current crisis.
>
> (European Commission official Brussels, November 2017)

In the 1950s and 1960s, the European Community (EC), as it was then known, was moving to progressively deepen levels of economic integration. The elaboration of a Common Market during the 1960s led to the elimination of barriers to trade between European countries, while providing for free movement for workers. The Single European Act of 1986 moved beyond this customs union to redefine the EU as an area without internal frontiers within which people, goods, services, and capital would be able to move freely. In 1985, Belgium, France, Germany, Luxembourg, and the Netherlands had already agreed to a system of passport-free travel in an agreement signed in the Luxembourg town of Schengen. This Schengen system of passport-free travel accompanied by the development of internal security mechanisms was later imported into the EU Treaty framework and is fundamental to regional migration governance in Europe (Monar, 2001).

Five distinct elements of the post-Cold War context after 1989 have been identified: greater intensity of migration flows to and within the EU; all EU member states becoming to some extent countries of immigration and emigration; a growing policy role for the EU; ostensibly new manifestations of the immigration problem, for example growing concern about irregular flows, people smuggling, and human trafficking; and, finally, a more intense politicization of migration at both member state and EU levels combining both increased issue salience and increased polarization (Geddes et al., 2020).

An immediate and specific effect of the end of the Cold War was to generate concern about the potential for large-scale migration flows to Western Europe from the ex-Soviet Union and its former satellite states in Central Europe. Sandholtz and Turnbull (2001) wrote that in the late 1980s security actors in national interior ministries and associated state-level agencies had already begun to connect their security concerns to potential large-scale flows from Eastern Europe. What is more, they began to understand potential flows in terms of a crisis or potential crisis. In their assessment, Sandholtz and Turnbull (2001: 196) take at face value the idea of a flood of immigrants moving to the EU:

> The primary component of the crisis was the fall of the Iron Curtain and the subsequent flood of immigrants into the EC, and especially into Germany, which became the chief protagonist in institutionalizing justice and home affairs cooperation in the EU. What made a new EC policy space appear necessary and appropriate was that the two contextual changes coincided. The abolition of national frontier controls within the EC raised concerns about controlling migration and transnational crime, just as several EC states, especially Germany, confronted an immigration crisis.

Germany was Europe's key destination country. Around 1.1 million ethnic German *Aussiedler* moved to Germany from Central and Eastern Europe and from the former Soviet bloc. As ethnic Germans, they had a right to return, although restrictions were later imposed. The break-up of the former Yugoslavia led to increased flows of asylum seekers, again with Germany as a preferred destination. Just over 1.5 million asylum seekers moved to Germany between 1989 and 1994. Framed by the idea of a migration crisis, the German government sought to 'export' the crisis to the EU level (Henson and Malhan, 1995). Neighbouring countries to Germany in Central and Eastern Europe with the incentive of EU membership were incorporated within the EU framework for migration controls via their designation as 'safe third countries' to which asylum applicants could be returned if they had passed through them on their way to an EU member state (Lavenex, 1999). The Dublin Convention of 1992 was particularly important because it established the principle that asylum seekers should make their application in the member states in which they arrived and not be able to move on to another member state. The convention began as an agreement in international law, but the Dublin regulation became a key legal instrument within what is now known as the Common European Asylum System (Lavenex, 2018).

By the end of the 1990s, the EU was beginning to elaborate measures on migration and asylum that, while dominated by intergovernmental cooperation as the modus operandi, showed that member states were also thinking collectively about migration and that their thinking about the causes and effects of migration—and, of course, who was doing that thinking—was having important effects on actions. The field has become more densely populated since, but it was national interior ministries that set the direction of EU cooperation on migration and asylum (Guiraudon, 2003). It has been difficult ever since to deviate from the course that was set and the associated repertoire. We can see underlying knowledge of the causes and effects of migration emerge during this period and become embedded at EU level and associated with the idea that there was a major challenge—both real and latent—to the external borders of EU member states posed by large-scale flows.

Concern about large-scale flows enacted a sensible environment that centred on certain representations of the causes and effects of migration that appeared plausible to key governance actors and motivated actions. A repertoire of migration governance developed that shaped both know-how and also expectations about role held by key actors in European migration governance systems. This repertoire, as in other regions, involved narrative claims, but was social, affective, performative, and ongoing. Even by the early 1990s we can see the emergent shape of the EU 'policy core', with a focus on stemming those flows defined as 'unwanted' by member state policies (Trauner and Servent, 2016). The 1990s were crucial because they had a powerful effect on what key governance actors knew how to do and also their expectations about their role. A Commission official reflected about how the complexity of the issue—the normality of complexity, as he tellingly observed—can lead to pressure caused by varying expectations about role:

> So, it is normal that the issue is very complex and the response is very complex. It won't change, it won't change. However, of course, there needs to be a correct understanding of what can be achieved and within what time span. Sometimes this is what is difficult. So expectations, what can be done and how, because, of course, there are different sets of expectations.
>
> (European Commission official, Brussels, November 2017)

This reflection refers directly to know-how and to expectations in a context within which complexity complicates things, but where decision-makers can look for 'shortcuts' using judgement heuristics. The 'normality' of EU cooperation on migration and asylum as it developed after the 1990s has been shaped by responses to intermittent crises that have centred on concern about real or potential migration flows and their controllability. This leads to confirmation bias, where information is favoured that supports views that are already held. This quote from an Austrian government official when reflecting on conversations with Dutch colleagues helps to illustrate this point about the influence of past events on current representations:

I didn't have the feeling that there was really a new discussion...I always remember my Dutch colleagues in Brussels, who had been around since the nineties, what we are discussing, what we consider as new ideas, they've already been discussing that in the early nineties...The difference now is with the crisis and this global attention that is being given with the [Global] Compact, I think this understanding now is also being created on the political level.   (Interior ministry official, Vienna, January 2018)

Similarly, an official from the German Interior Ministry put it like this:

we also feel kind of, yes, confirmed in the certain premises we always made. Unfortunately, sometimes not the right conclusions were drawn from the actual knowledge which was available here at the level of experts so that this enormous influx could take place in the dimension we have seen.
(Interior ministry official, Berlin, March 2018)

This quote exemplifies the importance of looking back not only to provide a frame of reference but also to provide confirmation of an account of the causes and effects of migration.

What kind of region?

Since the late 1980s, the EU and its institutions have produced countless documents about aspects of free movement, migration, and asylum. There have also been important institutional developments, particularly in the form of Treaty changes that mean that it is possible to identify not only a supranational system to support free movement but also a common migration and asylum policy. Of particular importance is the Maastricht Treaty of 1992, which created an intergovernmental 'pillar' covering immigration and asylum. In 1999, migration and asylum were brought into the Treaty framework by the Amsterdam Treaty, which also brought the Schengen *acquis* within the EU legal framework. A further important step was taken by the Lisbon Treaty of 2009, which subjected EU migration and asylum provisions to what is known as the EU's 'ordinary legislative procedure', which means co-decision between the Council of Ministers (representing the member states) and the directly elected European Parliament. The Commission is responsible for the management and implementation of policy, while the EU's Court of Justice has had full jurisdiction since the Lisbon Treaty entered into force (Acosta Arcarazo and Geddes, 2013). The caveat, as already noted, is that this common policy does not cover the numbers of migrants to be admitted or the legal substance of measures related to immigrant integration.

There are, however, significant policy continuities despite these institutional changes. We can see these by thinking about how a landmark document, the European Agenda for Migration (EAM), which sought to define the EU's response to the 2015 migration and refugee crisis, actually reflects a series of much longer-standing themes in EU regional migration governance whose origins can mostly be traced back to the 1990s. The EAM was a response to the surge in Mediterranean arrivals after 2015, but also built on twenty-five years of cooperation on migration and asylum and the associated policies and practices (CEC, 2015). The EAM rested on four pillars, encompassing the internal and external dimensions of policy, but, at its core, centred on stemming or deterring migration flows, particularly from Africa and the Middle East.

The first pillar focuses on reducing the incentives for irregular migration, with a focus on 'root causes behind irregular migration in non-EU countries', on 'dismantling smuggling and trafficking networks', and on 'the better application of return policies'. Here we see a tension between the need for short-term results and longer-term interventions, as noted by a European Commission official:

> If I say, 'We need to focus more, invest in root causes as a start, to provide alternative livelihoods or building socioeconomic infrastructure,' it's going to take forever... All the heads of state and governments sitting over there have a four-year term. They're not interested in what will probably be... in the long run. Instead, then, what we will do is that we will give them something on stepping up the training of officials, allowing Libyan coastguards to turn around ships within the Libyan territorial water. It'll have a direct effect... which is very, very communicable and a good deliverable for the public for the next European Council... sometimes the long-term solutions that you would think, personally and professionally, would be the right way to go about it will not fly politically. That's not only related to migration. That's basically everything we do.
>
> (European Commission official, Brussels, October 2017)

This focus on results and on the electoral horizon for national governments is reflected in this observation by an Austrian government official:

I'd say we operate under a lot of pressure to create results. So, the ideal way would have been to start with a pilot, see how it works, evaluate the pilot maybe in two or three countries, do the scientific evaluation, and then redesign the programme. Five or seven years later you can come up with a larger programme. It didn't quite work that way. That's why we do many things at the same time, which makes the work interesting and challenging.

(Austrian government official, Vienna, April 2018)

A particular focus of EU action has been on the external dimension of policy. This is a longer-standing theme, although the focus has shifted since the 1990s from Europe's more immediate 'neighbourhood', i.e. surrounding states, to countries beyond the neighbourhood in, for example, West Africa and the Horn of Africa (Boswell, 2003; Frowd, 2018; Lavenex, 2006).

The second pillar of the EAM was better management of the external border through 'solidarity' towards member states such as Greece and Italy that are the particular focus of arrivals via Mediterranean routes. The creation of 'hotspots' in Greece and Italy was an emergency response to the registration and processing of new arrivals (Beirens, 2018). The Commission identified solidarity as an element of future migration and asylum policy but this vertical or top-down convergence was unsuccessful because of the tensions caused between member states by increased politicization, particularly after 2015. In September 2015, EU member states agreed a two-year plan to move 160,000 asylum seekers from Greece and Italy to other member states, according to a distribution key based on population, national income, numbers of asylum applicants, and unemployment rates. Two years later, fewer than 30,000 people had actually been relocated. Political changes in EU member states are likely to have ramifications for solidarity. When announcing the priorities for the Austrian government's Council Presidency in the second half of 2018, Chancellor Sebastian Kurz said, 'Our aim is very clear – that in Europe there should not only be a dispute over redistribution (of refugees) but also at last a shift of focus towards securing external borders' (Euractiv, 2018).

The third pillar was the strengthening of the EU's common asylum policy, with the key issue being reform of the Dublin system. The basic problem was that there was disproportionate pressure on southern member states, particularly Greece and Italy, that were the first countries of entry for many asylum seekers. For those seeking asylum, procedures for registering and processing claims, as well as recognition rates, vary widely between member states, which, in turn, can lead to 'secondary movements' as asylum applicants try to move from one EU state to another (Beirens, 2018). These secondary movements became a central component of the crisis, as tens of thousands of people moved from Greece across central Europe—a 'reverse domino effect'—with new fencing and border controls introduced within the Schengen area to stop onward movement. A more fundamental challenge emerged at the intergovernmental level, where key member states led by the Austrian and Danish governments made a case couched in moral terms that the existing EU protection system had failed and that different kinds of protections systems needed to be put in place that were closer to the areas from which refugees were being displaced (Federal Ministry of the Interior, Austria, and Ministry of Immigration and Integration, Denmark, 2018). There is an underlying representation of the causes and effects of migration that informs this vision, namely that asylum migration has become a route for irregular flows and abuse of the system. On the basis of this kind of representation, there has been a strong emphasis in EU policy on clamping down on those who are seen to facilitate such migration, such as people smugglers, while also seeking to work more closely with non-EU member states to curb flows. This sensible environment is clearly evident in a vision paper by the Austrian and Danish governments that began by stating that 'the present asylum system is dysfunctional in many ways, not fit for a globalized world and needs to be mended' (ibid.:1). The document went on:

> Many citizens have lost trust in their governments' ability to deal with the challenges of irregular migration. In the current system it's not only the Member States of the EU that decide who enters the European Union but first and foremost smugglers (and to a lesser extent migrants themselves). The result is a massive loss of trust. Trust will not be restored simply by short-term partial strategies and measures at EU-level. There is an urgent need for an alternative, unifying vision. The priority must be to reassure our citizens by creating a sustainable policy framework that simultaneously has democratic support, meets our legal and ethical obligations, and is sufficiently prudent to avoid a legacy of regrets.   (ibid.:1)

The current asylum system was also condemned for being 'Darwinian' in that it favoured the strongest, who were more likely to be able to make it to Europe, and thus failed to protect the most vulnerable. The vision paper stated that the system confounded the rule of law by encouraging irregularity and illegality. There are major challenges actually putting into practice cooperation with third countries, as well as concerns about the protection of human rights, but these kinds of proposals are consistent with a well-established EU migration governance repertoire.

The fourth and least-developed pillar of the EAM was 'regular' migration, not least because EU competencies are extremely limited. The EU's so-called Blue Card targeted at migration into high-skilled employment, introduced in 2009, was significantly limited in its effects. Member states adopted very different approaches to its implementation. For example, salary thresholds ranged from €13,000 to €68,000 and conditions for labour market testing varied, as too did the permit's duration (ranging from one to four years). Even a revised scheme, as proposed by the Commission, would remain subject to member state controls over admissions (Cerna, 2018). It has been argued that openness to new migration via regular routes is predicated on effective controls, but without some regular pathways it is likely that pressure for entry will remain and that this could be channelled into irregular routes (Ruhs and Barslund, 2018).

The effects of crisis

Crises and the ways in which they are defined and understood are necessarily set against representations of the underlying causes and effects of migration, or, put another way, the normality of migration. As an example, consider this first paragraph of a 2017 statement from a European Commission document evaluating delivery of the EAM:

> In the last two years, Europe experienced the largest number of arrivals of refugees and migrants since the end of the Second World War. The Syrian crisis played an important part in generating this record number, as did conflicts, instability and poverty in many parts of the world. Migration, asylum and border management systems were put under huge pressure. The Union and its Member States were not sufficiently prepared to respond effectively. The scale of the crisis had a powerful impact across the EU. The integrity of both the Common European Asylum System and of the Schengen area of free movement for European citizens was put into question.
>
> (CEC, 2017a: 2)

This statement provides a representation of the reasons why people move to the EU and of EU actions. It refers to a lack of preparedness, high pressures on migration systems, and challenges to the integrity of these systems.

Migration itself is represented as an act of desperation driven by poverty, conflict, and instability. It is true that those who entered the EU by boat across the Mediterranean were fleeing desperate circumstances and were exposed to many dangers. But most migrants to Europe do not enter by boat across the Mediterranean; they enter via regular channels for employment, or to join family, or to study, motivated by hope, love, aspiration, and ambition (Eurostat 2018a). The point is that this kind of representation—of migration as an act of desperation—plays into longer-standing concerns about large-scale migration to the EU that can also be racialized. In this sense, the 'crisis' also represented powerful ideas about the causes and effects of migration. The practical effect is that a perception of what is normal about migration then enables certain actors and agendas to mobilize and to stake claims to resources that aim to stem or deter flows.

European responses to migration and asylum have been punctuated by intermittent events framed as crises. As already discussed, in the early 1990s this centred on flows—as well as the perceived potential for flows—to Germany and, in the late 1990s, refugee flows from Kosovo (Barutciski and Suhrke, 2001). In the 2000s, irregular crossings from Africa towards Spanish territories, including the enclaves of Ceuta and Melilla, as well as the Canary Islands, became the focus of attention. An EU official put it like this:

> it [the 2015 crisis] wasn't as new as it is sometimes perceived. If I make that historical link, when I started back in 2006 what we were all excited about at that time was the sea-borne irregular migration to the Canary Islands, which was the peak at that moment whilst there was rather little in the central Mediterranean or in Greece. Then the different peaks came and went, so to speak, but the problem itself of sea-borne migration in very difficult conditions from the African continent was the same, it was already there.
>
> (EU agency official, Brussels, February 2015)

When trying to work out what to do, officials and decision-makers look back at previous examples or instances that seem similar to the issue or problem that they face. An example of this is an EU official who in 2017 used the example of boat arrivals to the Canary Islands in 2005 and 2006 as a way of thinking about the post-2015 situation in Europe (Gabrielli, 2007; Lanni, 2016). Of particular importance is that, from an official point of view, the actions of the Spanish government were viewed as successful because they more or less ended the flow of migrants to the Canary Islands through agreements with Mauritania and Senegal:

Maybe on the European level the good example is Spain. I remember fifteen years ago when they were faced with big immigration waves from North Africa. They managed to get their own package with their neighbouring countries. This has often been cited as a role model how it could be solved, creating some kind of partnership that both sides have a vested interest in, so both are interested in keeping the situation stable.

(EU official, Brussels, February 2015)

The point is that this representation of migration to the EU in terms of crisis is not new. Such interpretations have been linked to real-world events in the form of actual flows, but also to representations of the potential for larger-scale flows and to concerns about uncontrollability.

We now consider EU responses to the hundreds of thousands of people that made perilous Mediterranean sea crossings during 2015 and 2016 and see how these drew from an established migration governance repertoire, the origins of which can be traced back to the late 1980s and early 1990s. In 2015, the number of people entering the EU via Mediterranean routes peaked at just over one million, of whom around 450,000 originated from Syria. Greece, with around 830,000 people arriving in 2015, became a visual and political focus for the crisis, with hundreds of thousands of people then moving on in seemingly haphazard ways through Central Europe towards Germany, which was the preferred destination for many migrants. In August 2015, the German Chancellor, Angela Merkel, decided to open the country's borders to refugees fleeing the Syrian civil war. This encouraged hundreds of thousands of people to move to Germany, but this also required them to cross the territory of other south-eastern and Central European countries en route. As flows across the Mediterranean increased in 2015 and into 2016, urgent measures were put in place by EU governments to try to reduce the numbers of arrivals and also to stop onward movement within the EU. An effect of this was the reimposition of border controls within the Schengen area—the EU's own system of passport free travel (Börzel and Risse, 2018).

Efforts were made by the EU to get non-EU member states such as Turkey to stop people moving to the EU or, if they did get to Europe, to return them to the countries they moved from. An EU-Turkey agreement of March 2016 contributed to major reductions in numbers of people moving across what was called the 'eastern Mediterranean' route from Turkey to Greece (Alpes et al., 2017). EU member states found it very difficult to reach agreement on a common approach within the EU, because front-line EU member states such as Greece and Italy wanted to see the relocation of asylum applicants to other

EU member states in the name of solidarity and responsibility-sharing, but there was strong opposition from other member states to the relocation of asylum applicants. Particularly vocal were the governments of the Czech Republic, Hungary, Poland, and Slovakia, which were firmly opposed to common EU measures on asylum that would require them to admit asylum applicants to their territory (Pachocka, 2016). While EU member states squabbled, public trust and confidence in governments declined and there was increased support for anti-immigration political parties (Dennison and Geddes, 2018b).

By 2019, the numbers of people crossing the Mediterranean to try to enter the EU had fallen significantly, although the death rate remained high. More than one million people entered the EU via Mediterranean sea crossings in 2015. This fell to 383,000 in 2016, 185,000 in 2017, and 141,000 in 2018 (UNHCR, 2019b). Notably, the death rate increased, with 3,771 people dead or missing in 2015, 5,096 in 2016, 3,139 in 2017, and 2,277 in 2018 (UNHCR, 2019b).

The dynamics of the crisis between 2015 and 2019 also shifted in ways linked to EU policy interventions. Following the EU-Turkey Statement of April 2016, the numbers of migrants moving along the 'eastern Mediterranean' route from Turkey to Greece fell from 176,000 in 2016 to 35,000 in 2017. The statement provided for the return of all irregularly arriving Syrian nationals from Greek Islands to Turkey; a mechanism for one vulnerable Syrian to move to the EU for every Syrian returned to Turkey; a €6-billion facility for refugees in Turkey; and designation of Turkey as a 'safe third country' to allow the return of asylum applicants from the EU who had passed through Turkey (Council of the EU, 2016). The 'Noori decision' of the Greek Council of State in September 2017 in the case of a 21-year old Syrian man upheld the provision within the EU-Turkey Statement that returns to Turkey were reasonable, albeit only by a knife-edge 13–12 majority (Alpes et al., 2017). There were concerns about lack of procedural safeguards to protect the rights of asylum seekers in Turkey and concern about the risk of refoulement (return to a country where an individual would be at risk of persecution) (Alpes et al., 2017). In March 2020, in the face of heightened conflict in Syria, thousands of refugees moved towards the Greek border. In response, Greece suspended asylum applications for a month with other EU member states, while other member states likened President Erdoğan of Turkey's actions to blackmail, as he sought increased funding from the EU (Wintour and Smith, 2020).

While the EU-Turkey agreement itself attracted a lot of attention, its effects on numbers were marginal. Between the signing of the EU-Turkey Statement in March 2016 and the end of 2018, it was calculated that there were 171,600 arrivals in Greece from Turkey. By the end of 2018, there were still 71,200 migrants and refugees in Greece, which left 100,400 people who had gone elsewhere. Using data from official Greek sources and from the UNHCR, the European Stability Initiative calculated that 63,325 people had left Greece. Of these a mere 1,806 were returned to Turkey using the provisions of the EU-Turkey agreement and a further 600 under the terms of an existing Greek-Turkish readmission protocol. A further 14,182 were other forced returns to Turkey, while 14,000 were voluntary returns facilitated by the IOM. Relocation to another EU member state accounted for a further 21,999 people, while 10,738 were transferred from Greece to another member state using the EU's Dublin protocol. This leaves a further 37,000 people, who, it would seem, are likely to have moved onwards irregularly from Greece (ESI, 2019).

After the EU-Turkey Statement came into effect and crossings via the eastern Mediterranean fell, the main point of arrival for Mediterranean crossings became Italy, where a total of 300,000 people arrived in 2016 and 2017, although this number fell back sharply to 23,000 in 2018 and to just under 11,500 in 2019 after Italy reached agreement with the Libyan authorities to prevent departures (Caponio and Cappiali, 2018). The scale of arrivals put significant pressure on systems for reception and processing of asylum applications. In Italy, for example, during a five-year period between 2013 and 2017 there were 427,000 requests for international protection, which compares to a total of 317,000 in the preceding thirty-seven years between 1985 and 2012 (Eurostat, 2018b). In 2017, 8 per cent of applicants were granted refugee status, 8 per cent a subsidiary protection status, 25 per cent humanitarian protection, and 58 per cent were rejected (Ministero dell'Interno, 2017).

At the official level, the focus was directed almost entirely to the data on numbers of arrivals, who would arrive on almost a daily basis during 2015 and 2016. A European Commission official conveyed the immediacy:

> It [our work] has been directly affected by the recent developments, let's say, over the last two and a half years because it basically dictates our everyday work...when the numbers are up, we are under pressure. When the numbers are down, we are less under pressure.

The effect of this immediacy was, in effect, a crisis bias that distracts from longer-term thinking:

> what people forget is that, first of all, there are a lot of people who can come legally to Europe, because we give them visas or work permits, and we have a need for legal migration because of our demographic. The debate is

completely biased by the crisis. The focus is still there, we still have the feeling that we are in crisis and politicians need to say, "We are getting out of the crisis and now is the time to talk about the future of our migration".'
(European Commission official, Brussels, November 2017)

This doesn't mean that there are not efforts to think beyond crises, but these are framed by representations of the normality of migration, particularly concern about the persistent pressure of large-scale flows. In a 2015 strategic note prepared by the European Political Strategy Centre—the European Commission president's in-house think tank—it was noted not only that the 'age of migration is here to stay' but that 'the current crisis is an opportunity for system overhaul' (EPSC, 2015: 1). Yet, as already noted, a well-established migration governance repertoire at EU level affects not only what is done, but also know-how and expectations. System overhaul is probably unlikely. Scepticism has been expressed about arguments for 'crisis as opportunity' because of the observation that a 'policy core' was established in the 1990s and that this has led to significant path dependencies, with initial policy choices driven by security concerns that have been difficult to shift (Guiraudon, 2018; Trauner and Servent, 2016). What did change as a result of the crisis was the level of politicization of migration, as the issue became salient across the EU, had important effects on election outcomes, and caused increased polarization within political systems, as we now discuss in the next section.

The politicization of migration governance

A distinctive aspect of the politicization of migration in Europe, certainly when compared to Southeast Asia and South America, is that it has occurred as both a national and a regional issue and is linked to deeper social and political changes in European politics marked by the emergence of a new dividing line or cleavage that has variously been described as pro- or anti-globalization or as a cosmopolitan versus communitarian divide (Hutter and Kriesi, 2019; de Wilde et al., 2019). This section focuses on two important characteristics of this politicization. The first is the composition of the field, with a wide range of new actors now involved in migration governance. The second is how decision-makers make sense of public attitudes to migration. Both affect know-how and social expectations about role.

First, some background: an effect of the crisis after 2015 was to focus attention even more strongly on the migration issue. Dominant images in 2015 and 2016 were of fear, human misery, danger, disorder, chaos, and death. As a European Commission official put it:

> because of the crisis...there was certainly at the corporate level, an increased level of attention, of resources mobilized, and also of tools which were launched. The new trust fund [for Africa] is one of those...it was a bit of the environment around giving increased priority to the topic.
>
> (European Commission official, Brussels, October 2017)

The crisis did not necessarily generate new thinking about the causes and consequences of migration, but did lead to more resources being channelled to deal with the challenge (as defined). In this sense, what was new was the dynamic of attention associated with the crisis rather than the thinking about migration.

There has been a self-conscious desire on the part of the EU institutions to think beyond the crisis and future-proof migration and asylum policies. Future-proof policies, according to the Commission should be 'built on strong foundations and clear values: a more effective and fairer approach based on solidarity and responsibility' (CEC, 2017b: 5). In December 2017, European Commission President Juncker called for a 'move away from crisis mode [because] migration will remain a challenge for a generation of Europeans. Europe urgently needs to equip itself with future-proof means of managing migration responsibly and fairly.' In its contribution to the EU leaders' thematic debate on a way forward on the external and internal dimensions of migration policy, the Commission identified two key aspects of a future-proof policy: developing a stable and integrated EU approach to migration and asylum; and ensuring that future-proofed policies are informed by values of solidarity and responsibility while inspiring trust and confidence (CEC, 2017b). Future-proof policy is also based on a representation of the likely future dynamics of migration and mobility both within and from outside the EU. In its March 2018 progress report on the EAM's implementation, the Commission provided a representation of these dynamics when it noted that the 'migratory challenge and pressure remains very high', that this was linked to 'geopolitical fragility and long-term demographic and socio-economic trends in Europe's neighbourhood and beyond', and that the 'situation remained fragile' (CEC, 2018: 1). This is an example of the retrospective element of sense-making: looking back to past experiences provides justification for a representation of a current challenge.

In Chapter 2, p. 35, reference was made to an interview with an EU official who referred to the idea of a 'new normal' which, as he saw it, would likely mean long-term, persistent migratory pressures at the EU's external frontiers. The phrase itself is, of course, a cliché, but its specific use in this context was interesting because it contains a diagnosis of the challenge: high migratory pressures understood as a 'new normal', coupled with a prognosis of required action: a new way of working with non-EU member states. As with all representations, this was also social in that it arose not only from discussions within the EU but also through contact with the US government. The importance of representations of migration generated within the migration governance system itself can be seen, particularly through this idea of a 'new normality' that sees continued high migration pressures as the shaper of EU migration policy in the years or decades to come. Whether accurate or not, this is the kind of view that enacts a sensible environment that makes sense to the actors involved. In such terms, EU migration governance cannot be understood solely as a response to flows of migrants and asylum seekers. The organization of migration governance and representations of migration (i.e. continued high pressures that can be racialized) define the challenges, enact a sensible environment, and, by doing so, shape responses.

Old and new actors

The migration governance field is now much more densely populated than ever before. In the 1990s, migration and asylum policy was dominated by the interior ministries of the member states, with EU institutions largely excluded. By the 2010s, immigration had become a 'whole of government' concern in most member states, involving other government departments such as foreign affairs and development. EU institutions, including the Commission, Court of Justice, and Parliament, were also fully involved in EU migration governance. The Directorate-General for Migration and Home Affairs increased considerably in size, while also delegating authority to new EU agencies responsible for border control (the European Border and Coast Guard Agency, previously known as FRONTEX) and asylum (the European Asylum Agency). At EU level too there was a diffusion of interest across the EU institutions so that, by the time of the refugee crisis, almost all Directorates-General of the Commission had staff working more or less directly on aspects of migration. There is also increased engagement by a range of other actors, including international organizations (some already well-established, of course, such as the IOM and the UNHCR), non-governmental organizations (NGOs), think tanks, and academic researchers.

This multi-actor and multilevel field creates a set of venues where data, information, and experiences can be shared. There are and are likely to remain major divergences within these kinds of cross-regional projects that are likely to be very difficult to resolve, not least because the EU's pursuit of enhanced mechanisms to control migration may well not fit with the priorities of non-EU member states. In the case of Tunisia, for example, migration is more likely to mean emigration, which is seen as an outlet for younger people and as a valuable source of remittances. There is also likely to be concern about the treatment of Tunisian migrants in European countries. Immigration has not been an important domestic political issue in Tunisia. This can make it more difficult for the EU to export its concerns when their basis is not shared (Geddes and Lixi, 2018).

Making sense of public attitudes

A key factor underlying the EU's desire to externalize migration controls and to involve non-EU member states has been the politics of migration in the EU and its member states. Perceptions of attitudes to migration and associated political mobilizations have shaped the representations by actors in migration governance systems of what's going on 'out there'. The events of 2015 and 2016 were seen as having important decisive effects on wider public perceptions. As a European Commission official put it:

> Then you see the massive flows and then you see people walking on roads in Hungary, thousands of people walking and people get afraid, 'What's going on? What have we done?', during 2015 and 2016 from an initial sympathy with the plight of migrants to a growing concern that things were getting out of hand.   (European Commission official, Brussels, November 2017)
>
> I think you can definitely see a shift within the European public perception. The way the refugee crisis was seen in the beginning, it was overwhelmingly positive. In the end, everyone saw that it was getting out of hand and really was a risk to the overall system, straining everybody's resources.
> (Austrian government official, Vienna, April 2018)

By 2016, migration had become a highly salient topic in European politics and, for example, played a key role in the UK's Brexit vote in June 2016, the strong first round vote in the 2017 French presidential elections for Marine Le Pen, the re-entry of the far-right Freedom Party into the governing Austrian coalition in December 2017, the growth in support for the Lega in the March 2018 Italian elections, the anti-migration focus of the victorious Fidesz campaign in the April 2018 Hungarian elections, the salience of the migration issue in the May 2019 European Parliament elections, and the emergence of the far right Vox party in Spain (Dennison and Geddes, 2018b; Dennison and Mendes, 2019).

These kinds of events have informed a particular representation among elite actors of what is going on 'out there' in terms of public attitudes to migration, whether accurate or not. Research shows that public attitudes to migration across the EU are relatively stable over time and, if anything, have actually become more favourable to both non-EU and EU migration. This trend towards favourability is evident in most EU member states even after the 2015 crisis. What did change was the issue salience of migration—the importance people attribute to it as a political concern—that rose steeply after 2015 and was a key factor in explaining growth in support for radical right, anti-immigration political parties in many EU member states (Dennison and Geddes, 2018b). Yet, among decision-makers, attitudes to migration are often represented as becoming more negative and as potentially driving support for populist parties that oppose European integration. As an example of this, the European Commissioner with responsibility for migration, Dimitris Avramopoulos, gave a speech to the EU Migration Forum in 2015 in which he said:

> We need to change the perception of the public opinion on migration. Our biggest concern is the rise of racism and xenophobia, fuelled by populist movements across Europe. To communicate the positive contribution of migration, I intend to launch an EU-wide campaign to improve the narrative about migration in cooperation with Member States later this year.
>
> (Avramopoulos, 2015: 2)

The issues of perceptions, of changing perceptions, and of changing or improving the narrative have been central to the ways in which governance actors, particularly those in an official role, made sense of migration and of how and why public attention became focused on the issue. As an official tellingly put it, solutions depend on perceptions of the problem:

> Yes, but where the light is on normally is also the problem in the sense that, if there is no public perception of a problem in the field of migration, there is no problem in itself. The problem is the public perception of the

problem...You decide how you perceive that issue and what makes it a problem. I need to provide solutions to your perceptions of migration.

(European Commission official, Brussels, October 2017)

There was broad agreement that the problem was a loss of control and that measures needed to be introduced to restore controls and, as a result, to restore public trust. This was a key claim of the Austrian and Danish vision paper on the asylum system referred to in the section 'What kind of region' above. Representations of public attitudes to migration play an important role in policymaking, as an official from the Austrian interior ministry put it:

You cannot deny that public opinion has an influence on what we do because of the interaction with the political level...So, we must be close to public opinion. We must not follow it, but we must be aware of it and we have to reach conclusions which are at least compatible with public opinion.

(Austrian government official, Vienna, January 2018)

The credibility of border controls is a key element of the response to public opinion, as understood. As an EU official put it:

Today I have minus 25 per cent arrivals on the Central Mediterranean route. Why? Because the borders are better controlled. So, in the short term it is a false assumption to tell me that the border controls do not work...The entire point...is we can discuss anything else once the border is up. Even the most neo-Nazi would accept if there are no irregular arrivals, that there are persons in need of protection.

(European Commission official, Brussels, October 2017)

The role played by public attitudes is complex. We know that interior ministries are key actors and that they favour a security-driven approach. Representations—whether accurate or not—of public attitudes also inform the ways in which governance actors enact a sensible environment within which a strong emphasis is placed on effective controls. There can be little doubt that this focus on controls has been a fairly constant component of the EU migration governance repertoire since its inception in the late 1980s, driven by concern about large numbers and also by fear of a public backlash.

In sum, the migration governance field has become much more crowded and more complex in terms of both participants and scale, although underlying representations of the migration challenge in Europe have remained relatively constant and focused on the potential for large-scale migration flows to the EU. The increased political salience of immigration means that public attitudes have also become part of the 'sensible environment', with border controls seen as the basis for an approach that addresses public concerns, as understood.

Conclusions

When assessing European and EU migration governance, we could swiftly become lost in the blizzard of initiatives, documents, laws, proposals, discussion documents, and the like. This chapter has sought to look beyond the more visible manifestations of migration governance such as laws and policies to think, instead, about how the constitution of the governance system itself has played a key role in defining both the migration challenge and forms of migration governance beyond the state. More particularly, it was shown that it is not crises that define EU and European migration governance but, rather, representations of what is normal about migration. Perceptions of normality shape what actors know how to do and also their expectations about role. This repertoire has a narrative component but, as this chapter has shown, is also social, affective, performative, and ongoing. More particularly, EU cooperation on migration and asylum by TCNs has been strongly driven by concern about large-scale and potentially uncontrollable flows that dates back to the end of the Cold War. In terms of the migration governance repertoire, this representation of the normality of migration has a powerful effect on what actors know how to do and also on their expectations about role. This has led to significant continuities in EU and European migration governance that also help to explain why, once established, such repertoires are difficult to shift or change.

6

North America

A Region without Regionalism

Introduction

This chapter gives a robust test to ideas of migration governance beyond the state by analysing developments in North America, where there is no formal regional migration governance and no realistic possibility of it developing. Between 2017 and 2020, a US President was determined to tear up existing norms and also use nativist and racist rhetoric on immigration and immigrants. The chapter looks back over more than forty years to identify a persistent regional migration governance repertoire in North America that derives from the views and actions of the US as the regional hegemon and shapes relations with Canada and Mexico. Through both the actions of its governments and the interests of capital, the US has had profound effects on the meaning and practice of borders; migration in its various forms; regionalism through NAFTA and its successor organization; and the politics of migration and migration governance. Immigration is deeply politicized in the US, with the 2016 election of Donald Trump a symptom of polarization on this and many other issues in US society (Abramowitz, 2018). Trump also expressed hostility towards formal structures for international cooperation that, while an extreme manifestation, particularly in the language used, reflected a longer-standing reluctance of US governments to participate in international frameworks that could compromise US sovereignty. In both Canada and Mexico there is awareness that it is necessary to try to work with the US government. In the absence of formal regional migration governance, this has led to bilateral relations, as well as some trilateral initiatives (Hadj Abdou, 2019).

A regional effect is evident not only in policies and practices associated with borders and migration, but also in the underlying perceptions of the causes and effects of migration and in the social expectations about role that are held by key migration governance actors in Canada, Mexico, and the US. This regional effect does not mean that there is a shared understanding; rather, it means the effects on migration governance of particularly influential

Governing Migration Beyond the State: Europe, North America, South America, and Southeast Asia in a Global Context.
Andrew Geddes, Oxford University Press (2021). © Andrew Geddes. DOI: 10.1093/oso/9780198842750.003.0006

representations. The resultant repertoire powerfully centres on and is driven by representations of the causes and effects of migration to the United States, in particular, on the role of pull factors exerted by the US economy and society and on deterrence measures that have been developed to prevent migration. While the focus on border security itself was not new, the 9/11 terror attacks had transformative effects on regional security. Racialized tropes and rhetoric in US immigration law and policy are also not new, but the Trump administration's anti-immigration and nativist approach has had important effects, particularly on Mexico. Only focusing on the US can, however, distract from wider regional dynamics and also effects on neighbouring countries, particularly Central American countries such as El Salvador, Honduras, and Guatemala. In fact, people fleeing violence in Central America towards the US have been the main focus for US interventions under Trump, but Mexico has for more than thirty years deported large numbers of Central Americans (FitzGerald, 2019).

To demonstrate a regional effect in the absence of regional migration governance, this chapter takes three steps. First, it shows how policies and approaches to immigration in the United States have been informed by particular representations of the causes and effects of migration that have been shaped by the idea that the US economy and society exert a powerful pull for migrants. While attitudes to immigration and immigrants are generally favourable, there has been growing concern since the 1990s about border security and the negative effects of migration that have been particularly evident in the Republican Party. A negative politicization of immigration has informed the development of deterrence-based approaches since at least the 1980s. Second, the chapter shows that, while there were no migration provisions in the NAFTA agreement or its successor, there has been cooperation on border issues that have been defined by security concerns and that have had important implications for migration governance. It becomes clear through the assessment of NAFTA and its successor organization—the variously named USMCA, CUSMA, or T-MEC, depending on whether viewed from the US, Canada, or Mexico, respectively—that regional cooperation can be a vehicle for economic integration but not political integration that allows participating states to achieve their sovereign objectives without countenancing political integration. While cooperation through NAFTA did create scope for enhanced rights for professional and business travellers, there were no substantive migration provisions within the agreement. Indeed, an underlying rationale for NAFTA was to promote economic development in Mexico and thus to stem migration flows, which, since the end of the 'guest worker' *bracero* labourer programme in 1964 had included large numbers of irregular migrants. After 1964, there was a growing population of irregular migrants in the US. By 2017, there were an estimated 10.7 million irregular migrants in the US (of whom half were from Mexico), although this was down from a pre-financial crisis peak of 12.2 million in 2007 (Pew Research Center, 2019). Finally, it is shown that migration governance has been punctuated by intermittent crises, particularly in the US, but that these have tended to affirm rather than shift the underlying representations. While the Trump presidency since 2016 is an extreme manifestation of a hard-line anti-immigration and anti-immigrant agenda, elements of its approach are consistent with a longer-standing focus on border security and deterrence, while the 'patchwork' quality of US immigration politics that sees a significant role for the courts as well as for variation in approach at state, county, and city levels limits the powers of the executive branch of the federal government (Reich, 2018).

Drivers and characteristics

The key migration relationship is between Mexico and the United States and is deeply entwined not only with the linked histories of these countries but also with complex border relationships. Figure 6.1 shows the scale of intra-regional migration and some, albeit modest growth, between 2010 and 2017. Figure 6.2 then breaks this down to show that migration from Mexico is

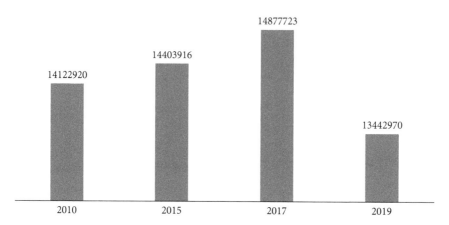

Figure 6.1 Trends in intra-regional migration in the ex-NAFTA region, 2010–19
Source: UNDESA 2019.

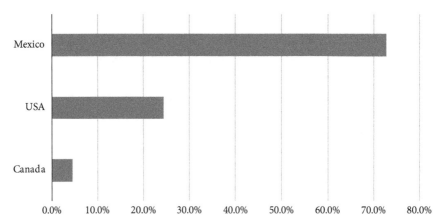

Figure 6.2 Share of intra-regional immigrants by country of origin, 2019
Source: UNDESA 2019.

the largest component of this intra-regional flow, while Canada has strongly extra-regional flows.

As in other chapters, the analytical focus is on how governance actors make sense of the context in which they operate. To orient to this approach in the North American context, consider this interview with a US government official responding to a question about how her organization—in this case the US Department of Justice—identifies and responds to risks:

> So, some things are crisis management, but then some things you can actually anticipate. I don't think you can anticipate 100 per cent of everything all the time, right? So, I think you do the best you can with the information you have at hand to make the best decisions that you can. Then you work with partners to see how you—I'm not a single player in this right? So, a lot of what we do and I do is looking at the whole, right, working with our partners to say, "'Hey, how can we as a whole unit make this process better?' Change in the government doesn't come fast but, you know, I think the dialogue is important.
>
> (United States Department of Justice official, Washington DC, July 2015)

In this response there is reference to how the interviewee's identity as an actor in this process is informed by her relations with other actors and how limits on information heighten the importance of relations with these other actors. It should be added that at an official level these partners tend to be within the US administration. There was little sense from our US interviews that, at an official level, 'we' included Mexico and Canada. There is also reference to how ways of knowing and ways of doing—repertoires—once established, are difficult to change. The result that 'Change doesn't come fast' is a recurring theme in this chapter.

Perceptions of the causes and effects of migration play an important role. As Jervis (2017: 21) put it, a 'subjective feeling of determinacy'—which here can be taken to mean representations of the causes and effects of migration and of risks and uncertainties associated with it—means that 'decision-makers can restrict their search for alternatives'. This can also include perceptions of how migrants perceive their own migration, as this official from the US Citizenship and Immigration Services (USCIS) put it, when referring to his view of the factors that motivated migrant decision-making:

> But the perception that now is the time to send your child out to get into the United States because the United States will accept these individuals, there is a lot of different instances of that perception. And individuals sending their children and putting them in harm's way in order to take advantage of what they perceive is a policy that will allow their children to come in. That happens all the time.
>
> (United States Citizenship and Immigration Services official,
> Washington DC, June 2015)

Without trying to overcomplicate things, this perception illustrates how representations of the drivers of migration through their effects on policy can then feed back to shape migration. To unpick this a little more, the idea in the quote above of US openness is seen as being taken advantage of by migrants and as having an effect on decisions by families to send children to the US. If this is what officials think is happening 'out there', then such a perspective suggests that it could be seen as necessary to try to deter such behaviour. The point here is not to evaluate whether this representation is accurate or not, but to observe that such representations have had powerful and persistent effects. This goes back to a recurring theme of this book: narratives can be deeply contested; but it is also the case that powerful perceptions held by powerful actors can have powerful effects.

Experiences of past events can also play a key role in shaping judgements, which can combine with the effects of uncertainty, as was put to us by an official from the US Department of Homeland Security (DHS):

> I think the more I've been in government, the more I realize that senior officials...are constantly making decisions with imperfect information. All

they can do is rely on their experience and their judgement, in an environment that is inherently uncertain and unpredictable, to be able to make the best decision that they can, at the time, with the information they have.

(United States Department of Homeland Security official,
Washington DC, June 2015)

The reference here is not only to limits on information, but also to how experience and judgement shape decision-making. Looking back to past experiences—as well as their limits—was captured by a Canadian government official, who said:

I think one of the challenges for us here and other departments is—and it's good—there's a large focus on evidence-based policymaking, which makes a lot of sense, but I find in a way is backward-looking by definition. You're measuring what has happened before and deciding what to do next based on how things were working.

(Citizenship and Immigration Canada official, Ottawa, March 2016)

This affirms a point that is central to a sense-making perspective, which is that the evidence that informs judgement necessarily means retrospection: to put it more intuitively, we look back to look forwards.

There was also keen awareness in the Canadian government and its provinces of the country's need to recruit economic migrants while also according with US priorities on border security marked by a concern that Canadian policy might be misconstrued as a lack of commitment to border security, as this official from the Canadian Border Services Agency (CBSA) put it:

So one of the great fears of the Americans if you can recall, I believe it was 2009, the Secretary of Homeland Security, Napolitano, was still operating under the belief that some of the 9/11 hijackers went through Canada to the US, which was completely false. So there are always these assumptions and fears that some individual may use Canada's generous immigration policies to enter Canada and then go to the US to commit terror attacks. So there's always a very strong security focus every time we deal with the US, but the pressure we have from stakeholders is always facilitation on the commercial side of things.

(Canadian Border Services Agency official, Ottawa, March 2016)

This affirms another point that is central to migration governance, which is that elite actors operate in an environment with competing and, at times, contradictory demands. For Canada, this means maintaining an openness to migration while satisfying US demands for tight border controls.

The US influence on the regional system is strong and evident through the political direction established by US leaders. A US State Department official compared the Obama and Trump administrations:

> Let's say there was a greater level of specificity and direction for particular policies because the incoming [Trump] administration had clearly given a lot of thought to this and had very, I would say, very solid ideas about what they wanted to pursue.
>
> (State Department official, Washington DC, September 2018)

Expectations of role can also play a part, particularly in how wider public expectations are understood. An interviewee from US Customs and Border Patrol in July 2015 put it like this:

> the 9/11 experience for us has been monumental in how the public sees the work, how we respond to their expectation. It certainly drove a lot of the policy in the early years of the department [in the mid-2000s]...But after 9/11, it became a national discussion...So instead of looking at it from a parochial security regime, we were looking at the whole national framework and the political will to do more and discuss what was only an internal discussion now became something that the American public, in our case, wanted to have answers on and wanted to see metrics and cared more about what we did.
>
> (United States Customs and Border Patrol official,
> Washington DC, July 2015)

This sense of the issues becoming a preoccupation for all Americans, who want 'answers', has powerful effects on the migration governance repertoire in the US and its regional effects on Canada and Mexico.

The 9/11 terror attacks had a powerful structuring effect on what governance actors in the US thought they should be doing. The importance of a lens—of a way of seeing the issues—was also evident in this quote from a representative of an international organization based in Mexico, referring to changing migration dynamics in central and North America and their effects on Mexico:

> Mexico is in a very difficult geopolitical position between Central America and the US, and the southern border is very difficult to control. Local

authorities estimate that almost half of the people that managed to enter regularly…have managed to reach the US. But also many ended up in Mexico and, due to the lack of an effective programme of regularization or through lack of information and access to the asylum system, they ended up living in cities without documentation.

(Representative of international organization, Mexico City, June 2016)

For a Mexican government official, this repatterning of migration dynamics fed directly into concern about how the US and to a lesser extent Canada perceive Mexico:

Mexico has the responsibility to keep working with the United States and Canada as partners. We need to accomplish and rescue some of these trilateral and regional initiatives in relation to migration that we were working on. Right now, the United States looks at Mexico as the problem and not as part of the solution, which we are.

(Mexican government official, Mexico City, July 2017)

Such quotes are not meant to validate particular representations of role and expectations, but to show how actors in influential positions interpret and respond to signals and cues from their environment. It's certainly the case that 9/11 was a compelling signal for the US, with powerful effects on regional security and migration governance. The election of Trump in 2016 simultaneously destabilized regional relationships while also heightening their importance.

While the 9/11 terror attacks certainly led to major and dramatic transformations in regional security, there was already an existing repertoire of migration governance at state, bilateral, and regional level that provided a template for subsequent responses and was powerfully influenced by perceptions—and their effects—particularly in the US.

Canada has maintained an open approach to immigration, although its border policy has been strongly influenced by the regional security context and its relations with the US. Canada has been characterized and frequently through policy and political communications sees itself as 'one of the few immigrant-receiving countries that has not discarded its welcome mat' (Woroby, 2019: 125). Between 2018 and 2021 the Canadian government and provincial authorities targeted the recruitment of 1.3 million new permanent residents with knock-on effects for family migration (Citizenship and Immigration Canada, 2018). Canadian policy has focused on selection, with criteria related to the economic potential of new migrants such as educational attainment and linguistic ability. While recruitment remains expansive, Gilbert (2019) shows that under US pressure the Canadian border has become more 'elastic' so that it can be accommodating of privileged travellers while snapping back into place to limit the ability of others to access Canadian territory. The distinctiveness of the Canadian position was put this way by a government official:

> We tend to come at it from different angles. For them [the US], security considerations tend to be primordial, and for us, it's about economic opportunities.
> (Canadian Citizenship and Immigration official, Ottawa, March 2016)

In Mexico, there has been a major reshaping of migration dynamics from being a country of emigration to a much more complex situation of immigration, emigration, transit migration, and return, but, as always, powerfully influenced by the US. Mexico's border with the US is a major international border of inequality across which there are intensive linkages (Selee, 2018). These deep influences between Mexico and the US have powerful historical antecedents. In 1848 the Treaty of Guadalupe Hidalgo ended the Mexican-American war of 1846–8 and saw almost half of Mexico's territory ceded to the US. This included setting the Mexico-US border in Texas on the Rio Grande and the ceding of California by Mexico to the US. The Mexican population in the ceded territory was given the choice of becoming American citizens or relocating to Mexico. The treaty established a 'pattern of inequality' between the two countries and a 'lopsided relationship' that has prevailed since (Del Castillo, 1992).

Since the 2000s, Mexico has transitioned from being primarily a sending country, with most migrants moving to the US, to a much more complex situation, with emigration from and immigration to Mexico, increasing numbers of Mexican returnees from the US, and a heightened focus on border security, as well as transit migration (or attempted transit migration), particularly by men, women, and children from Central American countries, many with protection needs. Tougher enforcement has played a crucial part in this, with greater effort made to control Mexico's southern border and also to contain migrants closer to this southern border. As a result, Mexico became a destination country (Alba, 2013). A new Mexican Migration Law in 2011 superseded the 1974 General Population Law, which was framed by the context of emigration. The 2011 law responded to these more complex migration dynamics and has had important effects on security cooperation with the United States, but also on Mexico's southern border and relations with Central American countries (Vera Espinoza, 2019). Marchand (2017) identified a regional focus on security that has turned Mexico into a buffer state protecting North American security interests. As an academic expert on Mexican migration put it to us, when referring to pressure from the United States:

> This means that you externalize the borders extending your security space beyond the administrative border. That is the case of Mexico. We live conditioned. I am not sure if threatened, but yes deeply influenced by the security policy of the United States.　(Academic expert, Mexico City, June 2016)

Mexican immigration to the US increased in the 1920s and reduced as an effect of the Great Depression in the 1930s. US entry to the Second World War led to labour shortages and, in 1942 to the *Bracero* ('Labourer') Accord between the Mexican and US governments for temporary entry by Mexican workers. These flows were 'circular' in that Mexican workers could move relatively easily across the border to undertake, for example, seasonal agricultural work. The *Bracero* scheme was extended on eight occasions and expanded during the 1950s. Between 1946 and the end of the programme in 1964, around 4.6 million Mexicans moved to the US (Calavita, 2010).

The end of the *Bracero* programme did not see the end of migration from Mexico to the US, but, instead, saw 'the *de facto* immigration policy of the United States devolved to a loose-fitting combination of limited legality and expansive tolerance' (Fernández-Kelly and Massey, 2007: 107). Migration flows continued in the form of irregular migration outside any formal agreement. In 1965 the US Immigration and Nationality Act had imposed a numerical quota for Mexican migrants. Increased irregular migration was in effect a move from a *de jure* guest worker programme regulated by the *Bracero* Accord to a *de facto* guest worker programme 'based on the circulation of undocumented labour' (Fernández-Kelly and Massey, 2007: 107). There were efforts to remove irregular Mexican migrants from the US. In 1954, during what was called 'Operation Wetback', just over one million irregular migrants from Mexico were apprehended (García, 1980). A combination of limited legality and expansive tolerance was characterized on the Mexican side as 'a policy of no policy', with *de facto* acquiescence to irregular flows and, on the US side, a permissive or benign neglect (Alba, 2016; Rosenblum, 2011).

By the 1980s, political momentum was growing in the US for further immigration law reform, but the issue was deeply contested, and progress towards agreement in Congress on legislation was slow and hard-fought. Ultimately, as Tichenor (2002: 261) notes, agreement was reached in Congress 'for compromise legislation behind closed doors, creating a sense of momentum that compelled business, ethnic and civil rights groups to pursue satisficing strategies on a measure they opposed'. The resultant Immigration Reform and Control Act (IRCA) of 1986 had three main elements: employer sanctions; border enforcement; and a legalization programme for those who had been in the US since 1982 and those who had worked as agricultural labourers for at least ninety days in 1986 (Donato et al., 1992: 40). Around 2.7 million people were legalized, of whom two million were Mexicans. IRCA was deeply contested, and no comprehensive immigration reform has been possible since. President Reagan's statement on the signing of the legislation highlighted the difficulties:

> The act I am signing today is the product of one of the longest and most difficult legislative undertakings of recent memory. It has truly been a bipartisan effort, with this administration and the allies of immigration reform in the Congress, of both parties, working together to accomplish these critically important reforms. Future generations of Americans will be thankful for our efforts to humanely regain control of our borders and thereby preserve the value of one of the most sacred possessions of our people: American citizenship   (Reagan, 1986)

Employer sanctions had limited practical effect and were referred to by Zolberg (2009: 383) as 'little more than a perfunctory law whose enforcement remained a largely dead letter, and the border itself remained a sieve'. Tichenor (2002: 262) argues that the Reagan (1981–8) and Bush (1989–92) administrations were 'less than zealous' in their enforcement of employer sanctions and, since the early 2000s, there is little to suggest that other administration have pursued tough labour market enforcement with greater zeal (Fine and Lyon, 2017).

A relatively expansive approach to immigration in terms of regularization and admissions continued with the Immigration Act of 1990, which increased the annual immigration cap and created H-1B visas for highly skilled temporary workers and H-2B visas for seasonal, non-agricultural workers. It also allowed for temporary protection status for people from countries experiencing armed conflicts, natural disasters, or 'other extraordinary and temporary conditions'.

The US policy focus increasingly shifted to the border with Mexico and the emergence of what Rosenblum (2011) refers to as 'prevention through deterrence', which became a mantra that developed during the Clinton administration after 1993 and also underpinned regional cooperation within NAFTA after 1994. This included efforts to make a show of force at the US-Mexico border as a way to deter migrants from even setting off. The first fence at the border was built in 1990 in the San Diego sector for 14 miles to separate San Diego from Tijuana. In the early 1990s there were also major enforcement operations by the US authorities in the form of 'Operation Hold the Line' in El Paso in 1993 and then, in 1994, 'Operation Gatekeeper' in San Diego-Tijuana (Bean et al., 1994; Nevins, 2001). In 1993 President Clinton expressed his intention to 'get serious' about border enforcement (Cornelius, 2001: 661). US Border Patrol commissioned a study that recommended deterring migrant journeys rather than relying on apprehension at the border (Cornelius, 2001: 662).

Prevention through deterrence made attempted border crossings costlier and riskier. These were not 'unintended consequences', as they were the specific intention of the prevention through deterrence approach (Cornelius, 2001: 667). Higher costs also meant that migrants from Mexico in the US were unwilling to return to Mexico, because the costs of getting back to the US were so high. It was also thought that forcing people into more dangerous routes would be a deterrent effect, which, again, was an intention, not an unintended consequence (Sanchez, 2016). There was scepticism expressed about the merits of a deterrence-based approach. Andreas (1998: 593) saw it has having more of a symbolic value that was 'less to do with actual deterrence and more to do with managing the image of the border and coping with the deepening contradictions of economic integration', while Gilbert (2009: 29) argued that 'deterrence as control and security risk management comes to legitimize the endless demand for wall technologies separating the USA and Mexico'. Nevertheless, deterrence remains a central component of the 'sensible environment' that informs US responses and that has a regional effect, as was put to us in 2015 by an official with US CBP:

People decided that post-9/11 we want to do something about the border. 2007, 2008, 2009, 2010, almost 700 miles of fencing on the south-west border and that's made a difference. People were always asking us, 'Does it work? Does it not work? You got all this investment. What are we getting for our return?' We've really gotten very good at protecting large pieces of border that were previously unprotected or unaffective [sic] in our response. People always ask, 'Well, is it the economy or is it what you guys do?' The economy is a big driver. If there is opportunity here, people are going to come, but also if they're caught and sent back, they stop coming. The economics don't work for them. You can only make a couple of attempts.

(United States Customs and Border Patrol official,
Washington DC, July 2015)

This statement clearly expresses a view on the economic pull exerted by the US but also the perceived power of deterrence if people are apprehended and sent back to Mexico. There was also a more insidious effect, because making another attempt at entry and being reapprehended were considered as illegal entry and a criminal offence. This perception is consistent with the direction of US policy established in the 1980s and that developed further after 1996 in the Illegal Immigration Reform and Immigrant Responsibility Act (IIRIRA), which increased enforcement efforts, but was also significant in that it marked a shift in the terms of domestic political debate away from the economic contributions of migrants towards a more pronounced focus on what was seen as migrants' use and abuse of public benefits and the idea that the US-Mexico border was porous (Freeman and Birrell, 2001). In terms of their place in the migration governance repertoire, perceptions of welfare abuse and a porous border have been key drivers of US actions, irrespective of whether the claims are true or not. These perceptions are contested but have taken root in policy and become part of a migration governance repertoire in the US.

By the end of the 1990s, the US had a large and growing population of irregular migrants from Mexico and an increased preoccupation with both border security and deterrence. As a presidential candidate prior to his election in 2000, George W. Bush had spoken of creating a new temporary migration programme for Mexican workers and a pathway for permanent legal residence for irregular migrants resident in the US, but, even prior to 9/11, there was vocal opposition to such ideas from within the Republican Party (Gutiérrez, 2007). After 9/11, the US focus changed to the fight against terrorism and reinforcement of border controls, with immigration firmly and decisively a matter of national security, not labour market regulation (Givens et al., 2008). This shift to immigration as a national security concern took bureaucratic form with the creation of the Department of Homeland Security to replace the Immigration and Naturalization Service (INS) that had previously been located in the Department of Justice. Even before the creation of the DHS there had been big increases in funding for enforcement. Andreas identifies a near threefold increase in the INS budget for enforcement between 1995 and 2002 to $2.5 billion (Andreas, 2003). The border hardened considerably after 9/11, with the effect that levels of return by Mexican migrants to

Mexico fell and the Mexican population in the US—both regular and irregular—grew. Illustrative of the key role played by economic factors in driving migration from Mexico to the US is that since the financial crisis of 2007–8, returns to Mexico have steadily grown. Between 2009 and 2014, the Mexican National Demographic Survey found that around one million Mexicans had returned from the US (cited in Vera Espinoza 2019, 171). Selee (2018) shows significant and growing connections across the border, but Mexico-US relations have also been dominated by what Fernández-Kelly and Massey (2007: 109) refer to as 'the growing militarization of a border separating the United States from a country that poses no strategic threat and is, in fact, an ally and major trading partner'. Trump's election in 2016 led to greater enforcement efforts. Between October 2018 and May 2019, 444,309 Central Americans were apprehended at the Mexico-US border, compared to 222,364 between October 2017 and September 2018 (Selee, 2019). This became part of what Trump referred to at the time of the November 2018 mid-term elections as a 'border crisis', assessed later in this chapter.

For Canada, the immediate effect of 9/11 was the December 2001 Smart Border Declaration, with the aim of creating a 'zone of confidence against terrorist activities' that would involve security measures at the Canada-US border related to the flows of goods and people, cooperation on infrastructure, and the sharing of information (Longo, 2016: 193). Also created were Integrated Border Enforcement Teams with US and Canadian officials working together.

The politicization of immigration in the US has meant that since IRCA, congressional deadlock has put paid to plans for immigration reform. In 2005, Democratic Senator Edward Kennedy and Republican John McCain proposed a bipartisan Secure America and Orderly Immigration Act that was subsequently reintroduced in 2006 and 2007 as the Comprehensive Immigration Reform Act and included a temporary migration programme, but this never became law. Kennedy provided a rationale for action in 2007, when he said:

> If we eliminate this programme, you will have those individuals that will crawl across the desert and continue to die as they do now. Or you can say, come through the front door and you will be given the opportunity to work for a period of time in the United States—two years—and return.
>
> (Senator Edward Kennedy speech to the US Senate, May 22 2007)

The IIRIRA of 1996 contributed to the development of 'immigration federalism' with greater scope for state- and city-level involvement in federal immigration law enforcement (Reich, 2018). A consequence of failure at federal level to legislate has been a growing role for state and city authorities to become more deeply involved and for greater politicization at state and city level. Arizona and Pennsylvania, for example, both passed ordinances designed to carry out strict document checks on people suspected of being irregular, preventing irregular migrants from access to housing, and imposing sanctions on employers (Archibold, 2010). The Personal Responsibility and Work Opportunity Reconciliation Act of 1996 was also important in the development of immigration federalism because, while it excluded immigrants from federal welfare benefits for their first five years in the US, states were given the ability to broaden coverage. This has led to divergence in access to welfare across states, with Arizona, Florida, and Texas among the least generous, while New York and California allow access to state-funded benefit programmes (National Immigration Forum, 2018).

Continual congressional deadlock stymied reform efforts, including the Development, Relief, and Education for Alien Minors (DREAM) Act that sought to provide a pathway to permanent residency for irregular migrants who entered the US as children, but which never became law. President Obama resorted to the use of an executive order in 2012 when he announced Deferred Action for Childhood Arrivals (DACA), which allowed young adults aged 15–30 who were brought to the US irregularly as children to apply for temporary deportation relief. DACA was seen as consolidating support for Obama amongst Hispanic voters (Barreto and Collingwood, 2015). In 2014, further executive orders were issued: Deferred Action for Parents of Americans and Lawful Permanent Residents (DAPA) and an expanded DACA Programme. DAPA allowed irregular immigrant parents who had been in the US for at least five years and had children who were US citizens or legal permanent residents to apply for deportation relief and a three-year work permit. It also expanded eligibility for DACA, with a series of conditions including age at time of entry, experience of education, and duration of residence. DAPA and DACA were ended by President Trump in June and September 2017, respectively, but 'amidst the policy cancellations, arrests, and threats, a dynamic of executive provocations and state and local counter-challenges [to Trump's measures] emerged that was reminiscent of the Obama years' (Reich, 2018: 381). In a movement dating back to the 1980s, more than 200 jurisdictions at state, county, and city level declared 'sanctuary' status, which means that they announced their intention to not comply with requests from Immigration and Customs Enforcement (ICE) to detain immigrants unless they were suspected of criminal violation of the law (Lasch et al., 2018).

There was also a hardening of the US position on asylum and refugee resettlement after Trump's election. The US has long been the world's leading destination for resettled refugees, but in 2017 President Trump proposed cutting to 45,000 the Obama administration's plan for 110,000 resettled refugees. In September 2017, the Secretary of State, Mike Pompeo, announced plans to further cap the numbers of resettled refuges at 30,000, which was less than a third of the number proposed for 2017 by Obama. In reality, just under 22,000 refugees were actually resettled in the fiscal year between October 2017 and September 2018 (Department of Homeland Security, 2019). The main origin countries for these resettled refugees were DR Congo, Iraq, and Syria.

In late 2017 and early 2018, the Trump administration also removed the temporary protected status from around 320,000 people mainly from Haiti, El Salvador, Nicaragua, and Honduras. In November 2017 the status was removed from around 59,000 Haitians, so that they would be expected to leave the US by July 2019 (Jordan, 2017).

Violence in Central America has led tens of thousands of men, women, and children to flee and to move north to Mexico, with many ultimately aiming to get to the US. In 2017, 26,500 people were granted asylum in the US, with the main origin countries being China, El Salvador, and Guatemala. In the same year, there were just under 140,000 asylum applications made in the US, a 150 per cent increase since 2014. Huge backlogs built up, with applicants stranded on the Mexican side of the border while they waited for their application to be considered. In June 2019, Trump threatened tariffs on Mexican goods if the Mexican government did not do more to stop migrants getting to the US. In response, President López Obrador announced the deployment of the National Guard to Mexico's southern border and also expanded the Migrant Protection Protocols to allow Central American migrants to be returned to Mexico while waiting to make an asylum application in the US. The Mexican government deployed 15,000 troops to its border with the US and added a further 2,000 troops to the 4,500 already deployed at its borders with Belize and Guatemala (Arias, 2019). In July 2018, an executive order from President Trump announced his intention to declare Mexico a 'safe third country', with the effect that people, including unaccompanied children, would not have a basis for an asylum claim in the United States unless the application had been rejected in Mexico. The underlying rationale of safe third country schemes is well known and has been a mainstay of EU approaches since the 1990s. The aim is to deter or delay would-be asylum applicants, although, as Fratzke (2019) argues, 'experience suggests that these may be false promises. The reality is that these arrangements have generally proven to be difficult to enforce, have played little role in deterring new claims, and have added new complexities to procedures for already over-whelmed asylum systems.' While Trump's measures were challenged in the courts, one effect—indicative of the performative component of migration governance repertoires—was to stir up his electoral base in the run-up to the 2020 presidential election (The Economist, 2019). Another is likely to be more pressure on the under-resourced Mexican asylum system. Between 2016 and 2017, there was a 66 per cent increase in asylum applications to Mexico, but there were only forty-eight staff members for the whole country, which gave rise to concerns about the capacity to protect asylum seekers (Fredrik, 2019; Vera Espinoza, 2019: 168). The human cost was made clear during the Covid-19 pandemic. On 1 April 2020, the Trump administration announced the suspension of all asylum hearings, leaving thousands of people trapped in camps on the Mexican side of the border with minimal medical provision and a high risk of exposure to the coronavirus (Villavicencio and Lee, 2020)

The intensified focus on borders and security during the Trump adminis-tration was accompanied by nativist and racist rhetoric. This included efforts to stem irregular migration ('Build the wall' was a relentless chant at Trump campaign rallies), but also to seal US borders to regular migrants. On 21 April 2020, during the Covid-19 pandemic, Trump announced via a tweet his intention to issue an executive order that would suspend all immigration to the United States. As always with Trump's policymaking via tweets, the devil was in the detail. Business groups immediately pushed back against the end-ing of work visas. The proposal was modified to a restriction on entry by green card holders. While the measures are distinctly more hard-line, there were underlying continuities in approach based on ideas about the pull factor exerted by the US and its society and economy and an attendant focus on deterring migrants. Suggestions were also made that more hard-line figures in the Trump administration saw the Covid-19 crisis as an opportunity in the run-up to the 2020 presidential election to signal Trump's anti-immigration credentials and build on his earlier targeting of migration from and via Mexico and further development of US-Mexico border security (Shear and Haberman, 2020).

While there is no formalized regional migration governance, representa-tions of the causes and effects of migration and of the risk and uncertainties associated with it that emanate from the US have exerted a powerful regional effect, while representations of the region have played a powerful role in US policy development. This becomes clear as we analyse NAFTA, its successor organization, and attempts to develop regional security cooperation.

What kind of region?

In September 2018, a US State Department official captured quite succinctly the key characteristics of North American regional migration governance, or, to be more precise, its absence:

> We're happy to say regionalism but in a very kind of not quite *ad hoc* but a looser sort of way. Happy to coordinate, happy to talk, happy to have standing structures to do it but there is no kind of coercion about it. That's something we would never accept, and I don't think most other governments in the region would either. Mexico has an exceptionally strong sense of its own sovereignty, doesn't like to be bullied by anyone.
> (US State Department official, Washington DC, September 2018)

While there is no formalized regional migration governance, there is a North American migration governance repertoire that has a clear regional effect. As has just been documented, this stems primarily from developments in US immigration politics that focus on border security and prevention of migration through what is understood as deterrence measures, including detention. A regional effect is made manifest through what Hadj Abdou (2019: 146) calls a 'double bilateralism' linking Canada and Mexico with the US that is not a vehicle for supranational integration, but functions 'as a tool to protect the interests of nation states in a globalised world'.

The centrality of borders is the defining characteristic of relations within the old NAFTA framework, with a strong focus on the US-Mexico border but also on what Andreas (2005) has called the 'partial Mexicanization' of the US-Canada border. NAFTA was replaced in 2018, but it is important to note that it was designed to stem, not facilitate migration flows. There was never an intention to create regional free movement or to promote 'mobility'; in fact, the opposite. As President Salinas of Mexico put it, 'the whole point of NAFTA for Mexico is to be able to export goods and not people'. There is an intensity to relations on all sides: 90 per cent of Canadians live within 100 miles of the border with the US, while there are around 350 million annual crossings of the US-Mexico border and around 110 million annual crossings of the Canada-US border (Sutcliffe and Anderson, 2018).

In the 1980s, US financial institutions faced very high levels of exposure to debt held by Latin American countries, including Mexico. At the same time, US companies were benefiting from lower wages to move their manufacturing operations outside the US, which then had major effects on employment in manufacturing in the US (Frieden, 1991). US interest rates were raised above 20 per cent by the Federal Reserve in the early 1980s in order to rid the US economy of stagflation, but this 'tightened the noose around the neck of Latin American economies' and precipitated the debt crisis of 1982 (Fernández-Kelly and Massey, 2007: 100). The US government then used international organizations such as the IMF to impose 'structural adjustment' on Latin American economics, with loans dependent on neoliberal economic reforms.

In 1986, Mexico had been admitted to the GATT system, as it moved from a strategy of import substitution to export promotion in GATT and then to regional economic integration within NAFTA (Sánchez-Reaza and Rodríguez-Pose, 2002). President Salinas was an eager and willing advocate of neoliberalism, which he saw as a way to integrate Mexico into the global economy, accompanied by neoliberal economic measures involving a familiar recipe of deregulation, privatization, and public spending cuts. There were also changes to property law. Of particular importance was the repeal of Article 27 of the Mexican constitution to end the *ejido* system of communal land used for agriculture and to authorize private ownership (Cornelius and Myrhe, 1998). The privatization of collective farms and the elimination of agricultural subsidies from the Mexican National Company of Popular Subsistence (CONASUPO), plus the effects of NAFTA, had a negative impact on the livelihoods of rural populations that contributed to increased migration to the US. This was because basic crop production in Mexico was labour-intensive, with low productivity levels, while basic crop production in the US was both more productive and also subsidized by the US government. In many agricultural sectors, Mexican producers were simply outcompeted by US producers.

NAFTA was designed to facilitate free trade and open markets and to expand opportunities for capital investment (Fernández-Kelly and Massey, 2007: 99). The regional framework reflected a commitment to market forces, with the presence of the US as a regional hegemon that had no willingness to participate in supranational structures (Duina, 2016). While Canada and Mexico retain a commitment to sovereignty, they know full well that their key relationship is with the US. For both, signing up to NAFTA was a reversal of a previous aversion to such agreements, with national identity defined in contrast to the United States (Golob, 2003). A Mexican government official put it like this:

In general, the relationship with the US and to a lesser extent Canada has been developed and institutionalized for several years . . . What we are trying to work now in the region is thinking in Mexico-US and Mexico-Canada and Canada-US. Each has their own issues and we are trying to improve those three bilateral relationships towards a regional perspective. However, migration is a complex topic and we haven't been able to talk about complete mobility and this will continue in the same way for several years.

(Mexican government official, Mexico City, July 2016)

There is clear recognition of the limits to cooperation and also a sense that any scaling up of relations is unlikely to occur any time soon.

While there was significant impetus from the US, as Fernández Kelly and Massey (2007: 101) note, 'NAFTA's architects are found on both sides of the US-Mexican border.' In 1965, following the ending of the *Bracero* programme, Mexico began a Border Industrialization Programme, the aim of which was to provide employment for returning migrants and to prevent emigration and also lead to the economic transformation of border towns. Of particular importance were manufacturing plants (*maquiladoras*) on the Mexican side of the US-Mexico border, owned and operated by US companies, with raw materials imported from the US to benefit from lower-cost manufacturing in Mexico to then be exported back to the US. Manufacturing in these northern Mexican border areas drew workers from rural areas, with a gendered division of labour as *maquiladoras* disproportionately hired women, which contributed to increased male irregular migration to the US (Cornelius and Martin, 1993).

Initial agreement on NAFTA occurred in 1991, when an agreement was signed by Presidents Bush and Salinas and Prime Minister Mulroney on 17 December 1992. Chapter XVI of the NAFTA agreement 'reflects the preferential trading relationship between the Parties, the desirability of facilitating temporary entry on a reciprocal basis and of establishing transparent criteria and procedures for temporary entry, and the need to ensure border security and to protect the domestic labour force and permanent employment in their respective territories'. This chapter is aimed at business travellers, traders and intra-corporate transferees, with no effect on national laws relating to permanent residence. As such Chapter XVI reflects 'the tension between the goals of preserving national autonomy, border security, and protecting the permanent employment of each Party's domestic labour force on the one hand, and encouraging the liberalization of trade on the other' (Yost, 1996: 211). Alba (2016: 47) argued that 'the spirit of NAFTA opened up spaces to "rationalise" the migration of Mexican workers to the USA', but hopes for the development of a common migration agenda were short-lived, because 9/11 ended any discussion of a 'NAFTA+' agreement that could include measures on migration.

The disjunction within the NAFTA framework between the freedoms granted to capital and the restrictions on migration contributed to a 'lopsided process of development' (Fernández-Kelly and Massey, 2007: 99). A regional NAFTA effect has been a huge expansion in trade but tighter restrictions on movement by people. Trade between the US and Mexico tripled after NAFTA was set up in 1994. The US is Mexico's largest trading partner, while Mexico is the US's third-largest trading partner after China and Canada (Villarreal, 2019). US exports to Mexico increased from $41.6 billion in 1993 (the year prior to NAFTA coming into force) to $265.0 billion in 2018. US imports from Mexico increased from $39.9 billion in 1993 to $346.5 billion in 2018 (Villarreal, 2019: 3). US foreign direct investment (FDI) in Mexico increased from $17 billion in 1994 to a record level of $109.7 billion in 2017 (Villarreal, 2019: 5). Fernández-Kelly and Massey (2007: 108) see this as indicative of the 'contradictory policy goals' of the US towards Mexico, with 'greater integration in markets for capital, goods, services, commodities and information while insisting on separation in labour markets'.

The regional effect is most clear on border relationships and border security both before and after 2011. In 2002, the US government introduced the Enhanced Border Security and Visa Entry Reform Act, which provided for the gathering of biometric data on travellers and the creation of interoperable databases for the various branches of the federal government. The US Homeland Security Act 2002 abolished the INS and transferred its functions to the DHS, including CBP, ICE, and the USCIS. The DHS became the key actor in US migration governance. In 2006, the US Secure Fence Act 2006 mandated the creation of a double-layered fence 700 miles long at the south-western border from California to Texas. In 2005, the Real ID Act established new requirements for eligibility to make an asylum application in the US, which was purported to be antiterrorism legislation but had the effect of 'specifically targeting asylum-seekers, a group of vulnerable non-citizens fleeing persecution to which the United States has historically offered protection' (Cianciarulo, 2006: 101).

For most of the twentieth century the US-Canada border had been 'low intensity, low profile and a low priority' (Andreas, 2005: 450). Prior to 9/11 there were only minimal enforcement efforts at the Canadian-US border. The 9/11 attacks led to what has been called the 'partial Mexicanization' of the Canada-US border, i.e. relabelling the border as a security threat, although there has been a much greater degree of trust and collaboration between the US and Canadian authorities (Andreas, 2005). In December 2001 a US-Canada Smart Borders Agreement included a thirty-two-point action plan, including provisions to enable access by frequent travellers under the NEXUS programme for air travellers.

In 2011, the Beyond the Border Agreement was reached between the US and Canada to create a more integrated border enforcement cooperation through interoperable technology and joint communication centres and a joint entry and exit system (Konrad and Nicol, 2016). This bilateral cooperation meant that people admitted to Canada did not need to be inspected again if travelling on to the US. Canadian willingness to cooperate was strongly driven by concern about the potential economic cost of not fitting in with US border security requirements, as this official from the CBSA put it:

And on the Canadian side, certainly in appreciation of that reality, but at the same time a concern that if the Americans had decided that Canada was the weak link or a weak link, that there was a significant economic risk. So the phrase that we often use is thickening the border. We wanted to protect against the Canada-US border becoming such a security feature that it would hinder trade and economic development.

(CBSA official, Ottawa, March 2016)

In 2009 Canada 'dramatically remapped its borders with Mexico' through the imposition in July of a visa requirement for Mexican travellers and in August 2009 announced a capacity building project with Canadian law enforcement officials working in Mexico with Mexican officials. The restriction was relaxed in December 2016, with short-term visitors for up to ninety days required to get an Electronic Travel Authorization (ETA) prior to travel.

The US administration also stepped up bilateral cooperation with Mexico. In October 2007 the Mérida Initiative was launched, with an initial focus on organized crime. In 2010 the Obama administration and the Mexican government agreed to a new framework for cooperation under the Mérida Initiative to create a 'twenty-first-century border'. Between 2008 and 2014 the US Congress approved over $2.4 billion for Mexico under the Mérida Initiative to also involve cooperation on Mexico's southern borders with Guatemala and Belize (Seelke and Finklea, 2010). Obama's 2012–16 National Strategy for Border Patrol sought to move to 'risk based approaches' that were not based on catching people on the border 'but on catching people before they come in, which is a form of deterrence' (the former head of CBP Gary Shiffman, cited in Longo, 2016: 191). The numbers of people deported from the US greatly increased under Obama, with more than three million removals during his presidency, most of them Mexican citizens.

In his election campaign, Trump had called for a renegotiation of NAFTA, which occurred in 2017 and into 2018. The USMCA/CUSMA/T-MEC (depending on whether its viewed from the US, Canada, or Mexico, respectively) was signed on 30 November 2018, but then required ratification in all three participating states. The new agreement did not affect the limited mobility provisions within NAFTA. The NAFTA Professional TN visa, which offers expedited work authorizations for professionals or skilled workers, remained unchanged. What did change was the US approach to relations with Mexico and ideas about 'smart borders' or 'risk-based approaches'. Instead, Trump based his election campaign around the pledge of building a wall at the border with Mexico and making Mexico pay for it, while in 2018 he threatened Mexico with tariffs on its exports unless it took action to stop migration to the US.

Beyond NAFTA there are also informal governance processes that connect North with Central America. The Puebla Process created in 1986 is a regional consultation process that links NAFTA members with eight Central American countries. The impact has been relatively small, and exposed divisions as much as it has eased them. A former US government official identified a trust-building benefit, 'talking about issues and getting familiar with the people, knowing each other' (Interview, former US government official, Washington DC, July 2015). The Puebla Process did facilitate the offer of temporary protection by the US and Costa Rica to people from Central America, particularly Honduras, displaced by Hurricane Mitch in 1998, but the more general orientation has been towards what Köhler (2011, 119) tellingly describes as 'informed' or 'coordinated divergence'. The result is that the Puebla Process reinforces power asymmetries. As a Mexican civil servant put it: 'nothing relevant has emerged in the last few years' (interview, Mexico City, July 2017). A Canadian government official highlighted a rather basic difficulty:

> When you're talking about a grouping that brings together countries as diverse as the United States and Nicaragua, you can appreciate that there's not always a lot of synergies in those relationships.
>
> (Citizenship and Immigration Canada official, March 2016)

Before 2016 and the election of President Trump, a migration governance repertoire can be identified that was not embedded in any formal regional migration governance arrangements but was evident as an effect exerted by the United States as a regional hegemon and attendant effects on migration, borders, and security. As we now see, intermittent crises are set against the ways of knowing and ways of doing that have developed over a considerable period of time.

Crises and their regional effects

In North America, as in the other regions that form part of this analysis, there have been intermittent crises that have both shaped and been shaped by international migration. The US reaction to the 9/11 terror attacks had particularly powerful effects and reshaped regional security, but, in so doing, drew from already established components of a migration governance repertoire.

There were intermittent migration and border crises before the 9/11 attacks. When evaluating events, governance actors often refer to past experiences or to the experiences of others, because, as already shown throughout this book, meaning is given to events through interactions with others. When asked about risks and uncertainties, this interviewee from US CBP highlighted that current events are not necessarily new.

> It's that way. It's always been like that; it's been like that since the 1990s. Having read and been able to talk to other people who had already been part of the federal government in the 1990s, they all told me the same thing: that it's cyclical.   (CBP official, Washington DC, June 2015)

It's also the case that when responding to events labelled as a crisis, actors will look back to past experiences. For example, when assessing child migration in 2014 and 2015, this official from the US State Department referred to experiences in the 1990s with migration from Cuba during the Clinton administration and the so-called 'wet foot, dry foot' policy:

> Any Cuban we interdicted would be brought to the US and once they got to US soil they were 'legal'...That, again, showed to me that where migrants had a sense that their chances of success actually getting to the US were high, they would do something illegal or something dangerous. So that, too,

showed me that we have to make clear that the chances of success are not high and we have to demonstrate that in the policy choices we make.

(State Department official, Washington DC, June 2015)

The lesson learned here about the success of a deterrence approach was then used to inform the assessment of current events. The point here is not to evaluate whether this assessment was or was not accurate, but to see how past experiences can frame representations by providing an anchoring bias that shapes response.

In Canada there is an aversion—perhaps self-conscious, given the high level of political attention devoted to the issue in the US—to refer to crisis and, instead, to highlight a preference for a 'steady-state' normality as a modus operandi likened to a Canadian national trait:

> It's not driven in our psyche by crisis to crisis or event to event, but just a steady state. A steady state, part of who we are and there's a plan for how many will come in every year. And there's a certain percentage that are refugees, so that might be where the reason for coming to Canada might be for a whole other set of reasons than those who have applied to come for economic or other reasons.
>
> (Citizenship and Immigration Canada official, Ottawa, March 2016)

It is, of course, political leaders that make decisions and set policy directions. In doing so they often use what in Chapter 1 was referred to as hedgehog-style thinking (knowing one big thing, compared to foxes who know many little things), with, for example, a tendency to draw from past experiences to inform the quest for 'solutions' (Tetlock, 2017). An official from USCIS nicely captured the tension between hedgehogs and foxes:

> I think, the policy process does sometimes want to find that single solution or a subset of one solution that can solve a problem, but we do always say, 'These problems are complex and multidimensional, and you may be able to tackle one aspect of it, but realize there are a lot of other factors that this one policy change won't solve.' We tell them that and their view, generally, is, 'We understand that, but we still need to do the one thing, or we need to have that one solution at least.'
>
> (United States Citizenship and Immigration Services official,
> Washington DC, July 2015)

This official from the DHS highlighted in response to falls in the number of unaccompanied child migrants the high level of risk that can be associated with actions and interventions at times of crisis:

> And when the flood sort of reduced, we don't know which of those measures, if any of them, was the one that did that. And we don't know—like everybody was waiting this spring to see if it was going to happen again. Nobody knew. And going into the future nobody knows, if we stop any of the things we did, will the flood start again?
>
> (United States Department of Homeland Security official, Washington DC, June 2015)

This DHS official was referring to the situation in 2014 when a 'surge' in unaccompanied child migrants between 1 October 2013 and 13 July 2014 saw around 63,000 children cross from Mexico to the US; two-thirds were from Guatemala, Honduras, and El Salvador. This 'surge' attracted significant attention from the highest levels of the federal government, including President Obama. There was abundant scope for the instrumentalization of the crisis, as Hernández (2014: 11) observes:

> The 'crisis' and 'surge' served all sides of the debate, demonstrating an unenforced and out-of-control border for anti-immigrant forces, a cruel and rushed detention apparatus for migrant advocates, and the urgent need for comprehensive immigration reform for the Obama administration.

The high level of attention can induce a sense of excitement among governance actors, as this congressional staffer recounted:

> Last summer [2014] was a really amazing time. It was probably the most important time I've had in my six years on the Hill because when the issue took over it was the first time that the issue that I was working on was legitimately national news; it was legitimately being treated, at least, as a national crisis. I mean CNN was covering it constantly.
>
> (Congressional staff member, Washington DC, July 2015)

An official from the DHS similarly highlighted the ways in which attention was focused on child migration:

> This was a crisis that consumed the US government for several months. So, there was a lot of attention and thought that went on with respect to it. So, in

some ways I think you might have gotten better decision-making because there were so many people.

(United States Department of Homeland Security official,
Washington DC, July 2015)

In response to the increased influx, the government passed a set of measures to stem the flow, including the reintroduction of family detention, as well as information campaigns that sought to deter migration. A letter from President Obama confirmed the continued resonance of deterrence-based approaches:

> we are working with our Central American partners, nongovernmental organizations, and other influential voices to send a clear message to potential migrants so that they understand the significant dangers of this journey and what they will experience in the United States. These public information campaigns make clear that recently arriving individuals and children will be placed into removal proceedings, and are not eligible for the Deferred Action for Childhood Arrivals process and earned citizenship provisions that are part of comprehensive immigration reform currently under consideration in the Congress…we will continue to use multiple channels to counteract the misinformation that is being spread by smugglers.
>
> (Obama, 2014)

Looking back at these events in September 2018, a State Department official reflected on the effectiveness of the interventions:

> Did it work? Well, at first nobody cared so much. The impulse was to show we are doing something and particularly if money is appropriated and this is how Congress says 'I love you', this is how they say they care, is by appropriating money…So they throw a lot of hot money after a problem, maybe it works, maybe it doesn't, but they try a lot of different things. Later on you figure out what actually worked and hopefully then you can focus your response.

What was noticeable at the time of the child migration 'surge' was a sense of increased willingness to develop cross-border cooperation with Mexico. US government officials told us that they had detected a greater willingness to cooperate:

> Mexico's real commitment to do things for a secure border on their side of the border, we've never seen that level of effort before…So I think Mexico

responded in a way that said, 'Hey, look. We have our own security challenge,' and so the world was watching, kind of thing, and they did more than they'd done before. Different leadership, I think, always matters but they really stepped up and they've made a big difference this year [2015].

(State Department Official, Washington DC, June 2015)

A key difference after 2016 is that the Trump administration saw events such as the EU 'crisis' after 2015 not as a worldwide crisis. From a US perspective, the specific issues were its sovereignty and its borders, as this State Department official put it:

I think the current [Trump] administration is less inclined to view this as a worldwide crisis and see it rather as, well, Europe has its problem and we have our problem on our southwestern border. We can certainly cooperate and help each other out on this, but to try and characterize these things which are quite different and have to be dealt with as local phenomena, to try and subsume them all under one broad heading of worldwide migration crisis, it obscures as much as it helps. I think that's their view of it.

(State Department Official, Washington DC, September 2018)

During his election campaign, Trump targeted Mexico and Mexican migrants, including this statement when announcing his candidacy:

When Mexico sends its people, they're not sending their best…They're sending people that have lots of problems, and they're bringing those problems with us. They're bringing drugs. They're bringing crime. They're rapists and some, I assume, are good people.   (cited in Hughey, 2017: 127)

A distinctive feature of the Trump administration has been both harsh, racialized rhetoric and hard-line enforcement measures such as the child separation policy, which was specifically designed to form part of a zero-tolerance approach, with the aim of deterring would-be migrants. In the summer of 2018, the DHS reported that 1,995 children had been separated from their parents, but these numbers were likely to be an underestimate, while it was argued that the treatment of the children amounted to torture (Amnesty International, 2018). In June 2018 a US federal court ruled against child separation and the US government's zero-tolerance policy.

Via social media at least, the response of Mexican and Canadian political leaders seemed robust. On 30 May 2018, the Mexican president, Enrique Pena

Nieto, tweeted directly to 'President @realDonaldTrump: NO Mexico will NEVER pay for a wall. Not now, not ever. Sincerely, Mexico (all of us)'. But what really changed? At the technical level, efforts were made to maintain existing arrangements, as this Mexican government official noted in the summer of 2017:

> This year we kept working with the US in the same way. I mean at the technical level, with low profile, there have not been changes…At least we have made sure that those agreements remain in place and are being accomplished.
>
> (Mexican government official, Mexico City, June 2017)

At a political level, in the face of Trump's threatened tariffs, Mexico acceded to US demands for much tougher migration controls.

On 28 January 2017, the Canadian prime minister, Justin Trudeau, responded to Trump's proposed travel ban on people from seven Muslim-majority countries by tweeting: 'To those fleeing persecution, terror & war, Canadians will welcome you, regardless of your faith. Diversity is our strength #WelcomeToCanada'. Canada has, however, long accepted the need to align its border security measures with the United States. The pressure has not been as significant as that faced by Mexico. Trump in his 2017 State of the Union speech actually expressed his desire to move towards what he referred to as Canada's 'merit-based immigration system', although the chances of the Trump administration enacting immigration reform shrank to essentially zero when the Democrats took control of the House of Representatives in the November 2018 mid-term elections.

Probably the most blatant example of a manufactured crisis was Trump's declaration of a southern border crisis in the run up to the November 2018 mid-term elections (Morales, 2019). Fear stoked about a 'caravan' of migrants from Central America was used by Trump to even question birthright citizenship, while he also deployed 5,000 troops to the US-Mexico border. While the Republicans actually suffered an electoral setback and lost control of the House of Representatives, this immigration scare foreshadowed a potential key theme of Trump's 2020 re-election campaign, albeit derailed by the Covid-19 pandemic.

Intermittent crises have been shaped by underlying representations of the 'normality' of migration, which, since the 1990s have focused on the porousness of borders, the powerful pull factor exerted by the US economy and society, and the subsequent need to deter migrants. While the Trump administration has been an extreme manifestation of what was labelled as 'prevention through deterrence' in the 1990s, its approach does retain elements of consistency with earlier approaches. After all, 'Death at the Border' was the title of an article published in 2001 (Cornelius, 2001). Its contemporary resonance may well be more pronounced, but the issue itself is not new. Similarly, regional cooperation has been shaped by US representations of the causes and effects of migration and of associated risks and uncertainties, which mean that while there is not and is unlikely to be formal regional migration governance, there is a powerful regional effect from the US migration governance repertoire.

Conclusion

In North America, a migration governance repertoire associated with a powerful hegemon means that migration governance remains state-centred, with little prospect of formalized migration governance beyond the state. Yet regional ties remain strong and have intensified in numerous ways that create close regional linkages that are clear evidence of regionalization. Migration has not formed part of the framework for formal regional cooperation, which was driven by economic concerns and has not had wider political ambitions. A limited form of regional cooperation can be a way to defend and to enhance sovereignty, not to pool, denude, or share it. Yet the operation and effects of this migration governance repertoire have and will continue to have powerful regional effects. They shape relations between the US, Mexico, and Canada, with an effect that stretches into South America too. Of particular importance were legislative changes in the US in the 1980s and 1990s that have given rise to a deterrence-based approach. While the efficacy and value of such an approach has been questioned, it remains a fairly stable component of the sensible environment of US policymakers that has operated for more than thirty years. While the Trump administration departed from established standards and ways of doing things in many important ways, there are also some consistencies with the actions of previous administrations. As under these previous administrations, the effects of 'immigration federalism' constrained to some extent the Trump administration, as they did its predecessors. It is these subnational dynamics in the US—but also in Canada and Mexico—of multilevel migration politics that seem as much if not more likely to shape North American migration governance than formalized cooperation at state level.

When they are compared to other regions, we can see some similarities, particularly in relation to a prevailing prevention logic that is also powerfully evident in Europe and is necessarily based on representations of the causes and effects of migration. US and EU officials do meet regularly and share views on migration and border security; plus, there are also bilateral ties that cross the Atlantic between European governments and the US, as well as Canada. In Southeast Asia too we saw a prevention logic that had developed in the region in relation to displacement but which was also given an external impetus by Australian involvement, albeit not within the formal ASEAN structures, but through the more informal Bali Process. In terms of formal regional structures, however, there is an enormous difference between Europe and North America; yet in both we do see evidence of regional governance effects. In Europe, these are associated with formal regional governance structures. In the US, they are much more closely associated with more informal regionalization.

7

Prospects for Global Migration Governance

Introduction

Attention now turns from the regional to the 'global' governance of migration, or, perhaps to be more accurate, its apparent absence if we take as a measure the fact that there is no single comprehensive global migration regime and one seems unlikely to emerge any time soon. That said, this is probably not the most appropriate measure, because there are many ways in which states cooperate in varying forms and types of migration governance beyond the state, which include global frameworks for refugee protection and to tackle specific issues such as human trafficking. There was also quite a lot of excitement in 2018 when 'global compacts' on migration and refugees were adopted by the international community (or most of it—some states were noticeably less excited). While the global level could include the creation of new rules that bind states, it is probably more likely that we would find measures to promote capacity building or the creation of venues where learning could take place through both formal and more informal processes. Taken together, these can all be understood as actually existing global migration governance that could change or constrain state behaviour and within which there is some substance, much activity, and scope for future development. There are also likely to be significant constraints on global migration governance, including the actual implementation of global standards, as well as the ways in which globalization is politicized both positively and negatively in national and regional politics. Of particular importance is a tension between the 'functional' demand for problem-solving mechanisms in areas where there is inter-state interdependence and a 'post-functional' dynamic where the 'global' and immigration are contested in some national political systems (Hooghe et al., 2019). Within much work on global migration governance there is a persistent, albeit often implicit assumption that the issue is how states and regions adapt to the global. In contrast, this book has shown that global norms and standards are rendered meaningful by their encounter with repertoires of migration

Governing Migration Beyond the State: Europe, North America, South America, and Southeast Asia in a Global Context.
Andrew Geddes, Oxford University Press (2021). © Andrew Geddes. DOI: 10.1093/oso/9780198842750.003.0007

governance at regional and state levels, with significant variation within and between them. This is consistent with the point made in Chapter 3, where the importance of what Acharya (2004) called 'localisation' is highlighted, but is a persistent theme across other regions too. States and regions make sense of, adopt, adapt, or reject global norms and standards.

The empirical material with which we work in this chapter has been characterized as 'a complex array' of institutional settings that allows states to 'selectively engage in different forms of informal cooperation with different partner states [which leads to] a complex and fragmented tapestry' (Betts, 2011: 2). Along similar lines, Aleinikoff (2007) identified 'substance without architecture', while Newland (2010: 331) noted that global migration governance tends to be 'portrayed simultaneously as a necessity and an impossibility'. In a March 2019 speech, the Deputy Secretary General of the International Organization for Migration (IOM), Laura Thompson, noted that 'for many years, global governance and cooperation on migration was fragmented, incoherent, and lacked an overarching vision' (Thompson, 2019). She went on to note that states have realized that there can be benefits from cooperation and that this has given rise to a 'proliferation of working groups, dialogues, processes, and reports on migration-related issues', including High-Level Dialogues on Migration in 2006 and 2013 and the creation in 2006 of the Global Forum on Migration and Development (GFMD) comprised of national governments with parallel processes for civil society groups, business, and mayors. Coordination at global level between UN and related agencies occurred through the Global Migration Group, which brought together twenty-two agencies and which was succeeded, following the adoption in December 2018 of the Global Compact for Safe, Orderly, and Regular Migration (GCM), by a new UN Network on Migration. While not directly using the term 'repertoire', although there are implicit references both to cognition and to social expectations about role, Thompson went on to note that a key contribution of these kinds of processes was that they enabled states 'to gain a better understanding of migration dynamics and policy options, while also engaging in trust and confidence-building'. This suggests that the 'global' can become part of what actors know how to do and also form part of their expectations about role. The word 'global' is put into inverted commas because it is important to bear in mind that it has many different potential meanings, with constellations of actors organized around particular meanings. This raises the question not only of *how* ideas travel, but also *which* and *whose* ideas travel. Is global migration governance a way for the practices and standards of major destination countries to prevail in the international system or can global migration governance lead to the inclusion of a wide range of voices and perspectives? If, however, there are more voices and perspectives, then consensus may also be more difficult.

How then to account for substance without architecture and for this fragmented tapestry? This chapter begins by looking more closely at the meaning of the 'global' and at the potential components of a global migration governance repertoire. This enables immediately the identification of both the potential for future development and important constraints. It also enables the unpicking of some of the 'functionalist' assumptions that underpin much work on global migration governance and, often implicitly, suggest that the creation of cooperation (usually at a technical and official level) can lead to momentum for the development of further global competencies. This could arise as a result of the development of trust and confidence that can be facilitated by the role of international organizations such as the UNHCR and the IOM, which have as a key part of their mandate the development of strengthened international cooperation. This is followed by an overview of the development of global migration governance since the 1990s, accompanied by a discussion of the role of key institutions, particularly the UNHCR, the IOM, and the ILO. The chapter then looks more closely at the global compacts on migration and refugees and suggests that, while these form part of an emergent global migration governance repertoire, they are simultaneously indicative of both the potential for and limits of more effective international cooperation on migration. Potential seems more likely to be realized in discrete areas in terms of either specific issues or geographical focus. A key constraint is what could be called the inevitability of politics: while some migration-related issues are technical and lend themselves to expert and official meetings, it is impossible to pretend that aspects of international migration do not also have a national and regional political resonance that can connect with concerns about 'sovereignty' and also with opposition to globalization and with differing regional perspectives on the issues. Going global is not a way to escape these concerns or pressures; it may intensify them.

The meaning of the global

This chapter deliberately adopts a broad understanding of the term 'global governance' that is interested less in the specific venue at which it occurs than in its effects. What this means is that the main focus for attention is the ways in which forms of governance beyond the state can be 'constraining or constitutive' of the behaviour of states (and transnational actors)' (Betts, 2011: 4). Rather than fixating on whether these processes are located in Geneva or New York and centre on the UN or specific international or global venues, the analysis that follows recognizes that forms of migration governance that constrain or are constitutive of the behaviour of states and other transnational actors can and do take many and various forms, can occur in many different places, and can be both formal and informal. There are also feedback effects, because the organization of governance can itself be constitutive of challenges by shaping or influencing the ways in which the migration issue (in all its diversity) is understood and the kinds of actions that should be pursued. Whether or not migration is seen as a global issue and the ways in which it is then understood as 'global' can be outcomes of governance. What are the global dimensions of the challenge? And once these are identified, what kinds of global solutions would be required? If it is thought about like this, it quickly becomes apparent that the various levels within the 'multilevel' system are closely connected, because it would be impossible to effectively operationalize global cooperation without the subnational, the national, and the regional as well as involvement by both public and private actors. To return to a familiar theme in this book, the regional level is important for three reasons. First, most migration occurs within regions. Second, there are already well-established—albeit highly diverse—forms of migration governance beyond the state at regional level. Third, the attainment of global objectives is likely to depend heavily on operationalization through regional organizations, and their non-attainment is also likely to have a regional dimension too. The region is a locus for action, mediates the relationship between the national and the global, and can produce as well as receive norms and standards. A good example of links across levels are the UN's landmark Global Compact for Safe, Orderly, and Regular Migration (GCM) and Global Compact on Refugees (GCR) (both formally adopted in December 2018), within which there is reference throughout to the regional level. Article 50 of the GCM, for example, notes that implementation of any measures that are agreed at a global level requires regional-level implementation because 'most international migration takes place within regions', and any agreed measures require involvement by regional, subregional, and cross-regional processes (United Nations, 2016). Similarly, the GCR devotes considerable space to the importance of regional, subregional, and cross-regional processes (UNHCR, 2016b).

It is highly unlikely that there will be a single comprehensive global regime for migration or that global supranational institutions will develop with law-making powers that override states. Instead, the focus of global cooperation is more likely to be on the potential of—and constraints upon—actually existing forms of migration governance beyond the state. There are venues that have been created where there is potential for norms, rules, principles, and decision-making procedures to be established and for these to potentially induce convergence in actors' expectations (Krasner, 1983). An outcome of this could be 'legalization', which has three dimensions: the extent to which states are bound by international rules; the precision of those rules; and the delegation to third parties of the power to implement those rules (Abbott et al., 2000). If the legalization of global migration governance occurs, then the evidence suggest that it is probably more likely in discrete issue areas (such as human trafficking, for example), where there is broad agreement between states and binding international standards can be incorporated into national law. On trafficking, the Protocol to Prevent, Suppress, and Punish Trafficking in Persons Especially Women and Children (the Palermo Protocol) was added to the UN Convention against Transnational Organized Crime (UNTOC), accompanied by a Protocol against Smuggling of Migrants by Land, Air, and Sea, also attached to the UNTOC. By April 2020, 146 countries had ratified the Palermo Protocol. In contrast, on labour migration, a UN Convention on the Rights of All Migrant Workers and their Families was agreed in 1990, but took thirteen years to reach the threshold of twenty ratifications that allowed it to come into force. By the end of 2020, fifty-five countries had ratified the convention, but these were mainly sending rather than destination countries. Meyers (2004) argues that this is because destination states can satisfy their need for migrant labour from available supply without global cooperation that could tie their hands. This means an aversion to wider commitments that can affect their ability to determine their own needs for the admission of migrant workers. States retain significant unilateral authority to determine admissions, residence, expulsion, and also the rules governing access to citizenship. Similarly, while there are international human rights standards that protect the right to family life, there is no right to family migration.

Regional migration governance in Europe provides the clearest example of the convergence of expectations around norms, rules, principles, and decision-making procedures, but there are constraints on EU actions on migration from outside the EU. For example, the EU has no say over numbers of non-EU migrants to be admitted. There is also evidence of continued divergence between member states, and this was exacerbated after the 2015 crisis. There is also a wider point about divergence, because not only is there divergence within the international system, but states are also conflicted about their own interests. Significant asymmetries in the international system can impede the development of governance beyond the state. Most obviously, these take the form of economic inequalities and divergent forms of political organization which, in turn, can also contribute to the positioning of states as countries that see themselves as primarily sending, destination, or transit countries, although these distinctions are seldom quite so clear-cut. Receptiveness to international cooperation will also be conditioned by existing forms of interstate cooperation and the norms and practices that underpin it.

A global migration governance repertoire?

If words like 'tapestry', 'patchwork', and 'fragmented' are used to describe global migration governance, then it might be rather difficult to identify a global migration governance repertoire. There is, however, actually existing global migration governance, albeit it does not—and probably will not—take the form of a single comprehensive regime. Actually existing global migration governance and the places where it happens can shape both what it is that actors know how to do and their expectations about role. This may occur in more geographically or functionally discrete ways, bringing together groups of countries—or to be more precise, specific actors from those countries—that are proximate or share interests where there is a more narrowly focused cooperation on specific issues. This is not to say that know-how and expectations converge on some single, shared representation, but the 'global' —or a representation of it—can become a component not only of the identity of actors involved in these processes but also of how they understand the nature of the challenge and potential solutions to it. This goes beyond the somewhat banal assertion that migration is a global issue that requires a global response. This is true to some extent, although migration is also a local, national, and regional issue and requires responses at those levels too. Also, asserting the global relevance of an issue says nothing too specific about the kinds of processes and responses that could or should develop. It also neglects that opposition to globalization is a driver of significant new forms of political mobilization, including in major immigration destination countries (Kriesi et al., 2006). There can also be a longer-standing reluctance to participate in potentially binding forms of international cooperation. In the US these two strands—the domestic political resonance of immigration and hostility to international cooperation—coalesced during the Trump presidency. This is made very clear in this quote from a US State Department official interviewed in 2018, who explained why the US would not sign up to the global compacts on migration and refugees:

> The Global Compact held itself out to be non-binding and a voluntary thing amongst states, to which my response is 'What good is it?' If it's just kind of a statement of principles, then why are people fighting so hard for it? The real answer is yes, it's just a statement of principles, but it's meant to be something more. It's meant to be the, say, kernel of a future body of international law on migration. The aspirations of the advocates is quite clear. If you look online, they say exactly what they're doing. It's just that they can't get it through the front door via international agreement or treaty-making process, so they're trying to do it via the backdoor strategy of transnational legal advance. From the US perspective and from this administration's perspective we saw this with the Paris agreement on climate change. I can say for purposes of getting the president [Trump] to agree to US withdrawal from the Global Compact, it was a relatively easy thing to liken it to the Paris Compact and we were done at that point.
>
> (State Department official Washington DC, September 2018)

Much of the attention to global migration governance adheres—either implicitly or explicitly—to a 'functionalist' perspective, or what the US official just cited might call a 'backdoor strategy of transnational legal advance'. Functionalism in the study of international relations emerged in the period between the First and Second World Wars and was motivated by concern about what was seen as the obsolescence of states marked by the erosion of their sovereignty. Alongside this was a perceived need for experts and scientists to become more involved in policymaking to avoid the perils of extreme nationalism. In his pioneering work written in the 1930s on functional approaches to international relations, Mitrany (1966) argued that cooperation can develop its own momentum as states cooperate with and learn to trust each other. A key proviso, however, is that cooperation is always vulnerable to states withdrawing support.

A functionalist perspective also implies the potential for a repertoire to develop that shapes what actors know how to do and their expectations about role, which has narrative, social, affective, and performative components. An issue is then the extent to which the actors—such as political leaders, officials, experts, and non-state actors—that are involved in these international processes could assume the 'global' (or various representations of it) as part of their identity. Identity and self-identification are central to sense-making because they shape what these actors know how to do and what they consider their role to be. Empirically, it is the case that interactions at a technical level between experts are a distinctive feature of much cooperation on global migration. This doesn't mean the automatic transmission of global norms and standards. State actors such as national officials can and do tend to remain state-focused.

This focus on technical cooperation is consistent with accounts of global migration governance that have adopted a functionalist perspective that identifies smaller steps such as cooperation on specific issues as building blocks that can generate shared representations. These could then form the basis for more developed types of cooperation (Koser, 2010; Martin and Weerasinghe, 2018; Newland, 2010). It has been argued that processes such as the GFMD have the potential to socialize states into a multilevel system of global migration governance by making it clear that migration is a global issue and also by bringing civil society perspectives into the process, with the resultant dialogue building trust by creating 'participatory spaces' (Rother, 2019). This is similar to the idea that migration governance beyond the state can also be built 'from below' by civil society as well as top-down by governments (Lavenex and Piper, 2019).

There are, however, limitations to the application of a functionalist perspective when analysing global migration governance, not least the central role played by states, the importance of 'localization', when translating the global to regional and national level, and a continued attachment to sovereignty. Moving to the global level does not mean being able to escape the political tensions that configure migration politics at other levels. While there is a vivid debate about the meaning and relevance of sovereignty in the face of global challenges, much of actually existing global migration governance is state- and/or regionally led. It is highly unlikely that states and state identities will somehow be socialized out of global migration governance, although it is more plausible that these state identities could change, with the 'global' becoming a more prominent within them. If this were to occur, then it is likely to be associated with the creation of global 'spaces' for dialogue and the development of cooperation on various forms and types of migration, but these are not empty spaces or, put another way, blank canvases onto which can be sketched visions of the global. They are constituted—and thus enabled and constrained—by the same kinds of social and political forces that shape regional and national migration governance, perhaps to an even greater extent.

To what extent can the 'global' shape the identities of actors? This also presupposes some attention to who these actors actually are. While states remain key actors, there are other prominent actors involved in global migration governance. The GCM, for example is a state-led process, but the GCR is led by the UNHCR. There are various international organizations, with particularly prominent roles played by the UNHCR, the IOM, and the ILO, although many other organizations within the UN system also have responsibilities that relate to migration. The United Nations Office on Drugs and Crime (UNODC) is, for example, enabled by the Palermo Protocol of 2000 to become closely involved in measures to counter trafficking and smuggling. As new venues across this and other migration issues have been created, there has also been much greater involvement by civil society organizations, as well as efforts to stimulate engagement by business and local government. The field has become more crowded and more organizational, although states remain key actors.

For a global migration governance repertoire to develop, it is required that the global—or some representation of it and its effects—becomes, to some extent, part of the identities of these actors, including states, and then manifests itself in specific ways that can be constitutive of or constraining upon state behaviour. To put it another way, actors such as—but not only—states can become socialized, which can be understood as 'a process of inducting actors into the norms and rules of a given community' that would be indicated by 'sustained compliance based on the internalization of these new norms' (Checkel, 2005: 804). As will become clear in the remainder of this chapter, a key word in this definition is 'process', because a lot of actually existing global migration governance takes the form of processes with a focus on the types of dialogues, information exchanges, and knowledge creation that can occur within them. These processes can be ways in which global norms and standards are 'localized' to be consistent with national and regional norms and practices. Global cooperation can give rise to new norms and rules that potentially change state behaviour. It can also lead to the consumption of an awful lot of energy going from meeting to meeting. The precise effects of all this activity could be difficult to judge: much actually existing global migration governance is specifically designed to be voluntary and non-binding, which means the effects of these processes in terms of changing in substantive ways the behaviour of actors, particularly states, can be quite difficult to detect. It is also possible that the extent of this internalization of new norms and thus of socialization can differ. Checkel (2005: 804) distinguishes between 'Type 1' socialization, which can be understood as role playing, and

'Type 2', which is more profound, with actors identifying strongly with the community or organizations and its norms and rules. Type 1 could mean turning up at a meeting because it's part of the job, while Type 2 would mean the global—or some representation of it—becomes part of the interests and identities of actors. Type 2 can also be consistent with an important component of sense-making whereby what actors know how to do and their understanding of role can develop as a result of interaction. Relatively sustained interaction over a period of time in an expert group of people from other countries and international organizations is likely to have a bigger effect than attendance at a large conference in a big hotel, where there may be less scope for sustained interaction and more temptation to sneak away to the swimming pool.

Following from this is the extent to which 'sensible' environments—in this case at global level—are enacted by dialogues and narratives through which people begin to understand what they think and to organize their experiences of migration accordingly. To understand what enactment might mean and also to see an implicit functionalist dynamic, we can look at the chapter on global migration governance in the IOM's 2018 World Migration Report, in which it is written that: 'The step-by-step process of consultation, cooperation and confidence-building that has taken place to date has shown that progress can occur, albeit in incremental ways. It remains the most promising path towards global migration governance' (Martin and Weerasinghe, 2018: 24). Similarly, Newland (2010: 335) portrays such processes as 'a bottom-up alternative that stitches together the common threads of governmental responsibilities for problem-solving purposes, often on the basis of intensive interactions among government officials (bureaucrats, regulators, legislators, judges) with similar functional portfolios'. Much of the history of global migration governance has involved creating settings that rely on voluntary participation, are non-binding, and are designed to promote dialogue that may, in the future, be scaled up in terms of scope and content, or may not. An early example of this was the establishment after the 1994 International Conference on Population and Development of the Intergovernmental Consultation on Migration, Asylum, and Refugees, which now has seventeen participating states, which are predominantly destination countries. There are, as documented in other chapters, many consultation processes at regional, subregional, and cross-regional levels (Thouez and Channac, 2006). There have also been efforts to create more coherence at a global level. Between 2003 and 2005 a 'Global Commission on International Migration' was convened, which produced a report entitled *Migration in an Interconnected*

World: New Directions for Action (GCIM, 2006). Among the important issues that were identified was the need to develop greater capacity within global migration governance and to promote greater policy coherence. As the report noted:

> government representatives from every part of the world have openly acknowledged the difficulties they encounter in formulating coherent migration policies. In many instances, they are confronted with competing priorities and short-term demands from different ministries within government and from different constituencies outside government. Important decisions taken in areas such as development, trade, aid and the labour market are rarely considered in terms of their impact on international migration.
>
> (GCIM, 2006: 2)

As extensively documented in earlier chapters, the impact of competing priorities and short-term political demands is a fairly standard feature of governance processes. The quote highlights that similar tensions also exist at the global level, which is not entirely surprising. In the pursuit of greater coherence, the Global Forum on Migration and Development was established in 2006 as a state-led setting, but it also developed to involve civil society, business, and mayors. As already noted, of great significance was the 2016 UN high-level meeting that led to the New York declaration and ultimately to the global compacts on refugees and migration which will be discussed in more detail later in this chapter. While not specifically referring to migration, Slaughter (2009) called these kinds of transgovernmental processes the potential 'building blocks of a new world order'. Viewed in this way, the path towards global migration governance is seen as incremental, where technical expertise often dominates and where small steps can lead to further development.

Functionalist perspectives were given new life by European integration after the 1950s and recast as 'neo-functionalism' to explain the specific role that supranational institutions, particularly the European Commission, could play in generating 'spillover' (Haas, 1966). To return to the point made by Aleinikoff (2007) about the global system possessing substance but lacking architecture, these kinds of functionalist perspectives suggest that architecture could follow substance. Given the absence of supranational institutions in other regions, similar dynamics appear unlikely. The EU also demonstrates the limits of intensive transgovernmentalism, i.e. official-level interactions bring states and other actors together at a lower and more technical level. The

EU demonstrates very vividly that 'functional' transgovernmentalism cannot escape 'post-functional' politics, particularly if cooperation occurs in areas of 'high politics' that are closely associated with state sovereignty such as migration. While new venues have been created at EU level, it is difficult to disguise cooperation on migration as merely a technical issue. Migration became politicized across the EU and was also closely associated with support for or opposition to European integration. Domestic political factors in member states have remained an obstacle to deeper integration at a regional level in Europe and cannot easily be overcome by assertions that national sovereignty is obsolete, when it remains an important component of the identities of key actors in migration governance systems and where sovereignty concerns expressed, for example, as opposition to globalization can be a significant mobilizing force in domestic politics (Hooghe and Marks, 2017).

These processes of interaction in forms and types of migration governance beyond the state are ongoing as participants both react to and shape their environments. A key stimulus for the New York Declaration of 2016 was the migration crisis in Europe but also large-scale displacement in Southeast Asia, South America, and Central America. This gave some momentum to the idea that a new impetus was needed at the global level to address these challenges. While the ideas themselves about the need for strengthened international cooperation were not new, they received further impetus as a result of crisis, but, as seen in earlier chapters, what crises tend to do is elicit responses that draw from established ways of dealing with issues. For example, this can involve claims that the scale, level, and extent of international migration mean that the issue has a global reach; it cannot be managed at national level; it leads to increased levels of vulnerability and exploitation; and it links to other key challenges such as climate change. To this can be added the supposed inexorable logic of globalization that requires global responses (Koser, 2010). While these arguments weren't in themselves new in 2016, there was the political will to at least begin a process of consultation at a global level. Doing so required the extraction of cues to decide what was relevant and what explanations were acceptable.

What became apparent after the initial steps in 2016 was the negative impact of the domestic political contestation in some countries on these global processes. This could be understood as the effect of anti-immigration sentiment and as a manifestation of a deeper concern among some sections of the population in economically developed countries about the adverse effects of globalization. It has been convincingly shown that pro- and anti-globalization has become an important dividing line in politics in European countries, with effects that have also been evident in countries such as Australia and the United States (Kriesi et al., 2006). This contestation presents a challenge to functionalist accounts. This has been most clearly the case in Europe, where it was argued that a 'permissive consensus' enabled cooperation and integration on largely technical issues until the early 1990s. After the end of the Cold War in 1989, the EU moved into areas of 'high politics' that impinged more directly on national sovereignty. This triggered a move from a permissive consensus to a 'constraining dissensus', with the effect that 'a brake on European integration has been imposed not because people have changed their minds, but because, on a range of vital issues, legitimate decision making has shifted from an insulated elite to mass politics' (Hooghe and Marks, 2009: 13). While there are some issues associated with migration that are quite technical, there are others that are intensely political. The effects of politics were identified by an official from the ILO:

> The unfortunate downside of this is that it's happening at the same time that the West and some countries are deeply entrenched on the migration issue. So we're seeing a political backlash, we're seeing a public backlash, we're seeing policies which are not particularly conducive to addressing the rights of migrants and irregular migrants and refugees, without mixing all of these up.
> (International Labour Organization official, Geneva, October 2017)

This section has sketched both the potential for and limits of a global migration governance repertoire by identifying the factors that can shape what actors of various types know how to do and also the expectations that they have about their roles. We now move on to look more closely at the origins and emergence of actually existing global migration governance.

Origins and emergence

There is a bifurcation in actually existing global migration governance between a global system for the protection of refugees that is associated with the work of the UNHCR and the remit of the IOM to promote, as it says on its website, 'the orderly and humane management of migration'. While the UNHCR and the IOM have differing histories and mandates, they have, since 2016, been within the UN system. Both are central to the global migration governance repertoire because of what they know how to do and also because of the expectations about role associated with both organizations. While they are closely associated, there is also scope for tension between them, given their very different histories and associated expectations about what they should be doing. In our interviews, people from the UNHCR were always keen to distinguish between refugees and asylum seekers (the UNHCR's concern) and migration (the IOM's concern).

The longest-standing and most significant component of the global migration governance system is that part related to the protection of asylum seekers and refugees for which the UNHCR has responsibility. This comprises the widely ratified (by 145 states as of the end of 2020) Geneva Convention of 1951 and a lead agency, the UNHCR, created in 1950. The 1967 New York protocol removed geographical restrictions on the 1951 convention to extend its remit beyond the consequences of statelessness in post-war Europe. The protection regime recognizes the right to seek asylum but imposes no corresponding obligation on states to accept asylum seekers, because there is no right in international law to enter the territory of another state. The UNHCR's role is to be the guardian of the 1951 convention but also to facilitate state policies towards refugees, because, as Loescher (2001: 2) observed, 'states did not establish the UNHCR through purely altruistic motives, but from a desire to promote regional and international stability and to serve the interests of governments'. This doesn't mean that the UNHCR has been a passive mechanism with no agenda of its own because 'the autonomy and authority of UNHCR has grown over the years and the office has become a purposive actor in its own right with independent interests and capabilities' (ibid.).

While the protection system and the UNHCR are legitimated by their moral purpose in defence of international human rights, it is also the case that they walk a tightrope, because the UNHCR is an intergovernmental organization and reliant on member state donors. Barnett (2001: 244) looked more closely at what it can mean to walk this tightrope to argue that in the 1990s a 'combination of state pressures and the normative principle of popular sovereignty enabled a more political and pragmatic UNHCR to widen its activities under the humanitarian banner and to become more deeply involved in the circumstances in the refugee-producing country'. He went on to argue that this generates 'the worrisome possibility that a more pragmatic UNHCR is potentially (though unwittingly) implicated in a system of [refugee] containment'. While the scale of the UNHCR and its responsibilities have grown, so too has the unwillingness or reluctance of key states to offer protection, with most of the displaced in poorer countries that border conflicts. As a UNHCR official put it:

At the present moment I think what is dramatic is the lack of capacity of the international system to prevent conflicts and to solve them. You have a multiplication of crises, more and more and more, and the old crises go on and go on and go on. The international system is totally unable to respond because, I mean, there is no global governance system that works. The power relations became unclear so there is total impunity, unpredictability, people trigger conflicts; nothing happens to them. Look at South Sudan. This is the most worrying factor for us. Then the fact that the international system is also not able to respond to the global threats of modern times: climate change is one, pandemics is another. It's quite ridiculous, no? So the international system is not prepared. National sovereignty, free market approaches and whatever undermine the capacity to establish global governance mechanisms to address these kind of issues and to form global consensus on them.   (UNHCR official, Geneva, November 2017)

This rather gloomy perspective is informed by the responsibilities that the UNHCR holds, but also by the major impediments to fulfilment of a protection mandate not only because of resistance by national governments, because of the 'traditional' ways in which that mandate has been viewed, but also as a result of new issues such as the climate crisis and pandemics such as Covid-19, which can generate new challenges and also require ways of working that cut across traditional divides between international organizations. Climate and disease have implications for migration that relate to the UNHCR, which also seeks to engage with other organizations with relevant responsibilities such as the World Health Organization (WHO) and the UN Environment Programme (UNEP).

Martin (2016) identifies reasons to be more optimistic because she observes that informal, non-binding, and state-led approaches are seen by states as a pragmatic approach to the development of norms, although she recognizes that they will only work if there is implementation. Implementation and compliance would seem to mean direct enforcement by supranational institutions, which could also require that there be punishment or sanctions for countries that shirk their responsibilities. In contrast, a managerial approach to implementation assumes that failure to comply is indicative of the need for states and international organizations to work together to improve capacity. This can then mean establishing ways to transfer knowledge and resources, as well as enforcement and management. A third approach to implementation is persuasion, which involves attempts to change the underlying norms and values that drive state actions (Hartlapp, 2007: 655–6). Actually existing global migration governance is much more focused on capacity building and persuasion than it is on the enforcement of binding rules.

We can see how these approaches play out in practice when considering the ILO's role through its Convention No. 97, which refers to various aspects of labour migration, including recruitment, migrants' rights, and their protections at work. Typically, the ILO is less likely to use direct enforcement mechanisms and more likely to seek to manage implementation through initiatives that involve states, employers, and trade unions and seek to develop capacity. This capacity-building component of actually existing migration governance is a good example of how a repertoire develops that informs what actors know how to do and also their expectations about their role. As an example, the Canadian government's Department of Foreign Affairs, Trade, and Development (DFATD) has supported the Tripartite Action for the Protection and Promotion of the Rights of Migrant Workers in the ASEAN Region (ASEAN TRIANGLE Project), which included efforts to improve labour migration statistics (Rother, 2018). The ASEAN TRIANGLE project takes a managerial approach to implementation and, to return to the 'Type 1' and 'Type 2' logics referred to in the section 'A global migration governance repertoire?' above when considering socialization, may involve role playing or could lead to more profound transformations of values and norms as actors are persuaded of the value of cooperation to develop national level systems in accordance with international standards. It is also likely to require 'localization' of international norms and standards to render them acceptable at national and regional level.

Compared to the UNHCR and the ILO, the IOM is a younger organization, but since 2016 it has been included as a 'related organization' within the UN system. While the IOM is a global organization, many of its activities have been and are associated with the practice of sovereignty and the development of capacity at a state level to manage or regulate migration or, in the IOM's own words to, 'ensure the orderly and humane management of migration, to promote international cooperation on migration issues, to assist in the search for practical solutions to migration problems and to provide humanitarian assistance to migrants in need, including refugees and internally displaced people'. The IOM was established in 1951 as the Provisional Intergovernmental Committee for the Movement of Migrants from Europe, which was then swiftly renamed just a few months later as the Intergovernmental Committee for Migration and was largely concerned with out-migration of Europeans to, for example, South America. This meant that its role was primarily logistical, acting almost as a travel agency. The role of the IOM was also closely linked to the needs of its member states, particularly the United States, because, as (Pécoud, 2018: 1624) put it, 'While formerly limited to technical tasks, IOM was from the start a politicized organization, closely associated with U.S. leadership, and with a homogeneous group of developed, "white", and capitalist Western states.' In 1989, the IOM acquired its current name. Questions were raised about how joining the UN system in 2016 would affect its role, because there are no commitments in its constitution to human rights, with the main focus being on the provision of 'migration services' to its member states (Guild and Grant, 2017: 15). There has been a huge expansion in the IOM's role, with important effects on migration policies and practices that have been linked to a 'market inspired' approach to migration management and also to the production of knowledge about migration by the IOM through its research capacity (Pécoud, 2018). In terms of knowledge production, Korneev (2018) shows how, in post-Soviet Central Asia, the IOM acquires 'reputational authority'. Similarly, Wünderlich (2012) shows IOM 'proactivity' in shaping migration governance in North Africa. The IOM's influence and reputational authority are also achieved through working closely with regional organizations.

International organizations also produce knowledge about international migration that can have framing effects and inform sense-making processes. Geiger and Pécoud (2010) identify how a framework with five elements has shaped the production of knowledge about migration by the IOM. These are that migration is a global issue that requires global cooperation; a 'triple win' is possible as a result of international cooperation that benefits sending and destination states and migrants; the global level can promote well-managed migration that is humane and orderly; there are important issue linkages to, for example, climate and development; and that international cooperation should adhere to universal principles such as human rights, but also to free market values.

The UNHCR, the IOM, and other international organizations are committed to the global and to the production of knowledge about migration that highlights the global nature of the challenges and the need for more effective international responses. Even more so than the UNHCR, the IOM must balance its intergovernmental roots and reliance on states as donors with wider international commitments, including the protection of migrants, although protection is not a prominent component of its constitution. While the IOM and the UNHCR work closely together, there can be tensions because of their different origins and mandates. A blurring of the legal distinctions between migration and refugee protection could legitimate the actions of governments that seek to want to return 'migrants' who are actually people that might have grounds for seeking protection as refugees.

Regime complexity

Global migration governance is necessarily an organizational process and, as the numbers of concerned organizations have increased, has become more intensely organizational. In their chapter in the IOM's 2018 World Migration Report, Martin and Weerasinghe (2018) observe that while there have been important developments at a global level, there is also fragmentation. Rather than being a deficiency that requires correction, it could be that it is and is likely to remain a characteristic of global migration governance rather than an impediment to its future development. By drawing from insights into what has been called 'regime complexity', it has been suggested that it might be more fruitful to work with existing institutions than to engage in possibly futile attempts to develop more comprehensive global settings (Betts, 2013; Keohane and Victor, 2011). Fragmentation means that actually existing global governance can occur in different frameworks and settings, with significant differentiation both in terms of the types of migration that are dealt with and in terms of the territorial scope. The result is a regime complex can be understood as comprising non-hierarchical and partially overlapping 'loosely coupled sets of partial regimes' (Keohane and Victor, 2011: 7).

If we try to unpick the main components of actually existing global migration governance, then it becomes apparent that there are various sources that inform this regime complexity. These include general multilateral instruments with relevance to migration such as the UN Declaration on Human Rights; texts governing access to nationality and statelessness such as the UN Convention relating to the status of stateless people; general instruments on refugees such as the Geneva Convention; texts produced by international organizations such as the ILO materials on protection in employment; measures and instruments at a regional level such as Council of Europe instruments such as the European Convention for the Protection of Human Rights, plus extensive EU measures relating to free movement, migration, and asylum; American treaties such as NAFTA; the MERCOSUR Treaty in South America; African treaties such as the creation of ECOWAS; and various other regional treaties (Plender, 2007). These all, to varying degrees, place some limits and constraints on the powers of states and are constitutive of the identities of these states as actors in the international system. Betts (2013: 71) identifies a consequence of this regime complex as being the rise of what he calls 'challenged institutions' because of institutional overlaps, which he understands as illustrating 'how, in the context of institutional proliferation over time, some policy fields come to be directly or indirectly governed by multiple institutions in different areas'. This point has already been made in relation to the various actors and organizations present in the migration field (broadly defined) and also to the important issue linkages that connect migration to other global challenges. Betts (2013: 79) argues that the UNHCR reinforces itself in this challenging environment by using issues linkages that connect, for example, displacement with climate and development to 'engage in the politics of overlapping regimes', thus expanding the scope of its work while reinforcing itself through overlaps such as with the human rights regime to improve efficiency. Another example of institutional overlaps is the Norwegian and Swiss governments-led 'Nansen Initiative' for disaster-induced cross-border displacement. This links displacement with climate and sustainable development with scope for learning in a non-binding setting (Gemenne and Brücker, 2015).

The Global Compacts

While the Global Compacts on refugees and migration that were formally adopted in December 2018 are non-binding commitments, there was optimism among advocates of stronger global governance that they could form the basis for more developed protection of migrants, asylum seekers, and refugees. The interviewee referred to earlier in this chapter from the US State Department who expressed scepticism about 'transnational legal advance' was identifying an ambiguity within the compacts, because advocates seemed to simultaneously highlight their potential while also playing it down: they could lead to important developments but, at the same time, were non-binding. This ambiguity could help to explain why the compacts became subject to intense politicization as some countries withdrew, particularly from the GCM, while the compacts were also subjected to online trolling via a far-right disinformation campaign that grossly exaggerated their scope (Politico, 2019). Playing on and exploiting underlying concerns led to a massive surge in anti-GCM tweets and disinformation from extreme right and anti-immigrant groups. One of the more dramatic examples was the collapse of the Belgian coalition government because of a dispute about the GCM.

The GCR was driven by experience of large-scale displacement. While things changed dramatically after Trump's election as US president in 2016, his predecessor President Obama had joined UN Secretary General Ban Ki-Moon and the leaders of Canada, Ethiopia, Germany, Jordan, Mexico, and Sweden in hosting in September 2016 a 'Leaders' Summit on Refugees' that sought to mobilize private-sector resources to help address mass displacement. The summit extracted commitments from fifty-two countries that increased their total 2016 financial contributions to UN appeals and international humanitarian organizations by approximately US$4.5 billion when compared to 2015 levels, while making an increased commitment to the resettlement of refuges, as well as considering other channels for admissions. When addressing the summit, President Obama highlighted the global nature of the challenge and, as he had done with the Paris Agreement on climate, indicated his preference for stronger global action, although consistent with a long-standing US preference this would be state-led. He said:

> It's a test of our international system where all nations ought to share in our collective responsibilities, because the vast majority of refugees are hosted by just 10 countries who are bearing a very heavy burden—among them Turkey, Pakistan, Lebanon, Iran, Ethiopia. Countries that often have fewer resources than many of those who are doing little or nothing.   (Obama, 2016)

His successor, Trump, refused to sign either the GCR or the GCM and, in a speech to the UN General Assembly in September 2018 demonstrated the major shift in the US approach:

> We recognize the right of every nation in this room to set its own immigration policy in accordance with its national interests, just as we ask other countries to respect our own right to do the same—which we are doing. That is one reason the United States will not participate in the new Global Compact on Migration. Migration should not be governed by an international body unaccountable to our own citizens. Ultimately, the only long-term solution to the migration crisis is to help people build more hopeful futures in their home countries. Make their countries great again.
>
> (Trump, 2018)

The GCR was endorsed by 181 UN member states, with only Hungary and the US not signing, while Eritrea, Libya, and Liberia abstained.The GCR reaffirmed a normative commitment to the existing system of refugee protection and was ostensibly designed to deal with a missing element of the 1951 convention, namely measures to ensure that responsibility was shared more fairly. The UNHCR drafted the GCR and is the lead agency responsible for its implementation (Türk and Garlick, 2016). The outstanding issue for the GCR is operationalization:

> So, actually there has been, right from the start of our work on refugee issues, a constant refrain, 'international solidarity', you need international solidarity, you need burden and responsibility sharing, you need to give content to what the preamble says in the [19]51 Convention, because it doesn't define the burden that states have when they receive large numbers of refugees.
> (UNHCR official, Geneva, November 2017)

The GCR is the beginning of a process, not its culmination. This process is designed to be extensive and involve a wide range of actors. Hathaway (2019: 594) expressed scepticism about the value of the process when arguing that the 'clearest output' of the GCR is 'lots and lots of meetings', with the result that the compact 'is all about process—a bureaucrat's dream perhaps, but nothing that comes even close to dependably addressing the operational deficits of the refugee regime'.

The GCM was signed by 152 countries, with five countries voting against (United States, Hungary, Israel, Czech Republic, and Poland) and twelve countries abstaining (Algeria, Australia, Austria, Bulgaria, Chile, Italy, Latvia, Libya, Liechtenstein, Romania, Singapore, and Switzerland). Slovakia did not vote. Switzerland delayed its decision. The far-right president of Brazil, Jair Bolsonaro, withdrew his government's support in January 2019 (Brumat, 2019b).

The GCM compact was a state-led process, with Mexico and Switzerland as co-facilitators, supported by the IOM and the UN Secretariat. The GCM is framed by the UN's Sustainable Development Goals, although the GCM changes the language from 'orderly, safe, regular and responsible migration' in the SDGs to 'safe, orderly and regular migration' in the GCM (Guild, 2019). The GCM contains twenty-three objectives with a review every four years, beginning in 2022. How these many objectives will be translated into on-the-ground effects has been much discussed. To take a practical example, objectives 5 and 6 focus on labour markets rights, protections, and recruitment. Martin and Ruhs (2019) argue that while the global compacts show strong commitments to increased labour market opportunities for migrant workers and increased protections as well as 'complementary pathways' to protection for refugees via labour mobility, they also see a gap between these ideals and what they call labour market realism, i.e. how labour markets actually function in major destination countries. They argue that a focus on migrants' rights has substituted for labour market realism. By this they mean that there has been a very important shift towards temporary migration programmes as the main method to recruit migrant workers, even in classic destination countries such as Australia and Canada. A problem would be that the GCM would turn these into permanent immigration programmes and thus be inconsistent with labour market realities (Martin and Ruhs, 2019). They conclude:

> These recommendations are unlikely to effectuate real improvements in the protection of migrant workers because they are not likely to be implemented. The GCM recommendations are policy aspirations that are not objectionable *per se*, but they do not address the well-known trade-offs and hard policy questions that arise in the regulation of the admission and rights of migrant workers, especially in countries that host large numbers of migrants.   (Martin and Ruhs, 2019: 4)

Resolving well-known trade-offs and hard policy questions may well be even more difficult in global forums, where there can be a huge diversity of interests grounded in actually existing repertoires of migration governance. These repertoires can and do contribute to migration governance beyond the state, but they may focus on specific issues or discrete geographical areas and need not necessarily be consistent with global migration governance. In such circumstances, it can be difficult to turn aspirations into effects, particularly if those aspirations are not grounded in the 'realities' of local contexts, although these realities too are likely to be contested.

Conclusion

Global migration governance is an intensely organizational process and, as such, requires these organizations to make sense of the phenomena with which they deal, as well as with both their own organization and the organizations with which they interact. Rather than focus on the unlikely prospects for a single, global regime to develop, this chapter has looked at the various forms and types of cooperation at an international level and the ways in which they can constrain the behaviour of states. This can be through the production of binding rules and their enforcement or through capacity building and persuasion; the last two are more likely than the first. Capacity building and persuasion are likely to occur in a fragmented and complex field, but these are not aberrations to be overcome, but are actually key systemic properties. From these fragmented processes have emerged a variety of outputs that can change the ways in which states and other actors behave, but, very often, the forums and venues that are created at an international level are designed to be non-binding and thus non-threatening to states. Building capacity and persuading fit closely with the idea of migration governance repertoire and the ways in which the 'global' can become part of what actors know how to do and also their expectations about role. It is highly likely that global norms, practices, and standards will require 'localization', which highlights that global migration governance may actually heighten the importance of regional processes through which global standards can be localized. At the same time, global cooperation cannot be written off as a largely technical process; global migration governance is necessarily political. To argue that migration is a global issue that requires global solutions is unlikely to make much headway with opponents of globalization, whose presence and voice in national politics across the world has been strengthened. As at the national and regional levels, the *politics* of global migration governance is inescapable.

8

Conclusions

This book has developed a comparative analysis of migration governance in four world regions and at a global level in order to study actually existing migration governance beyond the state as well as prospects for it. While the picture is uneven, there is, without doubt, significant evidence of forms of cooperation and even of integration that can constrain states through rules or change the way that they behave. The particular focus has been on how governance actors make sense of the structural factors that can cause or drive international migration and of how, in the shadow of uncertainty and in the face of risk, these governance systems as organizational processes through their perceptions and misperceptions, judgements, and misjudgements, actions and inactions, inclusions and omissions can actively shape the challenges that they face. Migration isn't something that simply 'happens' to governance systems; it is something they actively construct, constitute, and populate. Each of the four regions that were analysed is highly diverse both 'internally' in terms of its members and in its relations with other regions. Key elements of diversity include the patterns and dynamics of migration, the absence or presence of specific migration policies, and the structures of formal and informal regional governance. In all four regions, intra-regional migration is highly significant. In Southeast Asia and South America, flows are strongly intra-regional, although in South America there has been more regional-level cooperation than in Southeast Asia. In both Europe and North America there is a strong presence of extra-regional flows, but in both these regions there is evidence of significant regional effects through the EU free movement framework and in bilateral and trilateral ties between Canada, Mexico, and the US. By looking at each of these regions and how they make sense of migration, the book has attempted to demonstrate both the possibilities of and limits upon migration governance beyond the state.

The idea of governance and the practices that are both associated with it and enabled by it were central to the book's analysis. Governance can be a controversial term, because it may well be viewed as enabling the imposition of practices—usually from the more powerful actors in the migration governance system—on those in less powerful positions. There is certainly an

Governing Migration Beyond the State: Europe, North America, South America, and Southeast Asia in a Global Context. Andrew Geddes, Oxford University Press (2021). © Andrew Geddes. DOI: 10.1093/oso/9780198842750.003.0008

element of truth to this characterization. To develop an analysis of migration governance that was sensitive to context but also enabled the evaluation of four regions, a definition was developed that focused less on the content of governance (laws, policies, and associated practices) and more on the ways in which representations of the underlying changes in social and natural systems (political, economic, social, demographic, and environmental) can affect or shape migration governance. This is because representations of the effects of these potential drivers and of the interactions between them are central to migration governance, because migration governance is always, everywhere, and necessarily an organizational process. These organizations respond to signals and cues from the environment in which they operate and, depending on how they understand these signals and cues, decide what to do next. This was expressed in more intuitive terms in the form of two key dilemmas for governance actors: what's going on 'out there' and what should we do next? These responses are developed by situated actors in particular organizational settings with their own cultures and histories. The result is that governance systems themselves can be important drivers of migration through their (mis) perceptions, (mis)judgements, and the associated inclusions and exclusions that develop. The focus on regional governance was justified by the fact that regions are an important locus for actions, mediate the relationship between the national and the global, and are also themselves producers of highly significant norms and standards. By the end of this book it has also become clear that the 'global' needs to be rendered consistent with norms and practices at state and regional level. This reverses an implicit tendency to see the global as providing a template to which states and regions should adapt. The global acquires meaning through its encounters—both positive and negative—with the regional and national.

Central to the analysis of each region was the idea of repertoires of migration governance that enabled the development of a framework that captured the dual meaning of governance (Pierre, 2000). What was meant by dual meaning was that governance requires the conceptual representation of change in underlying social and natural systems and then efforts to manage or steer the effects of these changes (as understood). This dual meaning combines the perceptions that underpin the operation and effects of governance systems and the associated practices that develop. Repertoires contain two components: (i) what actors know how to do, which emphasized cognition but also the social context within which this develops; and (ii) what actors think they should be doing that focuses on expectations about role. Repertoires are *narrative* in that they involve the mobilization of knowledge claims; *social* in that they involve interaction with others; *affective* in that they can contain intuitive or emotional responses to issues; *performative* in that actions are embedded in day-to-day practices and can, at times, also be designed to have a more symbolic effect; and *ongoing* in that they do not have a beginning and an end. They capture the effects of decision-making under risk, of issue framing, and of sense-making. As noted in Chapter 2, actions, cognition, and expectations emerge from 'a culturally sanctioned and empirically limited set of options' that can induce a status quo bias (Tilly 1978: 151). Moving to the regional level does not create a blank canvas upon which new responses can develop that depart from established patterns of thought and action. More than that, the book has demonstrated throughout how migration governance is structured by uneven and unequal power relations that organize into the governance process certain representations, while organizing out or marginalizing others. The meaning of migration is deeply contested, but the representations of the powerful can and do have powerful effects. While the field is multi-organizational and multilevel and more complex as a result, it is state actors that remain the key actors.

In each region, while there was agreement that economic (relative inequalities of income and wealth) and political (conflict within or between states) factors were the key migration drivers, there was significant divergence in how these representations played out. This further emphasizes the need to develop regional analysis that is sensitive to context and, as noted in Chapter 2, pp. 52-4, in the section 'Is governance Eurocentric' with reference to the Tower of Hanoi puzzle, means that in ostensibly simple or similar task environments there can be significant variation in answer to the question 'What is learned?' This cannot be detached from the complex histories of migration and its interactions with social and political systems in each region.

In Southeast Asia, it was argued that repertoires have developed that centre on the imputed temporariness of migration, whether this be temporary foreign workers with gendered distinctions between male and female workers or the displaced seen by powerful actors as in need of, at best, temporary protection in the region and resettlement beyond it. While this representation is, of course, contested by some actors, it is a powerful and prevalent representation at state level that informs the scope and limits of regional cooperation. ASEAN, bound by principles of non-interference and strict adherence to consensus-based decision-making, has found it difficult to move beyond declarations. Schemes for intra-regional mobility are limited and have become mired in bureaucracy. More informal regional processes such as the Bali Process have been highly significant. The Bali Process brings Australia directly into Southeast Asian regional migration governance and serves as a mechanism for projection of its priorities, although it was also shown that there was an existing regional response that developed through the CPA in the 1980s and that had already reduced the status of asylum seekers and contributed to their irregularization and criminalization. Chapter 3 showed very clearly how outputs and outcomes of governance processes are configured by prevailing representations that have coalesced into know-how and expectations about role held by key migration governance actors in the region. These key actors are predominantly at state level, and there have been significant limits on the ability to contest prevailing views, for example, through civil society mobilization. International standards such as those related to refugee protection are weakened by low levels of adherence, while it was also shown that global norms and standards require localization to be rendered consistent with regional norms and standards (Acharya, 2004). Drawing this point out has shown that there has actually been an observable increase in temporary migration programmes elsewhere in the world, which suggests that not only is temporariness a specific issue for migrants in Southeast Asia, but temporary admission is a key component of admissions programmes in many middle- and high- income countries (Ruhs, 2018). This raises wider concerns that centre on the relations between openness and access to rights and various forms of vulnerability linked to occupation or to gender-based and/or racist discrimination.

In South America, a distinctive change in national and regional approaches was identified that was grounded in a distinct left-wing and progressive vision of migration and its relation to both national and regional governing projects. Both were set against particular negative representations both of the US as the regional hegemon and of EU regionalism. A regional repertoire was identified that centred on a distinction between *de jure* and de facto forms of openness that are closely linked to concerns about governability. In turn, governability connects with wider debates about state authority, legitimacy, and capacity within which regional cooperation can play an important role. The MRA both reflected and advanced a progressive representation of migration that developed in South America after the 2000s. The MRA developed at a time when emigration from the region was the predominant flow and was also driven by practical concerns in the regional migration hub, Argentina, about irregular flows from neighbouring countries. The MRA effectively resolved this issue for nationals of MERCOSUR states. In response to largescale displacement, it is also possible to see progressive and advanced regional standards in South America in the form of the Cartagena Declaration, which significantly goes beyond the provisions of the 1951 Geneva Convention and has been incorporated into national law in all MERCOSUR members and associates. Neighbouring states and other South American countries received large numbers of people displaced from Venezuela after its near total economic, social, and political collapse. Yet, while there have been some exceptions such as Brazil, relatively few of those displaced have been granted refugee status, with a variety of other statuses offered, including use of MRA provisions. This was identified as a governance effect linked to a repertoire within which concern about the governability of migration forms a powerful component of what key actors know how to do and what they think they should be doing. As was argued throughout this book, this helped to form a sensible environment—one that makes sense to key actors—that allowed them to proceed. A key point is that a sensible environment need not be an entirely accurate representation but that it is plausible and, because it is plausible, provides a basis to proceed. Within these repertoires knowledge claims can coalesce into narratives that centre on the causes and effects of migration. These representations are also social, as representations developed and were diffused within and between states and across the region by a variety of actors. In South America during the progressive wave of the 2000s we saw extensive involvement of a wider range of actors, including academic experts and NGOs, which was not a trend that was particularly evident in other regions. There was also a powerful affective dimension to representations, not least linked to the significant experience of displacement caused by oppressive authoritarian governments in the region. Finally, as in other regions, there was a performative dimension. This doesn't mean that migration governance is merely symbolic, but it does contain powerful symbolic elements that can take the form of inclusionary rhetoric. In South America this took the form of a notably progressive rhetoric about the right to migrate and non-criminalization. The link to underlying conditions of—and representations of—governability can, however, make rhetorical shifts more difficult to ground in day-to-day implementation and potentially vulnerable to the effects of economic and political change.

In the EU, it was shown that a highly developed form of regional mobility developed that is guaranteed by a supranational legal framework and attached to the rights of EU citizenship held by all citizens of an EU member state. A mobility repertoire for EU citizens is connected to visions of an integrated Europe but also to notions of market citizenship associated with the pursuit of closer economic integration via the EU's single market framework. This leads to a contrast between intra- and extra- EU migration regimes. For extra-EU migration, a repertoire has developed that centres on fear of large-scale and potentially uncontrollable migration flows. Whether well founded or not, this concern has contributed to the development of EU cooperation and also integration on aspects of migration and asylum and also to the 'externalization' of controls to third countries. Within the EU, there is clear evidence of a focus on deterrence—which was also evident in other countries and regions too, particularly Australia and the United States— which is grounded in a particular representation of the causes and effects of migration, namely that migration is 'pulled' by the economic benefits or social entitlements in destination countries. Whether accurate or not, this provides a plausible representation held by powerful actors that has powerful effects. It provides a very good example of a governance effect and of how governance systems can be constitutive through perceptions and misperceptions and through subsequent actions of the challenges that they face.

In North America we also saw considerable influence of a deterrence approach that developed in the United States and, as the regional hegemon, had major effects on Canada and, particularly, Mexico. While there is very weak regional migration governance and hardly any formalized provisions beyond limited scope for business and facilitated travel, there is a clear and evident regional effect that is linked to the constitution of migration as a governance concern that powerfully shapes intra-regional relations in the post-Trump incarnation of what was previously known as NAFTA. While the Trump regime engaged much more aggressively in putting migration onto the agenda with its neighbours and Trump was overtly nativist and racist in his pronouncements, this does not mean that nativism and racism only came onto the scene upon Trump's election. Concern about security and boundary build-up at the US southern border and also at its border with Canada was evident from at least the 1990s and even predates the September 2001 terror attacks on US targets. This involves knowledge claims advanced by powerful actors, has a social dimension in the way that lessons are learned, evokes affective concerns, and also has performative elements. While North America seemed an unlikely case for migration governance beyond the state, the argument developed is that there is a clear regional effect that actually militates against formalized regional migration governance.

The book then turned its attention to prospects for global migration governance and argued that it is highly unlikely that there will be a comprehensive integrated framework. It was also argued that this is probably beside the point. Instead, we can see forms of legalization at international level that relate to specific issues such as refugees, trafficked persons, or people smuggling on which there is widespread consensus. But, beyond this, there is clear evidence of two other crucially important components of migration governance: efforts to build greater capacity and more or less successful efforts to persuade countries to change their behaviour. A repertoire of global migration governance has developed that has been associated with an implicit functional dynamic that has privileged a bottom-up approach often centred on technical cooperation, with the aspiration or belief that scale-up is possible. In terms of knowledge claims, social effects, affective dimensions, and performative components, the global governance of migration is a restricted domain within which the transgovernmental has been enabled and within which the transnational in terms of participation by migrants and their civil society representatives has been present but more limited in its impact. A key tension was identified by the functional dynamics of technical cooperation often at an official level and post-functional dynamics that see the 'global' and immigration contested in the political systems of some major destination countries. Politicization had an effect on ratification of the global compacts, although the vast majority of states did ratify, but this politicization is a trend that predates these agreements and will continue to be a tension.

It is possible to also extract four more general observations evident across the regions. The first is the importance of 'localisation' (Acharya 2004), with evidence that it is important to assess how the global becomes regionalized rather than to assume that regions become globalized. There is significant variation in the ways in which international norms and standards take effect in regions. We also see that regions themselves as a locus for action, mediators between the national and global and, producers of norms and standards are constitutive of migration governance beyond the state. Any development of global migration governance will be strongly dependent on the regional.

Second, in all the regions we see that governance systems are powerfully constitutive of the challenges that they face, and thus governance is a driver of migration and not an *ex post* response to it. As noted frequently throughout this book, migration governance is necessarily an organizational process and, as such, it is crucial to understand how organizations relate to their environment (or what was termed their representation of 'what's going on out there') and how, on the basis of representations that develop, they decide what to do. These are general characteristics that also inform the significant variation across regions that this book has documented.

Third, an actor-centred approach that focused on how organizations understand the context in which they operate has demonstrated how, why, when, and with what effects perceptions matter. It was shown that governance necessarily involves an attempt to conceptualize the effects of change in underlying social and natural systems, but also that the resulting representations develop under conditions of uncertainty and risk. The use of a sense-making perspective enabled the analysis to show how the identities of actors are constructed through their interactions; governance is retrospective and ongoing, with actors always 'in the middle of things'; governance centres on relations between organizations and their environment; and governance involves the creation of sensible environments where plausibility can be more prized than accuracy. The idea of a repertoire allowed exploration of the comparative regional governance of migration in four major world regions and could also be applied to understand more about the representations, goals, and objectives of actors in migration governance systems across this multi-organizational and multilevel field.

Finally, and perhaps most centrally to the argument developed throughout the book, there is the relation between crisis and normality. The two obviously feed off each other, but it has been argued that what is perceived as normal about migration plays a powerful role in shaping responses to crises and can induce a status quo bias. Clearly, South American regionalism is distinctive because of the shift towards a more progressive vision of migration, although it was argued that underlying concerns about governability provide an element of continuity. In all four regions understandings and representations of the normality of migration are the basis against which crisis events are interpreted. This normality shapes ways of knowing, deciding, and acting. There were some common themes, such as those that represent migration as 'pulled' by wealthier economies and social rights provisions and that then motivate deterrence-based approaches. While questionable, it is clear that such representations have contributed to the creation of a sensible environment for key migration policy actors, i.e. one that makes sense to them and provides them with a basis to act. At the time of writing, the global Covid-19 pandemic had led to hundreds of millions of people living their lives under lockdown, with huge implications for migration and mobility to prevent contagion. While this led to the effective closure of borders and restrictions on individual mobility even at a local level, the crisis also revealed the key role played by migrants as essential workers in many countries. It's not possible to judge the future implications and whether or not the Covid-19 pandemic will shift the terms of debate about migration, but what this book has argued is that understandings and representations of migration are powerfully influenced by past experiences and that they shape understandings of the present and the future. If risk and uncertainty induce a tendency to look back, then it can be difficult to develop innovative forward-looking responses that challenge or adapt established ways of doing things. Because migration governance occurs in the shadow of uncertainty, where facts, values, and beliefs elide, what matters is the plausibility and not necessarily the accuracy of representations. This is why representations of what is normal about migration and of migration's normality are necessarily central to the opportunities for and limits upon migration governance beyond the state and to the political contests that will define future governance agendas.

Bibliography

Abbott, K., Keohane, R., Moravcsik, A., Slaughter, A.-M., and Snidal, D. (2000) 'The Concept of Legalization', *International Organization*, 54(3), 401–19.

Abramowitz, A. (2018) *The Great Alignment: Race, Party Transformation, and the Rise of Donald Trump*. New Haven, CT: Yale University Press.

Acharya, A. (1997) 'Ideas, Identity, and Institution-Building: From the "ASEAN Way" to the "Asia-Pacific Way"?', *The Pacific Review*, 10(3), 319–46.

Acharya, A. (2004) 'How Ideas Spread: Whose Norms Matter? Norm Localization and Institutional Change in Asian Regionalism', *International Organization*, 58(2), 239–75.

Acharya, A. (2012) 'Comparative Regionalism: A Field Whose Time Has Come?', *The International Spectator*, 47(1), 3–15.

Acharya, A. (2017) 'After Liberal Hegemony: The Advent of a Multiplex World Order', *Ethics & International Affairs*, 31(3), 271–85.

Acharya, A. (2018) 'Doomed by Dialogue: Will ASEAN Survive Great Power Rivalry in Asia?', in G. Rozman and J. C. Liow (eds.), *International Relations and Asia's Southern Tier: ASEAN, Australia, and India*. Singapore: Springer, 77–91.

Acosta Arcarazo, D. (2018) *The National versus the Foreigner in South America: 200 Years of Migration and Citizenship Law*. Cambridge: Cambridge University Press.

Acosta Arcarazo, D., Blouin, C., and Freier, L. F. (2018) *La emigración venezolana: respuestas latinoamericanas*, Madrid: Fundación Carolina.

Acosta Arcarazo, D. and Freier, L. F. (2015) 'Turning the Immigration Policy Paradox Upside Down? Populist Liberalism and Discursive Gaps in South America', *International Migration Review*, 49(3), 659–96.

Acosta Arcarazo, D. and Geddes, A. (2013) 'The Development, Application and Implications of an EU Rule of Law in the Area of Migration Policy', *Journal of Common Market Studies*, 51(2), 179–93.

Acosta Arcarazo, D. and Geddes, A. (2014) 'Transnational Diffusion or Different Models? Regional Approaches to Migration Governance in the European Union and MERCOSUR', *European Journal of Migration and Law*, 16(1), 19–44.

Adler, E. and Pouliot, V. (2011) *International Practices*. Cambridge: Cambridge University Press.

Alba, F. (2013) *Mexico: The New Migration Narrative*. Washington DC: Migration Policy Institute.

Alba, F. (2016) 'Changing Fortunes: Mexico and Mexican–US Migration', in D. Leal and N. Rodríguez (eds.), *Migration in an Era of Restriction and Recession: Sending and Receiving Nations in a Changing Global Environment*. Cham: Springer International Publishing, 39–55.

Alberdi, J. B. (1852) *Bases y puntos para l'organización política de la Republica Argentina*. Buenos Aires: Imprenta Argentina.

Aleinikoff, A. (2007) 'International Legal Norms on Migration: Substance without Architecture', in R. Cholewinski, R. Perruchoud, and E. MacDonald (eds.), *International Migration Law: Developing Paradigms and Key Challenges*. Rotterdam: Springer, 467–79.

Alpes, M. J., Tunaboylu, S., Ulusoy, O., and Hassan, S. (2017) *Post-Deportation Risks under the EU-Turkey Statement: What Happens after Readmission to Turkey?* (Policy Brief No. 2017/30). Florence: Migration Policy Centre, 1–10, http://cadmus.eui.eu//handle/1814/49005, accessed 10 August 2020

Amnesty International (2018) 'USA: Policy of Separating Children from Parents Is Nothing Short of Torture', https://www.amnesty.org/en/latest/news/2018/06/usa-family-separation-torture/, accessed 18 July 2019.

Andersson, R. (2014) *Illegality, Inc.: Clandestine Migration and the Business of Bordering Europe*. Oakland, CA: University of California Press.

Andersson, R. (2016) 'Europe's Failed "Fight" against Irregular Migration: Ethnographic Notes on a Counterproductive Industry', *Journal of Ethnic and Migration Studies*, 42(7), 1055–75.

Andreas, P. (1998) 'The Escalation of U.S. Immigration Control in the Post-NAFTA Era', *Political Science Quarterly*, 113(4), 591–615.

Andreas, P. (2003) 'Redrawing the Line: Borders and Security in the Twenty-First Century', *International Security*, 28(2), 78–111.

Andreas, P. (2005) 'The Mexicanization of the US-Canada Border: Asymmetric Interdependence in a Changing Security Context', *International Journal: Canada's Journal of Global Policy Analysis*, 60(2), 449–62.

Ansell, C., Levi-Faur, D., and Trondal, J. (2017a) 'An Organizational-Institutional Approach to Governance', in C. Ansell, J. Trondal, and M. Øgård (eds.), *Governance in Turbulent Times*. Oxford, New York: Oxford University Press, 27–76.

Ansell, C., Trondal, J., and Øgård, M. (eds.) (2017b) *Governance in Turbulent Times*. Oxford: Oxford University Press.

Ansell, C., Trondal, J., and Øgård, M. (2017c) 'Turbulent Governance', *Governance in Turbulent Times*. Oxford: Oxford University Press, 1–23.

A.R. (2019) 'America Closes the Doors to Asylum-Seekers from the South', *The Economist*, 16 July, https://www.economist.com/democracy-in-america/2019/07/16/america-closes-the-doors-to-asylum-seekers-from-the-south, accessed 10 August 2020.

Archibold, R. (2010) 'Arizona Enacts Stringent Law on Immigration', *The New York Times*, 23 April, https://www.nytimes.com/2010/04/24/us/politics/24immig.html, accessed 10 August 2020.

Arias, T. (2019, June 24) Mexico Sends Nearly 15,000 Troops to the US Border, *CNN*, https://www.cnn.com/2019/06/24/americas/mexico-sends-15000-troops-to-us-mexico-border-intl/index.html, accessed 4 July 2019.

ASEAN Secretariat (2004) *ASEAN Declaration against Trafficking in Persons, Particularly Women and Children*. Vientiane: ASEAN Secretariat.

ASEAN Secretariat (2007) *ASEAN Declaration on the Protection and Promotion of the Rights of Migrant Workers*. Cebu: ASEAN Secretariat.

Avramopoulos, D. (2015) 'Keynote Speech of Commissioner Dimitris Avramopoulos at the First European Migration Forum', http://europa.eu/rapid/press-release_SPEECH-15-3781_en.htm, accessed 14 June 2019.

Bali Process (2016a) *Bali Declaration on People Smuggling, Trafficking in Persons and Related Transnational Crime*. Bali: UNESCAP.

Bali Process (2016b) *Review of Region's Response to Andaman Sea Situation of May 2015*. Bangkok: Bali Process on People Smuggling, Trafficking in Persons and Related Transnational Crime.

Barnett, M. (2001) 'Humanitarianism with a Sovereign Face: UNHCR in the Global Undertow', *International Migration Review*, 35(1), 244–77.

Barreto, M. and Collingwood, L. (2015) 'Group-Based Appeals and the Latino Vote in 2012: How Immigration Became a Mobilizing Issue', *Electoral Studies*, 40, 490–9.

Barutciski, M. and Suhrke, A. (2001) 'Lessons from the Kosovo Refugee Crisis: Innovations in Protection and Burden-sharing', *Journal of Refugee Studies*, 14(2), 95–134.

Battistella, G. and Asis, M. (1998) 'The Impact of the Crisis on Migration in Asia. Conference Report', *Studi Emigrazione*, 130, 323–33.

Bean, F., Chanove, R., Cushing, R., Freeman, G., Haynes, C., and Spener, D. (1994) *Illegal Mexican Migration & the United States/Mexico Border: The Effects of Operation Hold the Line on El Paso/Juárez*. University of Texas at Austin: Population Research Centre, 137.

Beirens, H. (2018) *Cracked Foundation, Uncertain Future: Structural Weaknesses in the Common European Asylum System*. Washington DC: Migration Policy Institute.

Benford, R. and Snow, D. (2000) 'Framing Processes and Social Movements: An Overview and Assessment', *Annual Review of Sociology*, 26(1), 611–39.

Betts, A. (2011) *Global Migration Governance*. Oxford: Oxford University Press.

Betts, A. (2013) 'Regime Complexity and International Organizations: UNHCR as a Challenged Institution', *Global Governance*, 19(1), 69–81.

Bevir, M. and Rhodes, R. (2010) *The State as Cultural Practice*. Oxford: Oxford University Press.

Bianculli, A. (2016) 'Latin America', in T. Börzel and T. Risse (eds.), *The Oxford Handbook of Comparative Regionalism*. Oxford: Oxford University Press, 154–77.

Blitzer, J. (2019) 'How the U.S. Asylum System Is Keeping Migrants at Risk in Mexico', *The New Yorker*, https://www.newyorker.com/news/dispatch/how-the-us-asylum-system-is-keeping-migrants-at-risk-in-mexico, accessed 10 August 2020.

Boden, D. (1994) *The Business of Talk. Organisations in Action*. Cambridge: Polity Press.

Börzel, T. A. (2016) 'From EU Governance of Crisis to Crisis of EU Governance: Regulatory Failure, Redistributive Conflict and Eurosceptic Publics', *JCMS: Journal of Common Market Studies*, 54, 8–31.

Börzel, T. A. and Risse, T. (2016) *The Oxford Handbook of Comparative Regionalism*. Oxford University Press.

Börzel, T. A. and Risse, T. (2018) 'From the Euro to the Schengen Crises: European Integration Theories, Politicization, and Identity Politics', *Journal of European Public Policy*, 25(1), 83–108.

Boswell, C. (2003) 'The "External Dimension" of EU Immigration and Asylum Policy', *International Affairs*, 79(3), 619–38.

Boswell, C. (2008) 'Evasion, Reinterpretation and Decoupling: European Commission Responses to the "External Dimension" of Immigration and Asylum', *West European Politics*, 31(3), 491–512.

Boswell, C. (2009) *The Political Use of Expert Knowledge: Immigration Policy and Social Research*. Cambridge: Cambridge University Press.

Boswell, C., Geddes, A., and Scholten, P. (2011) 'The Role of Narratives in Migration Policy-Making: A Research Framework', *The British Journal of Politics & International Relations*, 13, 1–11.

Boucher, A. and Gest, J. (2018) *Crossroads: Comparative Immigration Regimes in a World of Demographic Change*. Cambridge: Cambridge University Press.

Bowker, G. and Leigh Star, S. (1999) *Sorting Things Out*. Cambridge, MA: MIT Press.

Brader, T., Valentino, N., and Suhay, E. (2008) 'What Triggers Public Opposition to Immigration? Anxiety, Group Cues, and Immigration Threat', *American Journal of Political Science*, 52(4), 959–78.

Braz, A. (2018) 'La gobernabilidad migratoria en Sudamérica: la difusión de abajo hacia arriba (ascendente) del Acuerdo de Residencia del Mercosur', *Revista de Administração Pública*, 52(2), 303–20.

Brumat, L. (2016) 'Políticas migratorias y libertad de circulación en el Mercosur (1991–2012)'. PhD Thesis, FLACSO, Buenos Aires, http://repositorio.flacsoandes.edu.ec/handle/10469/10634#.WjqJNlVKuUk, accessed 10 August 2020.

Brumat, L. (2019a) 'Venezuelans Are the First Nationality of Asylum Seekers Worldwide, but South American Countries Do Not Recognise Them as Refugees. Why?', *MPC Blog*, 1 July, https://blogs.eui.eu/migrationpolicycentre/venezuelans-first-nationality-asylum-seekers-worldwide-south-american-countries-not-recognise-refugees/, accessed 10 September 2019.

Brumat, L. (2019b) 'Migration and the 'Rise of the Right' in South America: Is There an Increasing Anti-Immigration Sentiment in the Southern Cone?', *Migration Policy Centre Blog*, 1 February, https://blogs.eui.eu/migrationpolicycentre/migration-rise-right-south-america-increasing-anti-immigration-sentiment-southern-cone/, accessed 30 July 2019.

Brumat, L., Acosta, D., and Vera Espinoza, M. (2018) 'Gobernanza migratoria en América del Sur: ¿hacia una nueva oleada restrictiva?', in L. Bizzozero Revelez and W. Fernández Luzuriaga (eds.), *Anuario de política internacional y política exterior 2017–2018*. Montevideo: Ediciones Cruz del Sur, 205–11.

Brunsson, N. (2003) *The Organization of Hypocrisy: Talk, Decision and Action in Organizations*. Copenhagen: Copenhagen Business School Press.

Burns, T. and Stalker, G. (2000) *The Management of Innovation*. Oxford: Oxford University Press.

Caetano, G., López Burian, C., and Luján, C. (2019) 'El Brasil de Bolsonaro, las orientaciones posibles de su política exterior y el futuro del regionalismo en Sudamérica', *Revista Uruguaya de Ciencia Política*, 28(1), 95–130.

Calavita, K. (2010) *Inside the State: The Bracero Program, Immigration, and the I. N. S.* New Orleans, LA: Quid Pro Books.

Camou, A. (2001) *Los desafíos de la gobernabilidad*. Mexico City: FLACSO Mexico.

Cantor, D., Freier, L., and Gauci, J.-P. (eds.) (2015) *A Liberal Tide?: Immigration and Asylum Law and Policy in Latin America*. London: Institute of Latin American Studies.

Cantori, L. and Spiegel, S. (1970) 'The International Relations of Regions', *Polity*, 2(4), 397–425.

Caponio, T. and Cappiali, T. M. (2018) 'Italian Migration Policies in Times of Crisis: The Policy Gap Reconsidered', *South European Society and Politics*, 23(1), 115–32.

Carling, J. (2002) 'Migration in the Age of Involuntary Immobility: Theoretical Reflections and Cape Verdean Experiences', *Journal of Ethnic and Migration Studies*, 28(1), 5–42.

Carling, J. and Hernández-Carretero, M. (2011) 'Protecting Europe and Protecting Migrants? Strategies for Managing Unauthorised Migration from Africa', *The British Journal of Politics and International Relations*, 13(1), 42–58.

Carranza, M. (2000) *South American Free Trade Area or Free Trade Area of the Americas*. Abingdon: Routledge.

Castles, S. (2004) 'Why Migration Policies Fail', *Ethnic and Racial Studies*, 27(2), 205–27.

CEC (2015) *Communication from the Commission to the European Parliament, the Council, the European Economic and Social Committee and the Committee of the Regions. A European Agenda on Migration* (No. COM(2015) 240 final). 1–22.

CEC (2016) *On Establishing a New Partnership Framework with Third Countries under the European Agenda on Migration* (No. COM(2016) 385 final).

CEC (2017a) *On the Delivery of the European Agenda on Migration.* Brussels: CEC.

CEC (2017b) *'Commission Contribution to the EU leaders' Thematic Debate on a Way Forward on the External and the Internal Dimension of Migration Policy* (No. COM(2017) 820 final).

CEC (2018) *Progress Report on the Implementation of the European Agenda on Migration* (No. COM(2018) 250 final).

Ceriani, P. and Freier, L. (2015) 'Migration Policies and Policymaking in Latin America and the Caribbean: Lights and Shadows in a Region in Transition', in D. Cantor, L. Freier, and J.-P. Gauci (eds.), *A Liberal Tide? Immigration and Asylum Law and Policy in Latin America.* London: Institute for Latin American Studies, 11–32.

Cerna, L. (2018) 'European High-Skilled Migration Policy. Trends and Challenges', in M. Czaika (ed.), *High-Skilled Migration: Drivers and Policies.* Oxford: Oxford University Press, 87–107.

Cerrutti, M. and Parrado, E. (2015) 'Intraregional Migration in South America: Trends and a Research Agenda', *Annual Review of Sociology*, 41(1), 399–421.

Chalamwong, Y. (2011) *Different Stream, Different Needs, and Impact: Managing International Labor Migration in ASEAN: Thailand (Emigration)* (Working Paper No. 2011–27). Makati City: Philippine Institute for Development Studies (PIDS).

Checkel, J. T. (2005) 'International Institutions and Socialization in Europe: Introduction and Framework', *International Organization*, 59(4), 801–26.

Cheung, S. (2011) 'Migration Control and the Solutions Impasse in South and Southeast Asia: Implications from the Rohingya Experience', *Journal of Refugee Studies*, 25(1), 50–70.

Chin, C. (1997) 'Walls of Silence and Late Twentieth Century Representations of the Foreign Female Domestic Worker: The Case of Filipina and Indonesian Female Servants in Malaysia', *International Migration Review*, 31(2), 353–85.

Cianciarulo, M. (2006) 'Terrorism and Asylum Seekers. Why the Real ID Act Is a False Promise', *Harvard Journal on Legislation*, 43, 101–43.

Citizenship and Immigration Canada (2018) 'Canada Extends Immigration Targets into 2021 with Prominent Roles for Express Entry, PNPs|Canada Immigration News', *CIC News*, 1 November. https://www.cicnews.com/2018/11/canada-extends-immigration-targets-into-2021-with-prominent-roles-for-express-entry-pnps-1111368.html, accessed 15 July 2019.

Cohen, M., March, J., and Olsen, J. (1972) 'A Garbage Can Model of Organizational Choice', *Administrative Science Quarterly*, 17(1), 1–25.

Constable, N. (2014) *Born out of Place: Migrant Mothers and the Politics of International Labor.* Berkley and Los Angeles: University of California Press.

Cornelius, W. A. (2001) 'Death at the Border: Efficacy and Unintended Consequences of US Immigration Control Policy', *Population and Development Review*, 27(4), 661–85.

Cornelius, W. A. and Martin, P. L. (1993) 'The Uncertain Connection: Free Trade and Rural Mexican Migration to the United States', *International Migration Review*, 27, 484–512.

Cornelius, W. and Myrhe, D. (1998) *The Transformation of Rural Mexico: Reforming the Ejido Sector.* Boulder, CO: Lynne Reiner.

Council of the EU (2016) *EU-Turkey Statement* (No. Press Release 144/16). Brussels: Council of the European Union.

Courtland Robinson, W. (1998) *Terms of Refuge: The Indochinese Exodus and the International Response*. London: Zed Books.

Courtland Robinson, W. (2004) 'The Comprehensive Plan of Action for Indochinese Refugees, 1989–1997: Sharing the Burden and Passing the Buck', *Journal of Refugee Studies*, 17(3), 319–33.

Crawley, H. and Skleparis, D. (2018) 'Refugees, Migrants, Neither, Both: Categorical Fetishism and the Politics of Bounding in Europe's "Migration Crisis"', *Journal of Ethnic and Migration Studies*, 44(1), 48–64.

Curley, M. and Vandyk, K. (2017) 'The Securitisation of Migrant Smuggling in Australia and its Consequences for the Bali Process', *Australian Journal of International Affairs*, 71(1), 42–62.

da Silva, T. (2019) 'La nueva política migratoria en la Argentina: la tensión entre el "derecho a migrar" y los "imaginarios sociales" históricamente construidos', *RDUno: Revista do Programa de Pós-Graduação em Direito da Unochapecó*, 1(1), 30–51.

Davies, S. (2008) 'Realistic yet Humanitarian? The Comprehensive Plan of Action and Refugee Policy in Southeast Asia', *International Relations of the Asia-Pacific*, 8(2), 191–217.

De Jaegher, H. and Di Paolo, E. (2007) 'Participatory Sense-Making', *Phenomenology and the Cognitive Sciences*, 6(4), 485–507.

De Vries, C. (2018) *Euroscepticism and the Future of European Integration*. Oxford University Press.

Del Castillo, R. (1992) *The Treaty of Guadalupe Hidalgo: A Legacy of Conflict*. Oklahoma City, OK: University of Oklahoma Press.

Dennison, J. and Geddes, A. (2018a) 'Brexit and the Perils of "Europeanised" Migration', *Journal of European Public Policy*, 25(8), 1137–53.

Dennison, J. and Geddes, A. (2018b) 'A Rising Tide? The Salience of Immigration and the Rise of Anti-Immigration Political Parties in Western Europe', *The Political Quarterly*, 90(1), 107–16.

Dennison, J. and Mendes, M. (2019) *When Do Populist Radical Right Parties Succeed? Salience, Stigma, and the Case of the End of Iberian 'Exceptionalism'* (EUI Working Papers No. RSCAS 2019/26). Fiesole: Robert Schuman Centre for Advanced Studies Migration Policy Centre, 1–19.

Department of Homeland Security (2019) *Annual Flow Report Refugees and Asylees: 2017*. Washington DC: DHS.

de Wilde, P., Merkel, W., Strijbis, O., and Zürn, M. (2019) *The Struggle over Borders. Cosmopolitanism and Communitarianism*. Cambridge: Cambridge University Press.

Domenech, E. (2013) '"Las migraciones son como el agua": Hacia la instauración de políticas de "control con rostro humano". La gobernabilidad migratoria en la Argentina', *Polis. Revista Latinoamericana*, 12(35), 119–42.

Donato, K., Durand, J., and Massey, D. (1992) 'Stemming the Tide? Assessing the Deterrent Effects of the Immigration Reform and Control Act', *Demography*, 29(2), 139–57.

Douglas, J. H. and Schloenhardt, A. (2012) *Combating Migrant Smuggling with Regional Diplomacy: An Examination of the Bali Process*, Brisbane: The University of Queensland Migrant Smuggling Working Group, 2–25.

Draude, A. (2007) *How to Capture Non-Western Forms of Governance: In Favour of an Equivalence Functionalist Observation of Governance in Areas of Limited Statehood*. Free University of Berlin: SFB Governance working paper series No.2, https://refubium.fu-berlin.de/handle/fub188/18490, accessed 10 August 2020.

Druckman, J. (2010) 'What's It All About? Framing in Political Science', in G. Keren (ed.), *Perspectives on Framing*. New York: Psychology Press, 279–301.

Duina, F. (2016) 'North America and the Transatlantic Area', in T. Börzel and T. Risse (eds.), *The Oxford Handbook of Comparative Regionalism*. Oxford: Oxford University Press, 133–53.

Dunlop, C. (2017) 'Pathologies of Policy Learning: What Are They and How Do They Contribute to Policy Failure?', *Policy and Politics*, 45(1), 19–37.

Durand, J. (2009) *Processes of Migration in Latin America and the Caribbean (1950–2008)* (No. HDRP-2009–24). Washington DC: United Nations Development Programme (UNDP).

Edelman, M. (1985) *The Symbolic Uses of Politics*. Urbana and Chicago: University of Illinois Press.

Elias, J. (2018) 'Governing Domestic Worker Migration in Southeast Asia: Public–Private Partnerships, Regulatory Grey Zones and the Household', *Journal of Contemporary Asia*, 48(2), 278–300.

EPSC (2015) *Legal Migration in the EU: From Stop-Gap Solutions to a Future-Proof Policy*. Brussels: European Political Strategy Centre.

Erisen, C., Vasilopoulou, S., and Kentmen-Cin, C. (2019) 'Emotional Reactions to Immigration and Support for EU Cooperation on Immigration and Terrorism', *Journal of European Public Policy*, 27(6), 795–813.

ESI (2019) *The EU-Turkey Statement Three Years on*. Berlin: European Stability Initiative.

Eule, T., Borrelli, L. M., Lindberg, A., and Wyss, A. (2018) *Migrants before the Law: Contested Migration Control in Europe*. London: Springer.

Euractiv (2018) 'Austria Plans to Put Immigration and Borders at Heart of EU Presidency', March 9, https://www.euractiv.com/section/justice-home-affairs/news/austria-plans-to-put-immigration-and-borders-at-heart-of-eu-presidency/, accessed 10 August 2020.

Eurostat (2017) 'People in the EU: Statistics on Demographic Changes', https://ec.europa.eu/eurostat/statistics-explained/index.php/People_in_the_EU_-_statistics_on_demographic_changes#EU_population_structure_and_historical_developments, accessed 18 May 2019.

Eurostat (2018a) 'Residence Permits: Statistics on First Permits Issued during the Year', https://ec.europa.eu/eurostat/statistics-explained/index.php?title=Residence_permits_-_statistics_on_first_permits_issued_during_the_year, accessed 10 August 2020

Eurostat (2018b) 'Asylum and Managed Migration Statistics', https://ec.europa.eu/eurostat/web/asylum-and-managed-migration/data/database , accessed 5 July 2019.

Eurostat (2019) 'Migration and Migrant Population Statistics', https://ec.europa.eu/eurostat/statistics-explained/index.php/Migration_and_migrant_population_statistics#Migrant_population:_22.3_million_non-EU_citizens_living_in_the_EU_on_1_January_2018, accessed 18 May 2019.

Everson, M. (1995) 'The Legacy of the Market Citizen', in J. Shaw and G. More (eds.), *New Legal Dynamics of European Union*. Oxford: Clarendon Press, 73–89, http://eprints.bbk.ac.uk/25583/, accessed 10 August 2020.

Faist, T. (2000) *The Volume and Dynamics of International Migration and Transnational Social Spaces*. Oxford: Oxford University Press.

Federal Ministry of the Interior, Austria, and Ministry of Immigration and Integration, Denmark (2018) *Vision for a Better Protection System in a Globalized World: Mending a Broken System*. Vienna and Copenhagen: Austrian Interior Ministry/Danish Ministry of Immigration and Integration.

Feller, E. (2005) 'Refugees Are Not Migrants', *Refugee Survey Quarterly*, 24(4), 27–35.

Fernández-Kelly, P. and Massey, D. S. (2007) 'Borders for Whom? The Role of NAFTA in Mexico-U.S. Migration', *The ANNALS of the American Academy of Political and Social Science*, 610(1), 98–118.

Fine, J. and Lyon, G. (2017) 'Segmentation and the Role of Labor Standards Enforcement in Immigration Reform', *Journal on Migration and Human Security*, 5(2), 431–51.

Finn, V., Doña-Reveco, C., and Feddersen, M. (2019) 'Migration Governance in South America: Regional Approaches versus National Laws', in A. Geddes, M. Vera Espinosa, L. Hadj-Abdou, and L. Brumat (eds.), *The Dynamics of Regional Migration Governance*. Cheltenham: Edward Elgar, 36–53.

Fisher, E. (2010) 'Risk Regulatory Concepts and the Law', in OECD (ed.), *Risk and Regulatory Policy: Improving the Governance of Risk*. Paris: OECD, 45–92.

Fiss, P. and Hirsch, P. (2005) 'The Discourse of Globalization: Framing and Sensemaking of an Emerging Concept', *American Sociological Review*, 70(1), 29–52.

FitzGerald, D. S. (2019) *Refuge beyond Reach*. Oxford: Oxford University Press.

Fitzgerald, D. S. and Cook-Martín, D. (2014) *Culling the Masses: The Democratic Origins of Racist Immigration Policy in the Americas*. Cambridge, MA: Harvard University Press, http://thesis.umy.ac.id/index.php?opo=bibliography&id=52410, accessed 10 August 2020.

Foley, L. (2016) *Women on the Move: Analysing the Gendered Governance of Domestic Worker Migration in Malaysia*. PhD Thesis, University of Sheffield.

Fratzke, S. (2019) *International Experience Suggests Safe Third-Country Agreement Would Not Solve the U.S.-Mexico Border Crisis*. Washington DC: Migration Policy Institute.

Fredrik, J. (2019) 'Mexico Is Overwhelmed by Asylum Claims as It Ramps Up Immigration Enforcement', *NPR*, 14 June, https://www.npr.org/2019/06/14/732485182/mexico-is-overwhelmed-by-asylum-claims-as-it-ramps-up-immigration-enforcement?t=1563433820100, accessed 10 August 2020.

Freeman, G. P. (1995) 'Modes of Immigration Politics in Liberal Democratic States', *International Migration Review*, 29(4), 881–902.

Freeman, G. P and Birrell, B. (2001) 'Divergent Paths of Immigration Politics in the United States and Australia', *Population and Development Review*, 27(3), 525–51.

Freier, L. F. (2015) 'A Liberal Paradigm Shift?: A Critical Appraisal of Recent Trends in Latin American Asylum Legislation', in J.-P. Gauci, M. Giuffré, and E.Tsourdi (eds.), *Exploring the Boundaries of Refugee Law*. Leiden: Brill, 118–45, https://brill.com/view/book/edcoll/9789004265585/B9789004265585-s007.xml, accessed 10 August 2020.

Freier, L. F. (2018) 'Why Latin America Should Recognize Venezuelans as Refugees', *Refugees Deeply*, 28 September, https://www.newsdeeply.com/refugees/community/2018/09/28/why-latin-america-should-recognize-venezuelans-as-refugees, accessed 24 March 2019.

Frieden, J. A. (1991) *Debt, Development, and Democracy: Modern Political Economy and Latin America, 1965–1985*. Princeton, NJ: Princeton University Press, https://www.jstor.org/stable/j.ctv39x8j5, accessed 10 August 2020.

Frowd, P. M. (2018) *Security at the Borders: Transnational Practices and Technologies in West Africa*. Cambridge: Cambridge University Press.

Fuller, T. (2014) 'Fearing a Junta Crackdown, Cambodian Workers Stream out of Thailand', *The New York Times*, 20 December, https://www.nytimes.com/2014/06/16/world/asia/after-coup-foreign-workers-stream-out-of-thailand.html, accessed 10 August 2020.

Fussell, E. (2010) 'The Cumulative Causation of International Migration in Latin America', *The Annals of the American Academy of Political and Social Science*, 630(1), 162–77.

Gabrielli, L. (2007) 'Les Enjeux de la sécurisation de la question migratoire dans les relations de l'Union européenne avec l'Afrique', *Politique européenne*, 22(2), 149–73.

Gallagher, A. and McAuliffe, M. (2016) 'South East Asia and Australia', in M. McAuliffe and F. Laczko (eds.), *Migrant Smuggling Data and Research: A Global Review of the Emerging Evidence Base*. Geneva: IOM, 211–42.

Gamble, A. and Payne, A. (1996) *Regionalism and World Order*. Houndmills: Macmillan.

García, J. (1980) *Operation Wetback: The Mass Deportation of Mexican Undocumented Workers in 1954*. Westport, CT: Greenwood Press.

GCIM (2006) *Migration in an Interconnected World: New Directions for Action: Report of the Global Commission on International Migration*. Geneva: Global Commission on International Migration.

Geddes, A. (2005) 'Europe's Border Relationships and International Migration Relations', *Journal of Common Market Studies*, 43(4), 787–806.

Geddes, A., Hadj Abdou, L., and Brumat, L. (2020) *Migration and Mobility in the European Union, 2nd edn*. London: Palgrave Macmillan.

Geddes, A., Hadj Abdou, L., Vera Espinoza, M., and Brumat, L. (2019) *The Dynamics of Regional Migration Governance*. Cheltenham: Edward Elgar.

Geddes, A. and Lixi, L. (2018) 'New Actors and New Understandings in European Union External Migration Governance? The Case of EU-Tunisian Migration Relations', in S. Carrera, L. den Hertog, M. Panizzon, and D. Kostakopoulou (eds.), *EU External Migration Policies in an Era of Global Mobilities: Intersecting Policy Universes*. Leiden: Brill Nijhoff, 60–80.

Geddes, A. and Pettrachin, A. (2020) 'Italian Migration Policy and Politics: Exacerbating Paradoxes', *Contemporary Italian Politics*, 12(2), 1–16.

Geddes, A. and Vera Espinoza, M. (2018) 'Framing Understandings of International Migration: How Governance Actors Make Sense of Migration in Europe and South America', in A. Margheritis (ed.), *Shaping Migration between Europe and Latin America: New Perspectives and Challenges*. London: Institute of Latin American Studies, 25–49.

Geiger, M. and Pécoud, A. (2010) 'The Politics of International Migration Management', in M. Geiger and A. Pécoud (eds.), *The Politics of International Migration Management*. London: Palgrave Macmillan, 1–20.

Gemenne, F. and Brücker, P. (2015) 'From the Guiding Principles on Internal Displacement to the Nansen Initiative: What the Governance of Environmental Migration Can Learn from the Governance of Internal Displacement', *International Journal of Refugee Law*, 27(2), 245–63.

Gilbert, E. (2019) 'Elasticity at the Canada–US Border: Jurisdiction, Rights, Accountability', *EPC: Politics and Space*, 37(3), 424–41.

Gilbert, L. (2009) 'Immigration as Local Politics: Re-Bordering Immigration and Multiculturalism through Deterrence and Incapacitation', *International Journal of Urban and Regional Research*, 33(1), 26–42.

Givens, T., Freeman, G., and Leal, D. (2008) *Immigration Policy and Security: U.S., European, and Commonwealth Perspectives*. London: Routledge.

Gleeson, M. (2017) 'Unprecedented but Unfulfilled: Refugee Protection and Regional Responses to the Andaman Sea "Crisis"', *Antropologi Indonesia*, 1, 6–20.

Goffman, E. (1974) *Frame Analysis: An Essay on the Organization of Experience*. Cambridge, MA: Harvard University Press.

Goldberg, J. (2018) 'The Border Wall Is a Symbol of our Symbolic Politics', *National Review*, 28 December, https://www.nationalreview.com/2018/12/border-wall-immigration-debate-political-symbol/, accessed 10 August 2020.

Golob, S. (2003) 'Beyond the Policy Frontier: Canada, Mexico, and the Ideological Origins of NAFTA', *World Politics*, 55(3), 361–98.

Guild, E. (2019) 'The UN Global Compact for Safe, Orderly and Regular Migration: What Place for Human Rights?', *International Journal of Refugee Law*, 30(4), 661–3.

Guild, E. and Grant, S. (2017) *Migration Governance in the UN: What Is the Global Compact and What Does It Mean?* (SSRN Scholarly Paper). Rochester, NY: Social Science Research Network.

Guiraudon, V. (2003) 'The Constitution of a European Immigration Policy Domain: A Political Sociology Approach', *Journal of European Public Policy*, 10(2), 263–82.

Guiraudon, V. (2018) 'The 2015 Refugee Crisis Was Not a Turning Point: Explaining Policy Inertia in EU Border Control', *European Political Science*, 17(1), 151–60.

Gurmendi, A. (2018) 'The Cartagena Declaration and the Venezuelan Refugee Crisis', *Opinio Juris*, 27 August, http://opiniojuris.org/2018/08/27/the-cartagena-declaration-and-the-venezuelan-refugee-crisis/, accessed 10 August 2020.

Gutiérrez, R. (2007) 'George W. Bush and Mexican Immigration Policy', *Revue Française d'Études Americaines*, 113(3), 70–6.

Haacke, J. (1999) 'The Concept of Flexible Engagement and the Practice of Enhanced Interaction: Intramural Challenges to the "ASEAN Way"', *The Pacific Review*, 12(4), 581–611.

Haas, E. B. (1966) 'The Uniting of Europe and the Uniting of Latin America', *Journal of Common Market Studies*, 5(4), 315–43.

Haas, E. B. (1970) 'The Study of Regional Integration: Reflections on the Joy and Anguish of Pretheorizing', *International Organization*, 24(4), 606–46.

Hadj Abdou, L. (2019) 'North America: Weak Regionalism, Strong Borders', in A. Geddes, M. Vera Espinoza, L. H. Abdou, and L. Brumat (eds.), *The Dynamics of Regional Migration Governance*. Cheltenham: Edward Elgar, 146–65.

Hainsworth, P. (2006) 'France Says No: The 29 May 2005 Referendum on the European Constitution', *Parliamentary Affairs*, 59(1), 98–117.

Hansen, P. and Hager, S. B. (2012) *The Politics of European Citizenship: Deepening Contradictions in Social Rights and Migration Policy*. Oxford: Berghahn Books.

Hartlapp, M. (2007) 'On Enforcement, Management and Persuasion: Different Logics of Implementation Policy in the EU and the ILO', *Journal of Common Market Studies*, 45(3), 653–74.

Hathaway, J. C. (1993) 'Labelling the "Boat People": The Failure of the Human Rights Mandate of the Comprehensive Plan of Action for Indochinese Refugees', *Human Rights Quarterly*, 15(4), 686–702.

Hathaway, J. C. (2019) 'The Global Cop-Out on Refugees', *International Journal of Refugee Law*, 30(4), 591–604.

Heffernan, M. (2011) *Wilful Blindness: Why We Ignore the Obvious*. London: Simon and Schuster.

Helbling, M. and Leblang, D. (2019) 'Controlling Immigration? How Regulations Affect Migration Flows', *European Journal of Political Research*, 58(1), 248–69.

Henson, P. and Malhan, N. (1995) 'Endeavours to Export a Migration Crisis: Policy Making and Europeanisation in the German Migration Dilemma', *German Politics*, 4(3), 128–44.

Hernández, D. (2014) 'Unaccompanied Child Migrants in "Crisis": New Surge or Case of Arrested Development?', *Harvard Journal of Hispanic Policy*, 27, 11–17.

Hitchox, L. (1990) 'Repatriation: Solution or Expedient? The Vietnamese Asylum Seekers in Hong Kong', *Asian Journal of Social Science*, 18(1), 111–31.

Hollifield, J. F., Martin, P. L., and Orrenius, P. M. (eds.) (2014) *Controlling Immigration: A Global Perspective*. Stanford, CA: Stanford University Press.

Hooghe, L., Lenz, T., and Marks, G. (2019) *A Theory of International Organization*. Oxford University Press.

Hooghe, L. and Marks, G. (2009) 'A Postfunctionalist Theory of European Integration: From Permissive Consensus to Constraining Dissensus', *British Journal of Political Science*, 39(1), 1–23.

Hooghe, L. and Marks, G. (2017) 'Cleavage Theory Meets Europe's Crises: Lipset, Rokkan, and the Transnational Cleavage', *Journal of European Public Policy*, 25(1), 109–35.

Hughey, M. (2017) 'Bad hombres? The Implicit and Explicit Racialization of Immigration', *Humanity & Society*, 41(1), 127–9.

Hugo, G. (2014) 'The Changing Dynamics of ASEAN International Migration', *Malaysian Journal of Economic Studies*, 51(1), 43–67.

Hurrell, A. (2007) 'One World? Many Worlds? The Place of Regions in the Study of International Society', *International Affairs*, 83(1), 127–46.

Hutter, S. and Kriesi, H. (2019) *European Party Politics in Times of Crisis*. New York: Cambridge University Press.

Igarashi, S. (2011) 'The New Regional Order and Transnational Civil Society in Southeast Asia: Focusing on Alternative Regionalism from Below in the Process of Building the ASEAN Community', *World Political Science*, 7(1).

International Organization for Migration (2012) *Integración y migraciones. El tratamiento de la variable migratoria en el MERCOSUR y su incidencia en la política argentina* (Cuadernos Migratorios n°3). Buenos Aires: IOM Regional Office for South America.

Jervis, R. (2008) 'Signaling and Perception: Drawing Inferences and Projecting Images', , in K. R. Monroe (ed.),*Political Psychology*. London: Lawrence Erlbaum, 293–312.

Jervis, R. (2017) *Perception and Misperception in International Politics*. Princeton, N.J: Princeton University Press.

Joint Statement: Ministerial Meeting on Irregular Movement of People in Southeast Asia. (2015) Putrajaya: Ministers of Foreign Affairs of Malaysia, Indonesia and Thailand.

Jones, D. (2008) 'Security and Democracy: The ASEAN Charter and the Dilemmas of Regionalism in South-East Asia', *International Affairs*, 84(4), 735–56.

Jones, D. and Smith, M. (2007) 'Making Process, Not Progress: ASEAN and The Evolving East Asian Regional Order', *International Security*, 32(1), 148–84.

Jones, L. (2011) *ASEAN, Sovereignty and Intervention in Southeast Asia*. Amsterdam: Springer.

Jordan, M. (2017) 'Trump Administration Ends Temporary Protection for Haitians', *The New York Times*, 20 November, https://www.nytimes.com/2017/11/20/us/haitians-temporary-status.html, accessed 10 August 2020.

Jurje, F. and Lavenex, S. (2015) *ASEAN Economic Community: What Model for Labour Mobility*. (No. 2). Neuchatel: NCCR–Swiss National Centre of Competence in Research.

Kahneman, D., Knetsch, J., and Thaler, R. (1991) 'Anomalies: The Endowment Effect, Loss Aversion, and Status Quo Bias', *Journal of Economic Perspectives*, 5(1), 193–206.

Kassim, Y. (2012) *Myanmar & ASEAN Community 2015: Are Member Countries Prepared?* Singapore: Nanyang Technological University.

Katzenstein, P. J. (2015) *A World of Regions: Asia and Europe in the American Imperium*. Ithaca, NY: Cornell University Press.

Kaur, A. (2007) 'On the Move: International Migration in Southeast Asia since the 1980s', *History Compass*, 5(2), 302–13.

Keohane, R. and Nye, J. (1977) *Power and Interdependence*. London: Longman.

Keohane, R. and Victor, D. (2011) 'The Regime Complex for Climate Change', *Perspectives on Politics*, 9(1), 7–23.

Kingsley, P. (2016) *The New Odyssey: The Story of Europe's Refugee Crisis*. London: Guardian Faber Publishing.

Kneebone, S. (2014) 'The Bali Process and Global Refugee Policy in the Asia–Pacific Region', *Journal of Refugee Studies*, 27(4), 596–618.

Kneebone, S. (2017) 'Australia as a Powerbroker on Refugee Protection in Southeast Asia: The Relationship with Indonesia', *Refuge: Canada's Journal on Refugees*, 33(1), 29–41.

Köhler, J. (2011) 'What Government Networks Do in the Field of Migration: An Analysis of Selected Regional Consultative Processes', in R. Hansen, J. Köhler, and J. Money (eds.), *Migration, Nation States and International Cooperation*. London: Routledge, 67–94.

Konrad, V. and Nicol, H. (2016) *Beyond Walls: Re-Inventing the Canada-United States Borderlands*. London: Routledge.

Korneev, O. (2018) 'Self-Legitimation through knowledge Production Partnerships: International Organization for Migration in Central Asia', *Journal of Ethnic and Migration Studies*, 44(10), 1673–90.

Koser, K. (2010) 'Introduction: International Migration and Global Governance', *Global Governance*, 16(3), 301–15.

Krasner, S. (1983) *International Regimes*. Ithaca, NY: Cornell University Press.

Kriesi, H., Grande, E., Lachat, R., Dolezal, M., Bornschier, S., and Frey, T. (2006) 'Globalization and the Transformation of the National Political Space: Six European Countries Compared', *European Journal of Political Research*, 45(6), 921–56.

Lanni, A. (2016) 'A Political Laboratory: How Spain Closed the Borders to Refugees', *Open Migration*, 2 March, https://openmigration.org/en/analyses/a-political-laboratory-how-spain-closed-the-borders-to-refugees/, accessed 14 June 2019.

Lapp, S. (2017) 'Migration Governance in Uruguay: An 'Adaptive' Approach or Something More?', *Migration Policy Centre Blog*, 4 December, https://blogs.eui.eu/migrationpolicycentre/migration-governance-in-uruguay-an-adaptive-approach-or-something-more/, accessed 24 March 2019.

Larking, E. (2017) 'Controlling Irregular Migration in the Asia-Pacific: Is Australia Acting against its Own Interests?', *Asia & the Pacific Policy Studies*, 4(1), 85–103.

Lasch, C., Chan, R., Eagly, I., Haynes, D., Lai, A., McCormick, E., and Stumpf, J. (2018) 'Understanding Sanctuary Cities', *Boston College Law Review*, 59, 1703–74.

Lavenex, S. (1999) *Safe Third Countries: Extending the EU Asylum and Immigration Policies to Central and Eastern Europe*. Budapest: Central European University Press.

Lavenex, S. (2006) 'Shifting up and out: The Foreign Policy of European Immigration Control', *West European Politics*, 29(2), 329–50.

Lavenex, S. (2018) '"Failing Forward" Towards Which Europe? Organized Hypocrisy in the Common European Asylum System', *JCMS: Journal of Common Market Studies*, 56(5), 1195–212.

Lavenex, S. and Piper, N. (2019) 'Regional Migration Governance: Perspectives "from above" and "from below"', in A. Geddes, M. Vera Espinoza, L. Hadj Abdou, and L. Brumat (eds.), *The Dynamics of Regional Migration Governance*. Cheltenham: Edward Elgar, 15–35.

Lee, S. and Piper, N. (2017) 'Migrant Domestic Workers as "Agents" of Development in Asia: An Institutional Analysis of Temporality', *European Journal of East Asian Studies*, 16(2), 220–47.

Levi-Faur, D. (2012) 'From "Big Government" to "Big Governance"?', in D. Levi-Faur (ed.), *The Oxford Handbook of Governance*. Oxford: Oxford University Press, 3–18.

Linares, M. D. (2017) 'Política migratoria y capacidad estatal: la Dirección Nacional de Migraciones (República Argentina) entre los años 2004 y 2015', *Polis. Revista Latinoamericana*, 16(48), 245–70.

Loebach, P. and Korinek, K. (2016) 'Crossing Borders, Crossing Seas: The Philippines, Gender and the Bounding of Cumulative Causation', *International Migration*, 54(1), 137–51.

Loescher, G. (2001) *The UNHCR and World Politics: A Perilous Path*. Oxford: Oxford University Press.

Lombaerde, P. D., Söderbaum, F., Langenhove, L. V., and Baert, F. (2010) 'The Problem of Comparison in Comparative Regionalism', *Review of International Studies*, 36(3), 731–53.

Long, K. (2013) 'When Refugees Stopped Being Migrants: Movement, Labour and Humanitarian Protection', *Migration Studies*, 1(1), 4–26.

Longo, M. (2016) 'A "21st Century Border"? Cooperative Border Controls in the US and EU after 9/11', *Journal of Borderlands Studies*, 31(2), 187–202.

Malamud, A. (2018) 'Book Review: Regionalism with Adjectives in Latin America. José Briceño-Ruiz and Isidro Morales (eds.). 2017. *Post-Hegemonic Regionalism in the Americas. Toward a Pacific–Atlantic Divide?* Abingdon and New York: Routledge', *Latin American Policy*, 9(1), 164–8.

Malamud, A. and Gardini, G. L. (2012) 'Has Regionalism Peaked? The Latin American Quagmire and its Lessons', *The International Spectator*, 47(1), 116–33.

March, J. and Olsen, J. (1976) *Ambiguity and Choice in Organizations*. Bergen: Bergen Universitetsforlaget.

Marchand, M. (2017) 'Crossing Borders: Mexican State Practices, Managing Migration, and the Construction of "Unsafe" Travelers', *Latin American Policy*, 8(1), 5–26.

Margheritis, A. (2016) *Migration Governance across Regions: State-Diaspora Relations in the Latin America-Southern Europe Corridor*. London: Routledge.

Mármora, L. (2010) 'Modelos de gobernabilidad migratoria. La perspectiva política en América del sur', *Revista Interdisciplinar da Mobilidade Humana*, 18(35), 71–92.

Marr, D. and Wilkinson, M. (2004) *Dark Victory: How a Government Lied its Way to Political Triumph*. Crows Nest, NSW: Allen & Unwin.

Martin, P. and Abella, M. (2014) *Reaping the Economic and Social Benefits of Labour Mobility: ASEAN 2015*. Bangkok: International Labour Organization.

Martin, P. and Ruhs, M. (2019) *Labour Market Realism and the Global Compacts on Migration and Refugees* (Working Paper). Florence: European University Institute, http://cadmus.eui.eu//handle/1814/62065, accessed 10 August 2020.

Martin, S. (2016) 'New Models of International Agreement for Refugee Protection', *Journal on Migration and Human Security*, 4(3), 60–75.

Martin, S. and Weerasinghe, S. (2018) 'Global Migration Governance: Existing Architecture and Recent Developments', in International Organisation for Migration (ed.), *World Migration Report 2018*. Geneva: International Organisation for Migration, 125–47.

Martínez, J. and Vono, D. (2005) 'Geografía migratoria intrarregional de América Latina y el Caribe al comienzo del siglo XXI', *Revista de Geografía Norte Grande*, 34, 39–52.

Martínez Pizarro, J. and Villa, M. (2005) 'International Migration in Latin America and the Caribbean: A Summary View of Trends and Patterns', Presented at the United Nations Expert Group Meeting On International Migration And Development, New York, 6 July: Population Division Department of Economic and Social Affairs, United Nations.

Massey, D., Arango, J., Hugo, G., Kouaouci, A., Pellegrino, A., and Taylor, J. E. (1993) 'Theories of International Migration: A Review and Appraisal', *Population and Development Review*, 19(3), 431–66.

Mayorga, F. and Córdova, E. (2007) *Gobernabilidad y gobernanza en America Latina*. Geneva: Working Paper NCCR Norte-Sur IP8, http://www.institut-gouvernance.org/docs/ficha-gobernabilida.pdf, accessed 10 August 2020.

McDermott, R. (2001) *Risk-Taking in International Politics: Prospect Theory in American Foreign Policy*. Ann Arbor, MI: University of Michigan Press.

Mendoza, D. (2015) *Shortage amid Surplus: Emigration and Human Capital Development in the Philippines*. Washington DC: Migration Policy Institute.

Mercer, J. (2005) 'Prospect Theory and Political Science', *Annual Review of Political Science*, 8(1), 1–21.

Mercier, H. and Sperber, D. (2017) *The Enigma of Reason*. London: Penguin.

Meyers, E. (2004) *International Immigration Policy: A Theoretical and Comparative Analysis*. Houndmills: Palgrave Macmillan.

Mincer, J. (1978) 'Family Migration Decisions', *Journal of Political Economy*, 86(5), 749–73.

Ministero dell'Interno (2017) 'Dati asilo 2016–2017', http://www.libertaciviliimmigrazione.dlci.interno.gov.it/sites/default/files/allegati/dati_asilo_2017_.pdf, accessed 5 July 2019.

Mitrany, D. (1966) *A Working Peace System*. London: Quadrangle.

Monar, J. (2001) 'The Dynamics of Justice and Home Affairs: Laboratories, Driving Factors and Costs', *JCMS: Journal of Common Market Studies*, 39(4), 747–64.

Morales, M. (2019) 'The Manufacturing of the US-Mexico Border Crisis', in C. Menjívar, M. Ruiz, and I. Ness (eds.), *The Oxford Handbook of Migration Crises*. Oxford: Oxford University Press, 145–62.

Moretti, S. (2018) 'Protection in the Context of Mixed Migratory Movements by Sea: The Case of the Bay of Bengal and Andaman Sea Crisis', *The International Journal of Human Rights*, 22(2), 237–61.

Moscovici, S. (2001) *Social Representations: Essays in Social Psychology*. New York: New York University Press.

National Immigration Forum (2018) 'Fact Sheet: Immigrants and Public Benefits', *National Immigration Forum*, https://immigrationforum.org/article/fact-sheet-immigrants-and-public-benefits/, accessed 10 July 2019.

Navarro, S. P. and Arechavaleta, B. O. L. de (2010) 'Heuristic Reasoning and Beliefs on Immigration: An Approach to an Intercultural Education Programme', *Intercultural Education*, 21(4), 351–64Routledge.

Nethery, A. and Gordyn, C. (2014) 'Australia–Indonesia Cooperation on Asylum-Seekers: A Case of "Incentivised Policy Transfer"', *Australian Journal of International Affairs*, 68(2), 177–93.

Nevins, J. (2001) *Operation Gatekeeper: The Rise of the 'Illegal Alien' and the Remaking of the U.S.–Mexico Boundary*. London: Routledge.

Newland, K. (2010) 'The Governance of International Migration: Mechanisms, Processes, and Institutions', *Global Governance*, 16(3), 331–43.

Nguyen, T. (2017) 'Labor Migration Flows from Vietnam to Thailand in the Context of ASEAN Regional Integration', *RUDN Journal of Economics*, 25(2), 272–82.

Norwegian Refugee Council (2020) 'Covid-19 Forces Migrants and Refugees back to Crisis-Ridden Venezuela', 7 April, https://www.nrc.no/news/2020/april/colombia-venezuela-press-release/, accessed 21 April 2020.

Obama, B. (2014) 'Letter from the President: Efforts to Address the Humanitarian Situation in the Rio Grande Valley Areas of our Nation's Southwest Border', 30 June, https://obamawhitehouse.archives.gov/the-press-office/2014/06/30/letter-president-efforts-address-humanitarian-situation-rio-grande-valle, accessed 8 July 2019.

Obama, B. (2016) 'Remarks by President Obama at Leaders Summit on Refugees', 20 September,https://obamawhitehouse.archives.gov/the-press-office/2016/09/20/remarks-president-obama-leaders-summit-refugees , accessed 30 July 2019.

Oelgemöller, C. (2011) 'Informal Pluralateralism: The Impossibility of Multilateralism in the Steering of Migration', *The British Journal of Politics & International Relations*, 13(1), 110–26.

Offe, C. (2009) 'Governance: An "Empty Signifier"?', *Constellations*, 16(4), 550–62.

OHCHR (2017) 'Italy-EU Search and Rescue Code Could Increase Mediterranean Deaths, UN Expert Warns', https://www.ohchr.org/EN/NewsEvents/Pages/DisplayNews.aspx?NewsID=21971&LangID=E, accessed 14 June 2019.

O'Leary, S. (2008) 'Developing an Ever Closer Union between the Peoples of Europe? A Reappraisal of the Case Law of the Court of Justice on the Free Movement of Persons and EU Citizenship', *Yearbook of European Law*, 27(1), 167–93.

Oltermann, P. (2016) 'EU Acting like "Human Trafficker" of Refugees, Says Austrian Minister', *The Observer*, 6 March, https://www.theguardian.com/world/2016/mar/05/rebel-austria-accuses-eu-human-trafficker-sebastian-kurz-angela-merkel, accessed 1 September 2020.

Pachocka, M. (2016) 'Understanding the Visegrad Group States' Response to the Migrant and Refugee Crisis 2014+ in the European Union', *Yearbook of Polish European Studies*, 19, 101–32.

Parent, N. and Freier, L. F. (2018a) 'The Venezuelan Exodus: Placing Latin America in the Global Conversation on Migration Management', *LSE Latin America and Caribbean*, 31 July,https://blogs.lse.ac.uk/latamcaribbean/2018/07/31/the-venezuelan-exodus-placing-latin-america-in-the-global-conversation-on-migration-management/, accessed 10 August 2020.

Parent, N. and Freier, L. F. (2018b) 'A South American Migration Crisis: Venezuelan Outflows Test Neighbors' Hospitality', 17 July, Migration Policy Institute, https://www.migrationpolicy.org/article/south-american-migration-crisis-venezuelan-outflows-test-neighbors-hospitality, accessed 24 March 2019.

Paul, R. (2019) 'The Political Ordering of Migrant Workers through Labour Admission Policies', in E. Carmel (ed.), *Governance Analysis: Critical Enquiry at the Intersection of Politics, Policy and Society*. Cheltenham: Edward Elgar, 93–111.

Paul, R. and Roos, C. (2019) 'Towards a New Ontology of Crisis? Resilience in EU Migration Governance', *European Security*, 28(4), 393–412.

Pécoud, A. (2014) *Depoliticising Migration: Global Governance and International Migration Narratives*. London: Springer.

Pécoud, A. (2018) 'What Do We Know about the International Organization for Migration?', *Journal of Ethnic and Migration Studies*, 44(10), 1621–38.

Pedroza, L. (2017) 'Innovations Rising from the South? Three Books on Latin America's Migration Policy Trajectories', *Migration Studies*, 5(1), 140–8.

Peel, M. and Pitel, L. (2019) 'EU Migration Chief Alarmed at Rise in Aegean Crossings', *Financial Times*, 3 October, https://www.ft.com/content/65516e3a-e5f7-11e9-9743-db5a370481bc, accessed 11 October 2019.

Petcharamesree, S. (2016) 'ASEAN and its Approach to Forced Migration Issues', *The International Journal of Human Rights*, 20(2), 173–90.

Petcharamesree, S., Hughes, P., Wong, S., McLeod, T., and Pudjiastuti, T. (2016) 'The Andaman Sea Refugee Crisis a Year on: Is the Region Now Better Prepared?', *The Conversation*, 26 May, http://theconversation.com/the-andaman-sea-refugee-crisis-a-year-on-is-the-region-now-better-prepared-59687, accessed 10 August 2020.

Peters, G. (2012) 'Governance as Political Theory', in D. Levi-Faur (ed.), *The Oxford Handbook of Governance*. Oxford: Oxford University Press, 19–32.

Petersen, M. and Schulz, C.-A. (2018) 'Setting the Regional Agenda: A Critique of Posthegemonic Regionalism', *Latin American Politics and Society*, 60(1), 102–27.

Pew Research Center (2019) 'Unauthorized Immigrant Population Trends for States, Birth Countries and Regions', https://www.pewhispanic.org/interactives/unauthorized-trends/, accessed 10 August 2020.

Pew Research Center (2020) 'More than Nine-in-Ten People Worldwide Live in Countries with Travel Restrictions amid COVID-19', https://www.pewresearch.org/fact-tank/2020/04/01/more-than-nine-in-ten-people-worldwide-live-in-countries-with-travel-restrictions-amid-covid-19/, accessed 10 August 2020.

Phillips, N. (2001) 'Regionalist Governance in the New Political Economy of Development: "Relaunching" the Mercosur', *Third World Quarterly*, 22(4), 565–83.

Pierre, J. (ed.) (2000) *Debating Governance: Authority, Steering, and Democracy*. Oxford: Oxford University Press.

Piper, N. (2010) 'All Quiet on the Eastern Front?—Temporary Contract Migration in Asia Revisited from a Development Perspective', *Policy and Society*, 29(4), 399–411.

Piper, N. and Roces, M. (eds.) (2004) *Wife or Worker?: Asian Women and Migration*. Lanham, MD: Rowman & Littlefield.

Piper, N., Rother, S., and Rüland, J. (2017) 'Challenging State Sovereignty in the Age of Migration: A Multi-Level Approach to Southeast and East Asian Migration', *European Journal of East Asian Studies*, 16(2), 191–2.

Plender, R. (2007) *Basic Documents on International Migration Law*, 3d rev. edn. Leiden: Brill.

Politico (2019) 'How the UN Migration Pact Got Trolled', 3 January, https://www.politico.eu/article/united-nations-migration-pact-how-got-trolled/, accessed 30 July 2019.

Pressman, J. and Wildavsky, A. (1973) *Implementation*. Berkley, CA: University of California Press.

Pugh, J. (2018) 'Negotiating Identity and Belonging through the Invisibility Bargain: Colombian Forced Migrants in Ecuador', *International Migration Review*, 52(4), 978–1010.

Pye, A. (2005) 'Leadership and Organizing: Sensemaking in Action', *Leadership*, 1(1), 31–49.

Quayle, L. (2015) 'Leading or Following? International Societies, Southeast Asia, and the Issue of Migrant Workers', *Global Discourse*, 5(3), 415–30.

Ramírez, J. and Ramírez, F. (2005) *La estampida migratoria ecuatoriana: crisis, redes transnacionales y repertorios de acción migratoria*. Quito: CIUDAD-ABYA YALA-UNESCO.

Rand Smith, W. (2014) 'The Left in Power: How Does It Govern? What Are the Consequences?', *Latin American Politics and Society*, 56(2), 163–72.

Ratha, D. and Shaw, W. (2007) *South-South Migration and Remittances* (No. 102). Washington DC: World Bank.

Raustiala, K. (2002) 'The Architecture of International Cooperation: Transgovernmental Networks and the Future of International Law', *Virginia Journal of International Law*, 43(1), 1–92.

Reagan, R. (1986) 'Statement on Signing the Immigration Reform and Control Act of 1986', https://www.reaganlibrary.gov/research/speeches/110686b, accessed 8 July 2019.

Recchi, E. (2017) *The Engine of 'Europeanness'?: Free Movement, Social Transnationalism and European Identification*, http://cadmus.eui.eu//handle/1814/53464, accessed 10 August 2020.

Redacción EC (2019) 'Cancillería: capacidad del Estado para atender el incremento de la migración venezolana ha sido sobrepasada', *El Comercio (Perú)*, 29 October, https://elcomercio.pe/peru/cancilleria-capacidad-del-estado-para-atender-el-incremento-de-la-migracion-venezolana-ha-sido-sobrepasada-venezolanos-en-peru-migracion-venezolana-noticia/, accessed 10 August 2020.

Reich, G. (2018) 'Hitting a Wall? The Trump Administration Meets Immigration Federalism', *Publius: The Journal of Federalism*, 48(3), 372–95.

Remmer, K. (1986) 'The Politics of Economic Stabilization: IMF Standby Programs in Latin America, 1954–1984', *Comparative Politics*, 19(1), 1–24.

Riggirozzi, P. and Tussie, D. (eds.) (2012) *The Rise of Post-Hegemonic Regionalism: The Case of Latin America*. Dordrecht: Springer.

Roberts, C. B., Habir, A. D., and Sebastian, L. C. (2014) *Australia's Relations with Indonesia: Progress despite Economic and Socio-Cultural Constraints?* Canberra: Australian National University National Security College.

Rochas Sánchez, A. (2019) 'Desde setiembre salieron del Perú más venezolanos de los que ingresaron: ¿cuáles son las razones? ', *El Comercio (Perú)*, 24 October, https://elcomercio.pe/peru/desde-setiembre-salieron-del-peru-mas-venezolanos-de-los-que-ingresaron-cuales-son-las-razones-venezolanos-en-peru-migracion-venezolana-venezuela-noticia/, accessed 4 November 2019.

Roe, E. (1994) *Narrative Policy Analysis: Theory and Practice*. Durham, NC: Duke University Press.

Romero, S. and Politi, D. (2017) 'Argentina's Trump-Like Immigration Order Rattles South America', *The New York Times*, 4 February, https://www.nytimes.com/2017/02/04/world/americas/argentinas-trump-like-immigration-order-rattles-south-america.html, accessed 11 August 2020.

Roos, C. (2018) 'The (De-)Politicization of EU Freedom of Movement: Political Parties, Opportunities, and Policy Framing in Germany and the UK', *Comparative European Politics*, 17, 631–50. doi.org/10.1057/s41295-018-0118-1.

Rosenblum, M. (2011) *Obstacles and Opportunities for Regional Cooperation: The U.S.-Mexico Case*. Washington DC: Migration Policy Institute.

Rother, S. (2012) 'Wendt Meets East: ASEAN Cultures of Conflict and Cooperation', *Cooperation and Conflict*, 47(1), 49–67.

Rother, S. (2018) 'ASEAN Forum on Migrant Labour: A Space for Civil Society in Migration Governance at the Regional Level?', *Asia Pacific Viewpoint*, 59(1), 107–18.

Rother, S. (2019) 'The Global Forum on Migration and Development as a Venue of State Socialisation: A Stepping Stone for Multi-Level Migration Governance?', *Journal of Ethnic and Migration Studies*, 45(8), 1258–74.

Rother, S. and Piper, N. (2014) 'Alternative Regionalism from Below: Democratizing ASEAN's Migration Governance', *International Migration*, 53(3), 36–49.

Ruhs, M. (2018) 'Labor Immigration Policies in High-Income Countries: Variations across Political Regimes and Varieties of Capitalism', *The Journal of Legal Studies*, 47(S1), S89–127.

Ruhs, M. and Barslund, M. (2018) 'Reforming Europe's refugee policies: Austrian-Danish plan will not work|View', *euronews*, 11 October, https://www.euronews.com/2018/10/11/reforming-europe-s-refugee-policies-austrian-danish-plan-will-not-work-view, accessed 14 June 2019.

Ruhs, M. and Palme, J. (2018) 'Institutional Contexts of Political Conflicts around Free Movement in the European Union: A Theoretical Analysis', *Journal of European Public Policy*, 25(10), 1481–500.

Samuelson, W. and Zeckhauser, R. (1988) 'Status Quo Bias in Decision making', *Journal of Risk and Uncertainty*, 1(1), 7–59.

Sanahuja, J. A. (2012) 'Regionalismo post-liberal y multilateralismo en Sudamérica: El caso de UNASUR', in A. Serbin, L. Martinez, and H. Ramanzani Júnior (eds.), *El regionalismo 'post–liberal' en América Latina y el Caribe: Nuevos actores, nuevos temas, nuevos desafíos*. Buenos Aires: Coordinadora Regional de Investigaciones Económicas e Sociales, 19–72.

Sanahuja, J. A. (2017) 'A "Rashomon" Story: Latin American Views and Discourses of Global Governance and Multilateralism', in A. Triandafyllidou (ed.), *Global Governance from Regional Perspectives: A Critical View*. Oxford: Oxford University Press, 181–208.

Sanchez, G. (2016) 'Women's Participation in the Facilitation of Human Smuggling: The Case of the US Southwest', *Geopolitics*, 21(2), 387–406.

Sánchez-Reaza, J. and Rodríguez-Pose, A. (2002) 'The Impact of Trade Liberalization on Regional Disparities in Mexico', *Growth and Change*, 33(1), 72–90.

Sandholtz, W. and Turnbull, P. (2001) 'Policing and Immigration: The Creation of New Policy Spaces', in A. Stone Sweet, W. Sandholtz, and N. Fligstein (eds.), *The Institutionalization of Europe*. Oxford: Oxford University Press, 194–220, http://www.oxfordscholarship.com/view/10.1093/019924796X.001.0001/acprof-9780199247967-chapter-10, accessed 11 August 2020.

Sbragia, A. (2008) 'Comparative Regionalism: What Might It Be? Review Article', *Journal of Common Market Studies*, 46, 29–50.

Scharpf, F. (1999) *Governing in Europe: Effective and Democratic?* Oxford and New York: Oxford University Press.

Schattschneider, E. E. (1960) *Party Government*. New Brunswick, NJ: Transaction Publishers.

Schön, D. (1983) *The Reflective Practitioner: How Professionals Think in Action*. New York: Basic Books.

Sears, D. (1993) 'Symbolic Politics: A Socio-Psychological Theory', *Explorations in Political Psychology*. Durham, NC: Duke University Press, 113–49.

Seelke, C. and Finklea, K. (2010) *U.S.-Mexican Security Cooperation: The Merida Initiative and Beyond* (No. CRS-7-5700). Washington, DC: Library of Congress Washington DC Congressional Research Service.

Selee, A. (2018) *Vanishing Frontiers: The Forces Driving Mexico and the United States Together*. London: Hachette.

Selee, A. (2019) 'Mexico's Migration Dilemmas. The Border Crisis South of the Border', *Foreign Affairs*, 8 July, https://www.foreignaffairs.com/articles/mexico/2019-07-08/mexicos-migration-dilemmas, accessed 11 August 2020.

Shear, M. and Haberman, M. (2020) 'Trump's Temporary Halt to Immigration Is Part of Broader Plan, Stephen Miller Says', *The New York Times*, 24 April, https://www.nytimes.com/2020/04/24/us/politics/coronavirus-trump-immigration-stephen-miller.html, accessed 11 August 2020.

Simon, H. A. (1955) 'A Behavioral Model of Rational Choice', *The Quarterly Journal of Economics*, 69(1), 99–118.

Simon, H. A. (1975) 'The Functional Equivalence of Problem Solving Skills', *Cognitive Psychology*, 7(2), 268–88.

Slaughter, A.-M. (2009) *A New World Order*. Princeton N.J: Princeton University Press.

Spaan, E. and Naerssen, T. van (2018) 'Migration Decision-Making and Migration Industry in the Indonesia–Malaysia Corridor', *Journal of Ethnic and Migration Studies*, 44(4), 680–95.

Sutcliffe, J. and Anderson, W. (2018) *The Canada-US Border in the 21st Century: Trade, Immigration and Security in the Age of Trump*. New York: Routledge.

Tetlock, P. (2017) *Expert Political Judgment: How Good Is It? How Can We Know?* Princeton, NJ: Princeton University Press.

Thompson, L. (2019) 'Keynote Address, GFMD Thematic Workshop: "Implementation of the Global Compact for Migration at the National Level"', 27 March. Geneva: International Organization for Migration, https://www.iom.int/speeches-and-talks/keynote-address-gfmd-thematic-workshop-implementation-global-compact-migration, accessed 11 August 2020.

Thouez, C. and Channac, F. (2006) 'Shaping International Migration Policy: The Role of Regional Consultative Processes', *West European Politics*, 29(2), 370–87.

Thurlow, A. and Helms Mills, J. (2009) 'Change, Talk and Sensemaking', *Journal of Organizational Change Management*, 22(5), 459–79.

Tichenor, D. (2002) *Dividing Lines: The Politics of Immigration Control in America.* Princeton NJ: Princeton University Press.

Tilly, C. (1978) *From Mobilization to Revolution.* Reading: Addison-Wesley.

Tilly, C. (1986) *The Contentious French: Four Centuries of Popular Struggle.* Cambridge, MA: Belknap.

Trauner, F. and Servent, A. (2016) 'The Communitarization of the Area of Freedom, Security and Justice: Why Institutional Change Does Not Translate into Policy Change', *Journal of Common Market Studies*, 54(6), 1417–32.

Triandafyllidou, A. (2018) *Handbook of Migration and Globalisation.* Cheltenham: Edward Elgar Publishing.

Trump, D. (2018) 'Remarks by President Trump to the 73rd Session of the United Nations General Assembly'. Washington DC: The White House, https://www.whitehouse.gov/briefings-statements/remarks-president-trump-73rd-session-united-nations-general-assembly-new-york-ny/, accessed 30 July 2019.

Tschoegl, A. and Armstrong, J. (2008) 'Review of: Philip E. Tetlock. 2005. Expert Political Judgment: How Good is it? How Can We Know?', *SSRN Electronic Journal*, http://www.ssrn.com/abstract=1153126, accessed 11 August 2020.

Tuccio, M. (2017) 'Determinants of Intra-ASEAN Migration', *Asian Development Review*, 34(1), 144–66.

Türk, V. and Garlick, M. (2016) 'From Burdens and Responsibilities to Opportunities: The Comprehensive Refugee Response Framework and a Global Compact on Refugees', *International Journal of Refugee Law*, 28(4), 656–78.

Tversky, A. and Kahneman, D. (1973) 'Availability: A Heuristic for Judging Frequency and Probability', *Cognitive Psychology*, 5(2), 207–32.

Tversky, A. and Kahneman, D. (1979) 'Prospect Theory: An Analysis of Decision under Risk', *Econometrica*, 47(2), 263–92.

Ugarte, M. (1922) *La patria grande.* Madrid: Editora Internacional.

UNASUR (2012) *Unasur/Cjeg/Decisión/No12/2012 por la cual el consejo de jefas y jefes de estado y de gobierno de la Unión de Naciones Suramericanas crea los consejos suramericanos de educación; de cultura; y de ciencia, tecnología e innovación en reemplazo del Coseccti.* Lima: UNASUR.

UNASUR (2014) *Fostering South American Integration through Development and Cooperation.* Santiago: UNASUR/UNECLAC.

UNDESA (2019) *International Migrant Stock 2019.* New York: United Nations Department of Economic and Social Affairs.

UNESCAP (2016) *Asia-Pacific Migration Report 2015. Migrants' Contributions to Development.* Bangkok: UNESCAP.

UNESCAP (2018) *Towards Safe, Orderly and Regular Migration in the Asia-Pacific Region: Challenges and Opportunities.* Bangkok: UNESCAP.

UNHCR (2016a) *Mixed Maritime Movements in South-East Asia 2015*. Geneva: UNHCR.

UNHCR (2016b) *The Global Compact on Refugees*. New York City: United Nations.

UNHCR (2019a) *Refugee Movements in Southeast Asia 2018–June 2019*. Geneva: UNHCR.

UNHCR (2019b) 'Syria Regional Refugee Response', *UNHCR Operational Portal*, https:// data2.unhcr.org/en/situations/syria, accessed 11 August 2020.

UNHCR (2020) '*Venezuela Situation*', https://www.unhcr.org/venezuela-emergency.html, accessed 11 August 2020.

United Nations (2018) Global Compact for Safe, Orderly and Regular Migration. Refugees and Migrants, https://refugeesmigrants.un.org/migration-compact#:~:text=In%20 September%202016%20the%20General,compact%20started%20in%20April%202017, accessed1 September 2020.

UN News (2019) 'UN Agency Hails Brazil 'Milestone' Decision over Venezuelan Refugees', *UN News*, https://news.un.org/en/story/2019/12/105292 , accessed 3 April 2020.

Vera Espinoza, M. (2019) 'Between Depoliticisation and Path Dependence: The Role of Mexico in Regional Migration Governance in North America', in A. Geddes, M. Vera Espinoza, L. Hadj Abdou, and L. Bruma (eds.), *The Dynamics of Regional Migration Governance*. Cheltenham: Edward Elgar, 163–85.

Vertovec, S. (2009) *Transnationalism*. London: Routledge.

Villarreal, M. (2019) *U.S.-Mexico Economic Relations: Trends, Issues, and Implications*. Washington DC: Congressional Research Service.

Villavicencio, K. and Lee, C. (2020) 'The Impending Mass Grave across the Border from Texas', *The New York Times*, 12 April, https://www.nytimes.com/2020/04/12/opinion/ matamoros-migrants-coronavirus.html?referringSource=articleShare, accessed 11 August 2020.

Vo, N. (2005) *The Vietnamese Boat People, 1954 and 1975–1992*. London: McFarland.

Watt, N. and Wintour, P. (2015) 'How Immigration Came to Haunt Labour: The Inside Story', *The Guardian*, 24 March, https://www.theguardian.com/news/2015/mar/24/ how-immigration-came-to-haunt-labour-inside-story, accessed 11 August 2020.

Weick, K. E. (1995) *Sensemaking in Organizations*. London: SAGE.

Wintour, P. and Smith, H. (2020) 'Erdoğan in Talks with European Leaders over Refugee Cash for Turkey', *The Guardian*, 17 March, https://www.theguardian.com/world/2020/ mar/17/erdogan-in-talks-with-european-leaders-over-refugee-cash-for-turkey, accessed 11 August 2020.

Woroby, T. (2019) 'Finding Commonalities amidst Increasing Differences in Canadian and U.S. Immigration Policies', in D. Carment and C. Sands (eds.), *Canada–US Relations: Sovereignty or Shared Institutions?*. Cham: Springer International Publishing, 125–50.

Wunderlich, D. (2012) 'Europeanization through the Grapevine: Communication Gaps and the Role of International Organizations in Implementation Networks of EU External Migration Policy', *Journal of European Integration*, 34(5), 485–503.

Yost, E. (1996) 'NAFTA—Temporary Entry Provisions—Immigration Dimensions', *Canada-United States Law Journal*, 22, 211–30.

Zolberg, A. (1989) 'The Next Waves: Migration Theory for a Changing World', *International Migration Review*, 23(3), 403–340.

Zolberg, A. (2009) *A Nation by Design: Immigration Policy in the Fashioning of America*. Cambridge, MA: Harvard University Press.

Zubrzycki, B. (2012) 'Recent African Migration to South America. The Case of Senegalese in Argentina', *International Journal of Humanities and Social Science*, 2(22), 86–94.

Index

Abbott, Tony 70
actors 12, 21, 33, 46–9, 136, 198, see also
    repertoires of migration governance,
    policymaking, processes
    academic researchers, see *experts*
    civil society organizations,
        see *advocacy*
    international and regional
        organizations, see *individual*
        organizations
    national governments, see *individual*
        countries
    think tanks 37
    environment creation 54
advocacy 101, 165, see also *human rights,*
    Global Compacts
Afghanistan 35, 81, 101
Africa, see *individual countries*
agreements, see *individual agreements,*
    see also *non-binding agreements*
agriculture, see *Bracero labourer*
    programme, seasonal migration
Alberdi, Juan Bautista 92
Algeria 191
ambiguity 32, 44–6, 189, see also
    narratives, representations
    bounded rationality 45
America, see *Central America North*
    America, South America
Andaman Sea crisis 2, 67–70, see also
    ASEAN, Southeast Asia
Andean Community (CAN) 104
anti-discrimination 65, 99, 105
anti-globalization, see *globalization*
anti-immigration 87, 140, 177, see also
    racism, xenophobia
Argentina 22, 90–104, 106–9, 197
Asia, see *individual countries, ASEAN*
Association of South East Asian Nations
    (ASEAN), see also *flexible engagement,*
    localization
    ASEAN Committee on Migrant Workers
        (ACMW) 78, 79

ASEAN Declaration against Trafficking
    in Persons, Particularly Women and
    Children 78
ASEAN Declaration on the Protection
    and Promotion of the Rights of
    Migrant Workers of 2007 (Cebu
    Declaration) 78
ASEAN Forum on Migrant Labour 78
ASEAN Human Rights Declaration 79
ASEAN Intergovernmental Commission
    on Human Rights 79
ASEAN Ministerial Meeting on
    Transnational Crime 69–70
ASEAN TRIANGLE Project (Tripartite
    Action for the Protection and
    Promotion of the Rights of Migrant
    Workers in the ASEAN Region)
ASEAN way 74–7
    multiplexity 71–2
assumptions 138, 145, 171, see also *biases,*
    eurocentrism, representations
asylum seekers 95 119–24, 155–6, see also
    Andaman Sea crisis, Bali process, forced
    migration, Global Compacts,
    policy, UNHCR
attitudes, see *public opinion*
Australia 22, 38, 48–50, 57, 65, 69–70,
    191–2, 199, see also *Bali Process*
    Operation Sovereign Borders 83
    Pacific Solution 83
Austria 22, 39, 50, 114, 123, 125, 126, 127,
    129, 137–8, 191
Austrian Freedom Party 137
Authoritarianism 95, 99, 110, 198,
    see also *dictatorial regimes, forced*
    migration
Avramopoulos, Dimitris 1, 137

Bachelet, Michelle 102
Bali Process (Conference on People
    Smuggling, Trafficking in Persons and
    Related Transnational Crime) 57, 70,
    80–4, 104, 170, 197

Bangladesh 67, 70, 101
Banzer regime 95
Belgium 50, 121, 189
Belize 155, 162
beyond the state, see *global migration governance*
biases 30, see also *perceptions, representations*
  anchoring bias 34, 164
  availability bias 34
  crisis bias 132, see also *crisis, normality*
  historical analogy 34
  representativeness bias 34
  status quo bias, see *status quo*
bilateral agreements 61
Blair, Tony 118
Blue Card 128, see also *high-skilled labour*
boat arrivals 63–7, see also *Bali Process, Mediterranean Sea, Southeast Asia*
Bolivia 91–5, 101, 104, 106
Bolsonaro, Jair 96, 101, 191
bottom-up approach 80, 180, 200, see also *migration governance repertoires*
Brazil 22, 91–99, 101, 104, 106–9, 198
Bracero Accord 142, 149–50, 159, see also *seasonal migrants*
Brexit referendum 112, 137
Brunei 56, 59
Bulgaria 191
bureaucracy 22, 73, 92, 152, 180, 191, 197, see also *processes*
Bush administration 150, 159
Bush, George W. 152, see also *Bush administration*
business
  business groups 156
  business and professional travellers 57, 77–8, 141, 148, 159–60, 162, 199, see also *high-skilled labour*
  human trafficking, see *human trafficking, smuggling*

Callamard, Agnès 116
Cambodia 56–65, 73
Cameron, David 119
camps, see *refugees*
Canada 21, 38, 48, 65, 140–8, 153, 157–64, 168–70, 190, 192, 194, 199

Canada-United States-Mexico Agreement (CUSMA), see *US-Mexico-Canada agreement*, see also *NAFTA*
capacity building 12–3, 24, 106, 161, 171, 186, 193
caravan of migrants 168, see also *Central America, Mexico, North America*
Cardoso, Fernando Henrique 107
Cartagena Declaration 95–8, 110, 198
Central America 95, 141, 147, 155, 162, 168, 182, see also *individual countries, North America*
Central Europe 118, 120, 121, 127, see *individual countries*
Chan-o-cha, Prayut 67
Chávez, Hugo 106
Chávez regime, see *Chávez, Hugo*, see also *Maduro regime, Venezuela*
child migration 144, 148, 155, 163–7, see also *ASEAN, DACA, family migration, narratives, North America, Palermo Protocol*
Chile 22, 91–7, 104, 106, 109, 191
China 65, 73, 90, 155, 160
climate change 18, 93, 177, 182, 185, 187, 189, see also *drivers of migration, Paris Agreement*
Clinton administration 151, 163
Clinton, Bill, see *Clinton administration*
Cold War 6, 13, 111, 121, 139, 183
Colombia 22, 91–7, 104, 109
Commission, see *European Commission*
Common Market of the South, see *MERCOSUR, South America*
complexity, see *perceptions, policymaking, uncertainty*
Comprehensive Plan of Action (CPA) 63–5, 69, 81, 84 197, see also *ASEAN, Bali process, Southeast Asia*
Mexican National Company of Popular Subsistence (CONASUPO) 158
Congo, Democratic Republic of 155
Correa, Rafael 100
Covid-19 pandemic 32, 97, 113, 156, 186, 201, see also *health care, mobility*
cooperation, 68, 191, see also *global migration governance, European Agenda for Migration European Union, South America*

multilateral 47, 70, 73–5, 188
partnerships 35, 130, 147, 153, 160,
    166, 172
trust 38, 161–2, 172–3, 177–8
Costa Rica 162
countries of destination, see *destination*
    countries
countries of origin 18, 58, 61, 63,
    92–3, 155
crime 64, 83, 122, see also *Bali Process,*
    trafficking, Palermo Protocol,
    smuggling, UNODC, UNTOC
crime narrative 17, 167
crisis, see also *normality, representations*
    financial crisis 75, 153, 158
    humanitarian crisis, see *Andaman Sea*
        crisis, Venezuela
    migration crisis, see *representations*
    political instability 94–5, 128–9, 184,
        see also *European Stability Initiative*
Cuba 163
Czech Republic 22, 118, 121, 191

decision-making, see *policymaking*
Deferred Action for Childhood Arrivals
    (DACA) 154
Deferred Action for Parents of Americans
    and Lawful Permanent Residents
    (DAPA) 154
Del Águila, Roxana 1
democracy, democratization 75–7, 80,
    see also *bottom-up approach*
demographic factors, see *gender, child*
    migration
Denmark 22, 127, 138
deportation 76, 141, 154, 162, see also
    forced return, repatriation
destination countries 9–10, 39, 91–93, 122,
    130, 143, 155, 173–6, 180, 187, 192, 199
deterrence 64, 116, 125, 141–2, 151–2,
    156–7, 162, 166–9, 199, see also
    security
Development, Relief, and Education
    for Alien Minors Act (DREAM
    Act) 154
dictatorial regimes 95, 100, see also
    authoritarianism, forced migration
directives
    Directive 2004/38/EC 118

Directive 2008/115/EC 102
discourse, see *narrative*, see also *framing,*
    rhetoric
discrimination, see also *anti-immigration,*
    racism, xenophobia
domestic workers 61–2, see also *female*
    migration, gender
Downer, Alexander 82
drivers of migration 10, 120, 128,
    see also *crisis*
    climate change, see *climate change*
    conflicts, see *forced migration*
    labour, see *labour migration*
    income and wealth inequalities 31, 34,
        59–62, 106, 176, 196
Dublin Convention 122, 132
Dublin system 126, see also *European*
    Agenda for Migration

Eastern Europe (*see* individual countries,
    see also Europe, European Union)
Eastern Mediterranean, see
    Mediterranean Sea
East Timor 73
economic migration, see *drivers of*
    migration
Ecuador 22, 91–2, 95–101, 104, 106
Egypt 47–8
elite actors 3, 4, 42, 105, 137, 183,
    see also *actors*
El Salvador 141, 155 ,165
employment, see *labour* migration
enlargement 117–8
environment, see *climate change, UN*
    Environment Programme, sensible
    environment
equal treatment, see also *inequality*
    migrants 100–1, 107, see also
        human rights
    EU citizens 118, see also *Schengen*
Erdoğan, Recep Tayyip 131
Eritrea 48, 101, 190
Estonia 118
Ethiopia 101, 190
eurocentrism 28, 52–4, 71
Europe, see *European Union*
European Agenda for Migration
    (EAM) 125–6, 128, 134, see also *crisis,*
    Dublin convention

EU Horn of Africa initiative 47–8, 126
European project 116, 119–20, see also
    European Union
European Single Market 77, 121, 198,
    see also *free movement, labour
    migration, mobility*
European Union (EU), see also *directives*
    European Asylum Agency 135
    European Border and Coast Guard
        Agency (FRONTEX) 135
    European Commission (EC) 112, 124,
        128, 181
    European Council 22, 117, 124–5
    European Court of Justice
        (ECJ) 124, 135
    European Parliament (EP) 22, 124,
        135, 137
    European Political Strategy Centre 133
    European Research Council 19
European Union treaties
    Amsterdam Treaty 112,124
    Maastricht Treaty 112, 124
exile 64, 88, 95, 110, see also *forced migration*
expectations 22–3, 26–30, 33, 36, 39, 41,
    45, 50, 53, 55, see also *public opinion,
    representations*
experts 94, 114, 149, 177, see also *actors,
    policymaking, technicalities*
exploitation 107, 182
externalization of controls 83, 136, 149,
    199, see also *safe third country*
ex-Yugoslavia 122, see also *individual
    countries*

family migration 10–1, 81, 128, 175,
    see also *child migration, UN*
    family reunification 62, 107, 120
female migration 62, 148, 155, 159, 196,
    see also *child migration, domestic
    workers, Palermo Protocol*
fencing 6, 27, 32, 151, 156, 162, 168,
    see also *narratives*
    US Secure Fence Act 260
Fidesz (Hungarian political party), *see also*
    European Union, Hungary 137
financial crisis, see *crisis*
flexible engagement 75–80, see also
    ASEAN way
free movement 94, 101, 117–9, 188, 194,
    see also *mobility*

forced migration 11, see also *asylum,
    drivers of migration*
    Southeast Asia 62–5, 69
    South America 95–9, see also *exile*
forced return, see *repatriation*
fox and hedgehog 9, 19, 164, see also
    policymaking
fragmentation, *see also* governance, X
framing 39, 50–2, 79, 84, 187, see also
    *representation, sense-making, signals
    and cues*
    components 33–36
    diagnostic framing 135
    discursive framing 34, see *narratives*
    judgement heuristics 123
    motivational framing 34
    prognostic framing 135
    strategic framing 34, 133
France 50, 65, 113, 119–21
FRONTEX, see *European Border and Coast
    Guard Agency*
functionalism 24, 173, 177–83, see also
    global governance
future developments 44, 134, 173, see also
    *Covid-19 pandemic, regionalization,
    uncertainty*
future-proof policy 134, see also
    policymaking

Gambia 69
gaps, see *policymaking*
gender 15, 18, 196–7, see also
    discrimination, female migration
Geneva Convention 95, 184, 188, 198
Germany 22, 39, 45, 50, 113, 119–22,
    129–30, 190
Global Commission on International
    Migration (GCIM) 181
Global Compacts
    Global Compact for Safe, Orderly, and
        Regular Migration (GCM) 172, 174,
        179, 189–92
    Global Compact on Refugees
        (GCR) 174, 179, 190–1
global cooperation, see *global migration
    governance*
Global Forum on Migration and
    Development (GFMD) 172, 178
global migration governance, see *capacity
    building, cooperation, Global*

Compacts, localization, non-binding agreements, processes, standards, sovereignty, UNHCR, IOM
globalization 133, 171, 173, 176, 182–3
  anti-globalization 193, see also *nationalism*
governability 53, 86–7, 96–8, 103, 109–10, 197–8, 201, see also *capacity building, MERCOSUR, politicization, South America, UNASUR*
  trust 127, 131, 134, 138, see also *political debate*
governance repertoires, see *migration governance repertoires*
Greece 39, 126–32, see also *cooperation, crisis*
Guatemala 141, 155, 162, 165
Guyana 104

Haiti 97, 155
health care 96–7, 119, see also *Covid-19 pandemic*
high-skilled labour 77, 84, 120, 128, 150, 162 see also *business*
Honduras 141, 155, 162, 165
Hong Kong 63
hostility, see *anti-immigration*
hosting countries, see *destination countries*
Howard, John 81
human rights 187 see also *narratives, refugees, UNHCR*
  European Convention for the Protection of Human Rights 188
  human rights protection 71, 75–7, 103, 105, 175, see also *ASEAN*
  human rights violations 67, 83, 95, 127
  UN Declaration of Human Rights 188
human trafficking, see *trafficking*, see also *smuggling*
Hungary 118, 131, 136–7, 190, 191

illegal immigration, see *irregular immigration*
Illegal Immigration Reform and Immigrant Responsibility Act (IIRIRA) 152, 154
immigration, see *migration*
Immigration and Customs Enforcement (ICE) 155
Immigration Reform and Control Act (IRCA) 150, 153

inclusion 194, see also *integration*
increase in immigration, see *migration flows*
Indonesia 22, 56–60, 57–70, 73–6, 81–4
inequality 93–4, 101, 148, see also *drivers of migration, equal treatment, neoliberalism*
information sharing 38, 50–1, 115, 153
innovation 88, see also *South America*
institutions, see *governance, actors*
integration, see also *cooperation, regionalization, global*
  economic integration, see *NAFTA, USMCA*
  integration of immigrations 112, 125
  political integration 104, 106, 111, see also *Europe, South America*
interdependencies 14–6, 75–6, 171
International Labour Organization (ILO) 21, 78, 173, 179, 183, 186, 188
International Monetary Fund (IMF) 60, 106, 158
International Organization for Migration (IOM)
interpretation, *see* representation
interstate cooperation, *see* cooperation
interviews 18–22
involuntary migration, see *forced migration*
Iran 190
Iraq 45, 155
Ireland, Republic of 22, 118
irregular immigration 78, 149, 197
Israel 191
issue-framing, see *framing*, see also *representations*
Italy 22, 113, 120, 126, 131–2, 191

Jafaar, Junaidi 67
Japan 69, 73
Jordan 190
Juncker, Jean-Claude 134

Kennedy, Edward 153
Kenya 101
key actors, see *actors*
Ki-Moon, Ban 190
Kirchner, Cristina 100
know-how, see *information sharing*
knowledge creation, see *processes*

Kosovo 129
Kurz, Sebastian 39, 126

labour migration 9, 11, 60–2, 94, 118,
    191–2 see also *ASEAN, business,*
    drivers of migration, female migration,
    high-skilled labour, ILO, lower-skilled
    labour, mobility, seasonal migration,
    temporariness, UN
Laos 56, 58–60, 64
large-scale displacement, see *migration*
    flows, see also *crisis, representations*
Latin America, see *Central America, North*
    America, South America
Latvia 118, 191
Lebanon 190
Le Pen, Marine 137
liberal tide 86–9, 94, 96, 99–105, see also
    South America
Liberia 190
Libya 125, 132, 190–1
Liechtenstein 191
like-mindedness, see *biases, perceptions,*
    see also *information sharing*
Lima Declaration 97, see also *Venezuela*
Lithuania 118
localization 74–5, 178, 186, 193, 197,
    see also *global migration governance,*
    regional migration governance
López Obrador, Andrés Manuel 155
lower-skilled labour 77, 97, 120, see also
    domestic workers
Luxembourg 121

Macri, Mauricio 101
Maduro regime 96, see also *Chávez regime,*
    Venezuela
Malaysia 56, 58–60, 67–9, 76, 84, see also
    Andaman Sea crisis
Malta 22
Manila process (Regional Seminar on
    Irregular Migration and Migrant
    Trafficking in East and South
    Asia) 81, see also *Bali Process*
Mauritania 130
McCain, John 163
Mediterranean Sea 39, 116, 120, 125–6,
    129–32, 138, see also *European Agenda*
    for Migration

MERCOSUR 100, 106–9, 188, see also
    individual countries, regional migration
    governance, South America, UNASUR
    Residence Agreement (MRA) 77, 88,
    97–8, 100, 106–7, 110, 197–8
Merkel, Angela 130
Mexico 21, 95, 140–62, 165–9, 190–1, 194,
    199 see also *NAFTA, USCIS*
Mexicanization of borders 157, 161,
    see also *North America*
Meza-Cuadra, Gustavo 1–2
Middle East 90, 125
migrants, see *forced migration, labour*
    migration, asylum, family migration,
    child migration, female migration
migration governance, see also *actors,*
    migration governance repertoires,
    policymaking, processes, signals
    and cues
    bottom-up approach 80, 180, 200
    cross-regional migration 15
    endogeneity 42–3
    extra-regional migration 113
    intra-regional 143, see also
        extra-regional
    regional migration 15, 74, 180, 194
Migration Protection Protocols (MPP) 2
misperceptions, see *perceptions,*
    representations
mobility 11, 31, 97, 118, 196, 198 see also
    business, Covid-19 pandemic, free
    movement, labour migration
motives, see *drivers of migration*
Mulroney, Brian 159
Murillo, Juan Carlos 100
Muslim minorities, see *Rohingya minority*
Mutual Recognition Arrangements 77,
    see also *lower-skilled labour*
Myanmar 56, 58–60, 65–7, 73, 76, see also
    Rohingya minority

narratives 3–5, 88, 144, 180, see also
    representations
    discourse 6, 74, 99, 101–2, see also *crime*
    plausibility 5, 49–51, 57, 64, 116, 198,
        see also *policymaking*
    symbolic measures 6, 30, 52, 114–5, 196,
        see also *political debate, politicization*
nationalism 105, 177

nativism, see *racism*
natural disasters, see *climate change*
neoliberalism 93, 105, 158, see also *North
    America, South America*
Nepal 101
Netherlands, the 22, 50, 121
New York Declaration 181–2
New Zealand 38, 48, 81–2
Nicaragua 155, 162
Nielsen, Kirstjen 2
Nigeria 101
non-binding agreements 82, 137, 179–80,
    see also *global governance, Global
    Compacts, standards*
non-interference 57, 66, 125, 166, 196,
    see also *ASEAN way*
Noori decision 131, see also *Greece*
normality 34–7, 43, 56, 65, 86, 110–1, 123,
    133–5, 139, 164, 168, 201–2, see also
    crisis, representations
'new normal' 35–6, 128–9, 135
North Africa 35, 130, 187, see *individual
    countries*
North America, see *individual countries*
North America Free Trade Area
    (NAFTA) 81, 98, 189, see also
    US-Mexico-Canada agreement
Norway 81, 98, 189

Obama administration 146, 154–5, 161–2,
    165–6, 190
Obama, Barack, see *Obama administration*
openness 15, 96, 99, 110, 144, see also
    South America
Operation Mare Nostrum 116, see also
    Mediterranean Sea
opposition to immigration, see
    anti-immigrantion
Orderly Departure Programme (ODP) 65
organizational process, see *processes* 8–10,
    23–6, 41, 114, 179, 188, 192, 195–6
Organization of American States (OAS) 108
overlapping 104, 188, see also *regionalism,
    global governance*

Pakistan 101, 190
Palermo Protocol to Prevent, Suppress and
    Punish Trafficking in Persons Especially
    Women and Children (Palermo

Protocol) 65, 175, 179, see also *ASEAN
    Declaration against Trafficking in
    Persons, Particularly Women and
    Children*
Papua New Guinea 73, 83
Paraguay 91–96, 104, 109
Paris Agreement 177, 190
partnership, see *cooperation*
path dependency 106, 133, see also
    representations
Patria Grande 102, 119 *see also*
    MERCOSUR, South America
Patria Grande-MERCOSUR
    programme 108
Peña Nieto, Enrique 168
perceptions 36–7, 86–8, 117, 136–40
    see also *governability, representations,
    signals and cues*
performance 5–7, see also *repertoires of
    global migration*
permanent migration
    permanent residence 119, 148, 152, 154
    permanent employment 159–60, 192
Peru 1, 91–97, 101, 104, 109
Philippines 22, 56, 58–60, 63, 65, 73, 78
Pitsuwan, Surin 67, 75–6
plausibility, see *narratives*
Poland 22, 118, 131, 191
polarization 121, 133, 140, see also
    politicization
policymaking, see also *environment,
    framing, perception, performance,
    technicalities*
    gaps 42, 86, 90–1
    implementation 40, 45, 124, 128, 134,
        171, 174, 186
    policymakers, see *actors*
    policy failure 8, 40, 46
policy choices, *see* repertoires of global
    migration
political debate, see *politicization*
politicization 82, 178, 182, 187, 189, 200,
    see also *migration governance*
    South America 86–8, 91–9
    Europe 113, 118, 121, 126, 133–41
    North America 152–4, 171
Pompeo, Mike 155
populism 105, 137
poverty, see *drivers of migration*

prevention, see *deterrence*
principles 175, 177, see also *ASEAN, Cartagena Declaration, Global Compacts, non-binding agreements, standards, governance*
problem setting, see *framing*, see also *representations*
processes 171–4, see also *bilateral agreements, migration governance*
  informal processes 48–9, 115, 149, 185 see also *non-binding agreements, Bali Process*
  information exchange, see *information sharing*
  knowledge creation 179
  multilateral, see *cooperation*
  multilevel 16, 32, 47–9, 136, 169, 174, 178
  transgovernmental 181–2
  organizational processes 8–10, 23–6, 41, 114, 179, 188, 192, 195–6
professionals, see *business travellers*
progressive attitudes, see *liberal tide*
Prospects for International Migration Governance (MIGPROSP) 19–20
public opinion 36–9, 41, 137–8, 141, see also *perceptions, politicization*
Puebla Process 162

Qatar 69

racism 92, 99, 105, 137, 140, 156, see also *anti-immigration, xenophobia*
  nativism 140–1, 156, 199
Reagan, Ronald 150
receiving countries, *see* destination countries
refoulement 65, 131, see also *deportation, repatriation*
refugees, see also *asylum seekers human rights, Refugee convention, Rohingya minority, UNHCR*
  refugee camps 32, 64, 66, 156
  Refugee Convention 65, 66, 71, 73
regionalism 16, 57, 70–4, 83, 86, 104–10, see also *regionalization*
regional migration governance, see *migration governance*
regionalization 13, 57, 80, 88, 109, 170, see also *cooperation, localization*

absence of regionalization, see also *North America*
strong regionalization 88, 109, see also *South America*
reluctance, see also *ASEAN way, North America, sovereignty*
repatriation see also *deportation, refoulement*
  forced return 64, 69, 132
  voluntary return 132
repertoires of global migration 5–6, 27–8, 177, 196–9, see also see *narratives*
  affective component 110, 123
  knowledge claims 196–9
  ongoing component 49–51, 123, 139, 182
  performative component 42, 46, 123, 156, see *narrative, performance*
  social component 139
representations, see also *liberal tide, narratives, signals and cues, uncertainty*
  beliefs & values 7–9, 18–9, 26–7, 40–2, 114
  bias, see *biases*
  cognitive dissonance 114
  collective representations 30
Republican Party 141,152, 168
residence, see also *permanent migration*
resilience 6, 47
restrictions to mobility, see *mobility*
return policies, see *repatriation*
rhetoric, see *narratives*, see also *representations*
rights, see also *human rights*
  right to migrate 86, 100, 103, 198
risk, see also *uncertainty*
Rohingya minority 66–70, 74, 82
Romania 191

safe third country 2, 131, 155
Salinas de Gortari, Carlos 157–9
Saudi Arabia 69
Schengen Area 43, 113, 121, 124, 127–30, see also *mobility, Covid-19 pandemic*
sea border, see *Mediterranean Sea*
sea crossings, see *boat arrivals*
seasonal migration 93, 149–50, 158, see also *Bracero labourer programme, temporary migration*

Second World War 92, 128, 149
security 31–33, see also *narratives,*
    representations
  Europe 121, 133, 138
  North America, see *North America,*
    terrorism
  South America 105–7
  Southeast Asia 83, see also *ASEAN*
Seehofer, Horst 1
self-identification
sending countries, see *countries of origin*
Senegal 90, 121, 130
sense-making 5, 10, 25, 37–8, 50–2, 73, 89,
    135–9, 145, 178, 180, 187, see also
    framing, signals and cues
sensible environment 49, 50, 57, 84, 98,
    109, 116, 123, 127, 135, 138–9, 151,
    169, 180, 198, 201
Singapore 56, 59, 60, 191
Single Market, see *European Single Market*
signals and cues 10, 18–9, 27, 39, 42, 72,
    115, 147, 182, 195, see also *framing,*
    perceptions, public opinion,
    sense-making, representations
Slovakia 118, 131, 191
Slovenia 118
smuggling 48, 60, 72, 115–16, 121, 166,
    200, see also *Andaman Sea crisis, Bali*
    Process, crime, European Agenda for
    Migration, Manila Process Palermo
    Protocol, trafficking, UNTOC
social benefits, see *welfare,* see also
    Covid-19 pandemic, health care
socialization 71, 83, 180, 186
solidarity, see *cooperation*
Somalia 101
South America 11, 13–6, 86–110, 119, 133,
    see also *individual countries,*
    MERCOSUR
South Korea 73
South Sudan 185
Southeast Asia 56–85, 104, 133, see also
    individual countries, ASEAN
Southern Common Market (MERCOSUR),
    see *MERCOSUR,* see also
    South America
sovereignty, see also *cooperation*
  global migration governance 173,
    177–8, 182–6
  North America 140–1, 157, 167

South America 109, 111,
    see also *UNASUR*
Southeast Asia, see *ASEAN way*
Soylu, Süleyman 1
Spain 22, 100, 113, 120, 129–30, 173
stability 5–6, 87, 91, see also *perceptions,*
    security, uncertainty
  instability, see *crisis*
standards 15, 71, 100, see also *Cartagena*
    declaration
  European standards 111, 118
  global standards 52, 171–8, see also
    global governance
  international standards 186, 197
status quo, status quo bias 4, 27, 42–4, 56,
    87, 114, 196, 201, see also
    representations, uncertainty
Strössner regime, see *dictatorial regimes*
student migration 10, 97, 108, 120, 129
Sub-Saharan Africa (*see* individual
    countries)
Suharto 75
Surinam 104
Sweden 22, 39, 50, 118, 190
Switzerland 189, 191
symbolic measures, see *narrative,*
    performance
Syria 50, 128, 130–1, 155

technical issues, technicalities 32, 39, 117,
    173, 178, 180–3, 193, see also
    politicization, political debate
temporariness, see *ASEAN*
tensions 125–6, 159, 181 see also
    politicization, stability
terrorism 95, 153, see also *security*
  9/11 terror attacks 23, 141, 145–7,
    152–3, 163, 199
Thailand 22, 56, 59–63, 66–9, 73,
    82, 84
Third-Country Nationals (TCNs) 112,
    117, 139
Thompson, Laura 172
Tower of Hanoi puzzle 54, 196, see also
    eurocentrism
trafficking 17, 115, 125, 175, 199, see also
    smuggling
transit migration 148, 176
transnational processes, see *migration*
    governance

Tratado entre México, Estados Unidos y Canadá (T-MEC), see *US-Mexico-Canada agreement*, see also *NAFTA*
travel restrictions, see *mobility*
travellers
  business, see *business and professional travellers*
  Enhanced Border Security and Visa Entry Reform Act 160
  Electronic Travel Authorization (ETA) 161
  restrictions, see *mobility, Covid-19 pandemic*
  travelling of ideas, see *information sharing*
Trudeau, Justin 168
Trump administration 2, 6, 23, 101, 140–2, 146–7, 153–56, 162–3, 167–9, 177, 190, 199
Trump, Donald, see *Trump administration*
trust
  among States, see *cooperation*
  in governments, see *governability*
Tunisia 136
Turkey 1, 69, 120–2, 190
types of migration, see *individual types: family, female, forced, irregular, labour, seasonal, student, permanent, temporary, voluntary*

Union of South American Nations (UNASUR) 108–9, see also *MERCOSUR*
uncertainty 1–4, 18–22, 43–4, 88–91, 113–4, 169, 194 see also *risk, stability, status quo*
understandings, see *representations*
undocumented immigration, see *irregular immigration*
unemployment, see also *drivers of migration*
United Kingdom (UK) 22, 38, 48, 50, 112–4, 118–20, 137
United Nations (UN), see also *Global Compacts*
  UN Convention against Transnational Organized Crime (UNTOC) 175

UN Convention on the Rights of All Migrant Workers and their Families 175
UN Global Compacts, see *Global Compacts*
UN Economic and Social Commission for Asia and the Pacific (UNESCAP) 57–8, 62
UN Environment Programme (UNEP) 185
UN Office on Drugs and Crime (UNODC) 82, 179
United Nations High Commissioner for Refugees (UNHCR) 2, 64–70, 82, 96–7, 136, see also *global migration governance*
United States (US), see *North America, USMCA*
  US Citizenship and Immigration Services (USCIS) 160
  US Department of Homeland Security (DHS) 152, 160, 167
  US-Mexico border, see *NAFTA, USMCA*
United States-Mexico-Canada Agreement (USMCA) 141, 162, see also *NAFTA*
Uruguay 91–100

Vázquez, Tabaré 102
Venezuela 92–101, 104, 106, 109–10, 198, see also *solidarity, South America, Lima Convention*
Venezuelan crisis, see *Venezuela*
Vietnam 56, 58, 60, 63–5, 121, see also *forced migration*
violence, see *Central America, crime, drivers of migration*
visa, see *labour migration, travellers*
voluntary commitments, see *non-binding agreements, global compacts*
Vox (political party) 138, see also *European Union, Spain*
vulnerable migrants, see *child migrants, female migrants, trafficking*

walls, see *fencing*, see also *anti-immigration, narratives*
Washington Consensus 106

welfare
    abuse 119, 152, 154, see also *narrative,
        security*
    benefits 9, 112, 116, 118, see also *health
        care, social benefits*
women, see *domestic workers, female
        migration, gender*
World Bank 106

World Health Organization
    (WHO) 185

xenophobia 98, 105, 137, see also
        anti-immigration, racism

Yugoslavia, see *ex-Yugoslavia,* see also
        individual countries